Should I Stay or Should I Go?

A Guide to Knowing if Your Relationship Can— and Should—Be Saved

Lundy Bancroft and JAC Patrissi

BERKLEY BOOKS, NEW YORK

THE BERKLEY PUBLISHING GROUP
Published by the Penguin Group
Penguin Group (USA) Inc.
375 Hudson Street, New York, New York 10014, USA
Penguin Group (Canada), 90 Eglinton Avenue East, Suite 700, Toronto, Ontario M4P 2Y3, Canada
(a division of Pearson Penguin Canada Inc.)
Penguin Books Ltd., 80 Strand, London WC2R 0RL, England
Penguin Group Ireland, 25 St. Stephen's Green, Dublin 2, Ireland (a division of Penguin Books Ltd.)
Penguin Group (Australia), 250 Camberwell Road, Camberwell, Victoria 3124, Australia
(a division of Pearson Australia Group Pty. Ltd.)
Penguin Books India Pvt. Ltd., 11 Community Centre, Panchsheel Park, New Delhi—110 017, India
Penguin Group (NZ), 67 Apollo Drive, Rosedale, Auckland, 0632, New Zealand
(a division of Pearson New Zealand Ltd.)
Penguin Books (South Africa) (Pty.) Ltd., 24 Sturdee Avenue, Rosebank, Johannesburg 2196,
South Africa

Penguin Books Ltd., Registered Offices: 80 Strand, London WC2R 0RL, England

While the authors have made every effort to provide accurate telephone numbers and Internet addresses at the time of publication, neither the publisher nor the authors assume any responsibility for errors, or for changes that occur after publication. Further, the publisher does not have any control over and does not assume any responsibility for author or third-party websites or their content.

PRINTING HISTORY
Berkley trade paperback edition / November 2011

Library of Congress Cataloging-in-Publication Data

Bancroft, Lundy, date.
  Should I stay or should I go? : a guide to knowing if your relationship can—and should—be saved / Lundy Bancroft and JAC Patrissi.
    p. c.m.
  ISBN 978-0-425-23889-9 (pbk.)
  1. Interpersonal relationships. 2. Couples—psychology.
3. Man-woman relationships. 4. Sex role. I. Title.
  HM1106.B365   2011   2011023702
  646.7'8082—dc22

PRINTED IN THE UNITED STATES OF AMERICA

10 9 8 7 6 5 4 3 2 1

For Rythea, Patrick, and the little one
—Lundy Bancroft

For you whose courageous spirit asks the question,
"Should I stay or should I go?"
And for Heidi Ehrenreich and Jeremiah McGillicuddy,
who helped me reset the stones of my foundation.
—JAC Patrissi

ACKNOWLEDGMENTS

As always, I owe deep gratitude to my early mentors and teachers on healthy relationships and gender justice, including Bettina Aptheker, David Adams, Carole Sousa, Susan Cayouette, Ted German, and MBM. For their more recent support and friendship in the domestic violence cause I thank Sarah Cortes, Janice Levinson, and SS.

For love, support, and encouragement in recent years I want to especially thank Jay Silverman, Rythea Lee, Patrick Crowley, Amy Waldman, Molly Maguire, Flip Rosenberry, Chris Boulton, Daniel Moss, Kate Bancroft, Eunice Rodrigues, Jennifer Hartley, Carlene Pavlos, Susie Hurlbert, and my children Fabienne and Lhiam.

My thanks always to my agent, Wendy Sherman, who always watches over me, to Denise Silvestro at Berkley Books who has been such a terrific person to work with through three titles now, to Denise's friendly and helpful assistant, Meredith Giordan, and to Martin Karlow for copyediting the manuscript.

My deep thanks to JAC Patrissi for her tireless work as we shaped various versions of this book before finally finding one that we could get the publishing world to get behind, and then more than two years hashing out the ideas and bringing them into the form you now hold. JAC is a stalwart, kind, and sharp ally to women and she has many profound offerings left to give to the world in the years ahead.

—L.B.

Over the past twenty-two years, I have had the privilege of collaborating with numerous women toward our greater clarity and healing. This work rests on their hard-won wisdom. I would like to honor the experience of particular women whose presence remained with me while writing: Gina R., Ginger T., Melissa V., Deb M., Kim G., Kendra M., Dawn L., Jackie S., Lisa T., and Barbara W.

I would like to express my gratitude to Jeri Martinez, whose brilliant and utterly compassionate treatment of the Stockholm syndrome during that basement volunteer training so many years ago inspired me to deepen my thinking and expand my role working on behalf of abused women and their children.

I would like to thank the members of the support group for healing from destructive relationships in Ware, Massachusetts. These women and their facilitator, Jackie Sweeney, worked with the concepts in this book, providing valuable feedback and suggestions for ways to make the book as useful as possible.

I would like to thank Barbara Whitchurch, Sherry Burnette, Marie Brodie, Deb Morin, Chani Waterhouse, Meg Kuhner, Margaret Mcguire, Michael Perreca, Avery Russell, Will Roberts, Gary Wolf, Frank D. Cernese, and Jason Patrissi for their many astute insights that have strengthened this work.

I am grateful to my coauthor, Lundy Bancroft, both for his numerous gifts, and for the ongoing dialogue over the course of our friendship that brought this work forward.

I am grateful to Denise Silvestro, whose editorial clarity not only made a much better book, but improved the way I facilitate and present these ideas. I thank our agent, Wendy Sherman, for taking me on and finding this work the right home.

—J.P.

CONTENTS

PART III
ENTERING THE NEW PHASE

PART IV
MAKING THE BIG DECISIONS

PART V
LIFE BEYOND

INTRODUCTION

Y OU ARE HOLDING a book that has been written for women who are going through repeated conflicts, frustrations, and dissatisfactions in their relationships, and are beginning to wonder what the root of the problem might be. You may be asking yourself whether your partner and you are just not a good match, and perhaps considering whether all this struggle is worth it. See if any of the following questions strikes a chord for you:

- Do you find it hard to figure your partner's behavior out, so that you end up confused about what he is actually feeling and thinking?
- Do you find yourself wondering whether he really loves you?
- Do you repeatedly feel that your partner keeps you at a distance or makes you a low priority? Are you missing the days when he seemed to put a higher value on spending good time with you?
- Is he failing to take good care of himself and his responsibilities, and you end up having to deal with the consequences?
- Do you feel like he's more attached to his buddies, or to his partying, than he is to you?
- Does he interact flirtatiously with other women in a way that keeps you off balance or makes you insecure? Does he insist that you shouldn't be bothered by it?

- Does he put you down or speak to you in a tone that makes you feel stupid?
- Does his anger sometimes make you nervous?

If you had some "yes" answers, this book can help you find out what has gone wrong, and what steps you need to take to get your relationship back on track. We will also guide you in figuring out if your relationship can't be saved—or shouldn't be—and how you can move yourself decisively toward a happier life *whether you and your partner succeed in staying together or not.*

Everyone enters a relationship with high hopes. In those early months of excitement and newness, of giddiness and lost sleep, it's natural to paint a picture in your mind of the years to come, sharing love and laughter with a partner who is thrilled to be with you. We all do it.

So when you discover that your relationship is not going to be a storybook one—in fact that it may be in serious trouble—you can find yourself feeling the shock of a bucket of ice water in the face. You may say to yourself, "I can't believe this is happening to us. This can't be real? Where did those great early days go?" And if some days you start to question whether you'll even be able to stay together, you can feel like the earth is dropping out from under you.

You are going to be okay, whatever happens. In this book, we will guide you in how to give the best possible chance to your relationship while also making sure to take equally good care of yourself. Some days you may feel that your life depends on fixing your current relationship, but it doesn't; if you go through the steps and exercises that we lay out in the pages ahead, you will find yourself able to handle the challenges that lie ahead for you.

The issue we address right away in Chapter 1—because we think it will be at the forefront of your mind—is whether the difficulties you are having are just the typical ones that all relationships go through, or whether they are symptoms of something deeper. We'll ask you to examine your expectations, to answer the question "Do I just expect too much from a relationship?" (We're already guessing that you don't; we meet more women who expect too little than too much.)

We believe there are basics that *all* relationships need to have, indispensable elements such as:

- love, affection, and kindness
- mutual respect

- freedom of both partners to express their true opinions and feelings
- safe, loving physical intimacy
- equality
- making each other a high priority (though not necessarily the only priority)
- accepting responsibility for one's own actions
- each partner caring about how his or her actions affect the other person

Nothing on this list is pie-in-the-sky. If your relationship is missing any of these elements, you have good reason to want that gap to be attended to—and to insist on it.

Did the list above include "a relationship that has no struggles"? Of course not. Tensions, difficulties, even heated arguments are all part of normal and healthy relationships. But we will show you how to sort out a relationship's ordinary growing pains from the signs that something deeper has to change.

If your challenges are the ordinary ones, the solutions are mutual ones. Each partner needs to work on improving communication, and to develop awareness of where their "buttons get pushed." The decision of whether to stay in the relationship is not based on the question "Is this relationship doing me harm?"; instead, it's about issues along the lines of "Is this relationship giving me what I need? Do we have enough in common? Are our feelings for each other strong enough?"

Next we will take you a chapter at a time through sources of difficulty that are *not* problems that you can share responsibility for, but rather that are pieces of work your partner would have to do on himself. We look primarily at the four most common causes of unhealthy relationship behavior in men: (1) immaturity; (2) addiction; (3) mental health problems; and (4) abusiveness. We examine how these factors can operate alone or in combination, and how a woman can best respond if her partner has any of these issues. However, we will be reminding you from time to time that you can't make your partner change; you can ask him to, you can even demand it, but you can't do the work for him. Some men decide to do serious work on themselves and some don't; if over time you find that your partner still refuses to dig deep, that's not your fault.

We refer throughout to women's partners as "he"; our area of greatest expertise is in relationships between men and women, and gender plays a leading role in relationship dynamics. However, a woman whose partner is female can still find a great deal of helpful information and guidance in these pages; we regret not having the background to speak to her more directly in what we've written here.

We do not attempt to address in much detail those relationships between men and women where the woman is the one whose unhealthy behavior or failure to grow is the primary problem. This book is directed at women, especially those who have a sense that their partner's behavior is a big part of why the relationship isn't working. If you suspect that your own conduct or emotional problems are in the way, you will find much help in this book in sorting out which of you is responsible for what (particularly in Chapter 6) and finding resources for working on your own issues.

The bulk of the book is about working toward solutions, not about analyzing problems. We encourage you to use a journal and work carefully through the exercises that are offered in each chapter.

About half of the women who read a book like this one have children, so we've made several references to issues that parents have to deal with. If you don't have children, we hope you will still find these examples useful.

Finally, Chapters 9 and 11 are somewhat different from the rest, because they cover in detail the work that *your partner* needs to do and how he should go about it. Slightly modified versions of these chapters, tailored to make them appropriate for him, are available free at our book's Web site, ShouldIStayOr ShouldIGo.net. We have put these on the Web because we don't recommend that you share the actual book with your partner; we want it to be just for you. Besides, the Web versions of those chapters are more helpful to him than the ones in the book because they have been modified to help him understand them and take them in.

Welcome, then, to a process of healing and clarification. We believe you will gain insights that will build your strength, increase your faith in your own thinking, and help you to love yourself. Along the way, you will learn how to give your partner a great gift: the opportunity to experience tremendous growth, and to make his relationship with you a vibrant and satisfying one. If he chooses not to do the work, he will be punishing himself. And whether he does or not, your growth will leap forward, and you will come out feeling in charge of your life and relationships.

PART I

FOCUSING ON THE ROOT ISSUES

ONE

Don't All Relationships Have Problems?

A WOMAN NAMED SHELLEY was on the telephone, hoping that we would have advice for her regarding what to do next:

"Ezra can be so loving—it seems like he's crazy about me. He really pursued me at the beginning of our relationship, saying he had never felt this way about someone before and that he wanted to spend the rest of his life with me. But now he does a lot of push and pull. When we get really close and in love, it only lasts for about two weeks, and then he pulls away. He says that I'm being too intense for him and he needs more space. It hurts my feelings, because I feel like he is the one that pulls me in, and then he acts like I'm too dependent on him. So I'll pull back for a while and feel disappointed, and then he comes in hot pursuit again, saying he wants me to make a deeper commitment to our relationship, he wants us to grow closer, he wants our relationship to be more sexual. I can't figure out what he wants."

Marianne called with quite a different story:

"My boyfriend is really kind to me, for the most part. I mean, he never gets super angry or nasty. So maybe I shouldn't even be complaining. But to me he seems different after he's had two or three drinks—and that's

pretty much every night. He starts the evening acting all sweet and sexy, but then he starts drinking and zones out and goes off into his own world. Then he gets kind of preoccupied with his ex-wife, complaining about her and how she messed up his life. He totally pulls away from me and just falls asleep. But it's not like he gets drunk exactly. I mean, he's not slurring his words or making a fool of himself or anything. Maybe I'm overreacting, but I'm wondering if maybe he has a drinking problem. I don't think I want to marry him until I've figured out what's going on with him."

Leah called us when she was on a break from work:

"My husband is a kind man—he's not like a lot of the mean people you've been talking about. But it's a different kind of problem. He acts a little . . . strange sometimes. Like he gets anxious if the magazines and drink coasters in the living room aren't in exactly their 'right' places, or if a picture is a little tilted on the wall—strange things. He'll say I moved things around when I didn't, and get cranky and blaming with me because somebody changed how little things were arranged. And it isn't just with me. I'm pretty good friends with his sister, and she told me a couple of months ago that she's worried about him, because he has started to ask her these questions over and over again about their inheritance from their mother—like he thinks his siblings are moving money around or something. He's a good guy, but there is something . . . wrong."

Alicia tells us:

"I feel like I've tried everything. I've made it very clear to my husband that I'm sick of feeling controlled by him. He has to win every argument, it's his way or the highway. And I don't mean just with decisions involving the two of us; even when it has to do with my own life and it's really none of his business, he's still so insistent that I have to do what he thinks is going to work best for me. He wants to decide when it's time to hang up on my mother, when I should file a complaint against my boss, you name it. I don't want him running my life anymore!

"I'd say there have been four different times when he agreed to stop telling me what to do, and things between us got better for a couple of months.

But then he goes back to his old ways, and he gets mad when I point out that he's doing the same stuff he always has. And when I say that maybe he should go to a counselor, he says I'm the one who needs therapy because I'm so stubborn and I can't make good decisions for myself. That maybe if I was more sensible he wouldn't have to take care of me. That's his view . . . And sometimes I wonder if maybe he's right. Maybe I'm just not smart enough about some things and he's just looking out for my best interest. But it really gets annoying at times. I'm a grown woman, for goodness' sake! And I did a pretty good job of taking care of myself before I met him.

"Am I going to have to end my marriage? I really don't want to, and I don't want my kids to go through that. But sometimes I just get so sick and tired of him trying to control my life."

What do these four women, with their sharply contrasting experiences, have in common? A number of similarities exist, despite the differences.

- **A partner who was loving and positive at first has turned increasingly unhealthy.** Each of these women is struggling with behaviors on the man's part that are hurting her, and that are leaving her frustrated and unsatisfied in her relationship.
- **The partner is insisting that nothing is wrong.** In each case, the man is insisting that she shouldn't be bothered by his behavior. In fact, they are all saying that if she doesn't like what he's doing, that's a sign that something is wrong with *her,* and she should stop complaining and make changes herself.
- **The woman wants to know how to get him to face his problems and change.** Each of these callers is looking for ways to get through to her partner and get him out of his denial. She loves her partner, but she is getting hurt more and more over time, and the relationship is starting to take a toll on her.
- **She's wondering whether the time may be drawing near when she will have to break up with her partner.** These women all expressed not being ready to take that kind of step—which for Alicia and Leah would mean a divorce—but they are hungry for ideas about what to do next. And they are concerned about the time that is passing as they devote their lives to trying to make their relationships work.

Ending a relationship is a huge decision for a woman, whether she has children or not. Building a relationship takes energy and time; who wants to have to start all over again, building closeness from scratch with another person? Breaking up is painful, too. The feelings of loss at ending a relationship can last a long time, and run deep. When you have been in love with your partner, you find yourself thinking, "Will I ever find someone else? Am I ever going to feel this strongly about someone again?"

And a relationship involves entanglements that are hard to leave behind. You may own a house together, you may have children. You may have grown close to his relatives and come to feel part of his family. You may have made plans that you care about for your future together.

So it's natural that you want to put work into saving your relationship. We will not be pressuring you anywhere in this book to leave your partner; we are behind you on making your decisions carefully, taking your time, and doing what's right for you.

At the same time, we don't want you to sell yourself short. Your own needs, feelings, and dreams need to be a high priority. Time is precious, and we don't want you to end up later with regrets, feeling that you let too many years go by. So although we are not going to ask you to leave your partner, we are going to encourage you to take a number of important steps to retake control of your life and make yourself your own centerpiece. Your own life is important, and you are worth it.

"ARE WE JUST DEALING WITH THE REGULAR STRUGGLES THAT EVERYBODY GOES THROUGH?"

This is the first question on the minds of so many of the women we speak with. All relationships have tensions and difficulties—or at least almost all of them do—and some fighting and arguing come with the territory. Any two people have their different needs, preferences, and opinions, and negotiating those gets complicated—and, at times, unpleasant. So how do you know whether you are living with the normal challenges of a healthy relationship, or if you are in a relationship that is unhealthy and has to change?

We'll help you answer this question by looking first at the predictable cycles and difficulties that couples in healthy relationships go through, and then examining the signs that you are involved with a partner who has serious problems.

The Three Stages of a Healthy Relationship

Every relationship is unique, but most healthy relationships follow a fairly typical pattern composed of three stages. There are no hard-and-fast rules for when a couple enters these stages or how long each stage lasts, but we can make some generalizations for the purpose of enabling you to determine where your relationship may be.

The Romantic Stage of a Healthy Relationship

If you've ever fallen in love—or if you've seen it happen in the movies—you know about the expansive, consuming, all-enveloping high of love's "Flaming June." It's during this Romantic Stage that you can't wait to make your plans to move in together—or even start naming your future grandchildren. It's a heady state of mind. You are beyond food and water—you practically don't need air. The mere thought of your newfound passion makes you feel stronger, more attractive, smarter, and funnier.

The Conflict Stage

All the openness and intimacy of the Romantic Stage predictably lead to your feeling a bit exposed and vulnerable. The next stage is when partners start to realize, perhaps unconsciously, how vulnerable they have become by allowing themselves to feel so strongly about someone. They start to have feelings such as *What if my partner leaves me? What if something happens to him or her? What if he or she starts to have feelings for someone else?* And finally, love tends to trigger some of people's earliest experiences in life, including their early wounds. It has been said that love reveals what needs to heal.

People manage this vulnerability in sharply different ways: by pulling away a little, or by becoming clingy, or by trying to get reconnected to the life goals and interests they had before the lightning struck, to name a few. Partners begin to turn back to the activities that made them feel more "centered." You go to a drumming circle to get back to who you are, and he wants to go back to church. Perhaps you want to feel more connected and feel the need to talk about it all. Your partner wants to drop down into the wilderness like Bear Grylls of the popular television series and books *Man vs. Wild* to remind himself how to live. Your individual interests clash and crash. His love of sports seems like an immature obsession. Your preference for foreign films seems boring and pretentious to him. Significant differences concerning things like how to use resources like money, gender roles, children, and long-term goals rise to the surface. You find yourselves having tense conversations about values and what matters most to you in life. Does either of you have much skill in negotiating all of these places where your beliefs collide? Six weeks ago, you felt so happy. The conflict stage is a buzz kill. How are you going to share your life, or at least accept and understand the other person? Facing these conflicts leads you to the next stage.

The Evaluating-the-Commitment Stage

After spending some time discovering that differences are inevitable—and starting to notice whether the differences and ensuing struggles between the two of you tend to lead eventually to good places or not—deeper questions will follow: Do we actually have enough in common? Is that nice mix of the magic of attraction, laughter, romance, and shared dreams going to be strong enough to carry us through the times when one of us hurts the other's feelings, or the times when our beliefs collide? Do we feel enough fulfillment that we believe we belong together? If so, what are the rules we agree to? For example, how much are we together, and how much apart? What kind of arguing is okay and what kind isn't? Are we monogamous or are we still seeing other people?

The good news is that if you successfully clarify your commitment together, the Romantic Stage can be yours again—only this time it will have legs.

Over the course of the months and years of your relationship, a healthy relationship will go through these predictable cycles. The cycles won't seem to exactly repeat one another, however; with each round you are spiraling higher up, growing closer on a deep level and developing a way of being together that works for both of you. Your Evaluating-Your-Commitment Stage may become

The Three Stages of a Healthy Relationship

Romantic Stage *"I could just stare at you all day—I've never felt this way before."*

- Usually lasts one to four months.
- Everything seems perfect.
- Differences seem trivial.
- You feel expansive and filled with joy.
- Both partners seem to be diving in headfirst.

Conflict Stage *"I need a little space. We're two different people. I'm not that into you."*

- You're working out communication styles, ways of expressing irritation.
- You're trying to understand each other's values and ethics.
- You begin to feel the impact of gender roles.
- You need to negotiate how to share money, time, and other resources.
- You feel the need to reconnect with your life direction or spiritual center.
- You begin to feel vulnerable.

Evaluating Commitment Stage *"Is this working?"*

- You reflect on whether the relationship is satisfying to you.
- You wonder if the growth and happiness are outweighing the hurt.
- You consider what kinds of change are needed.
- You ask yourself whether the time is coming to move on.
- You decide (perhaps silently) to renew your commitment.

one of celebration and fine-tuning most times around. The Romantic Stage deepens, and you can navigate the Conflict Stage more skillfully.

THE UNHEALTHY RELATIONSHIP

An unhealthy relationship also goes through stages, but instead of evolving and growing closer, the couple experiences severe disappointment, anger, and hurt as the relationship spirals downward until it crashes and burns, damaging one or both partners.

The Romantic Stage happens in an unhealthy relationship, too. In fact, it is sometimes extremely powerful, because men with destructive patterns can sometimes be especially charming individuals with highly developed capacities to make their dating partners feel special, understood, and cherished—*in the early period of a relationship*. But when the relationship enters the Conflict Stage, it gradually—or abruptly—becomes apparent that you are not a team, working and struggling together for mutual well-being. Something different is happening. Among the most common symptoms are the following:

- Conflicts seem to be more about who can win, and who can hurt the other person more effectively, than about how to have a constructive struggle to work out a problem.
- One or both partners turns out to be explosive, and those explosions can come at unexpected times.
- You start to notice that your partner is really thinking almost exclusively about what is good for *him,* not about what's good for you or what's good for your relationship.
- Nothing ever seems to be his fault, and he seems to have an excuse for everything; or, alternatively, he apologizes frequently, but then the same behavior from before continues right on as if the apology had never happened.
- He says and does mean things sometimes, or at the very least you find yourself getting blamed repeatedly for things that are not at all your fault.
- You discover that he is being secretive or dishonest about some important issues such as money, his relationships with other women, or his use of substances.
- You find yourself worrying often about how your partner is harming himself, because he's drinking and drugging, or he's suicidal, or he's abusing his health.
- He is making your relationships with other people more difficult by saying bad things about you to them or by interfering with your contact with people. He seems to have very little space for your complaints or grievances, or even becomes distant and punishing when you bring

them up; you find yourself increasingly concerned about how he will react if you bring certain subjects up.

- You find yourself spending a lot of time trying to figure out what is bothering him and what you are doing wrong, and your self-esteem is perhaps suffering as a result.
- You are winding up feeling starved for love and affection; this is perhaps (but not necessarily) combined with your partner having a lot of excuses for being distant or for making you a low priority. You end up working even harder to keep the attention he does give you.

If in reading through the characteristics above you found yourself thinking a few times—or several times—"Yes, that feels like it's going on in my relationship," please don't despair. We will help you sort out the roots of your partner's behavior—and there may be more than one—and make a plan for getting your relationship back on course if possible. And whether you succeed in turning your relationship around or not, working through this book will make sure that *your own life* gets back on course, and stays that way.

The first crucial point we would like to share is:

Conflicts and difficulties in destructive relationships have to be understood *differently* from the ones that happen in healthy relationships.

You may get advice from friends, or from books about relationships, that not only will not help you, but that could actually make things worse; advice that makes sense for a healthy relationship can point you down exactly the wrong road if you apply it to an unhealthy one. This off-the-mark advice may include people telling you that if you would just behave absolutely perfectly yourself and handle your partner in just the right way, you could manage, or even solve, the problem. And it's just not so.

THE JOURNEY WE ARE ABOUT TO SET OUT ON

In the chapters ahead, we will be walking you through a process, step-by-step, that will help you move toward greater and greater clarity. Each part will contain important concepts, combined with exercises that will help you digest these ideas and decide what they mean for you. We encourage you to set aside time for the writing, reflecting, and other exercises we offer; while it's true that knowledge is power, much greater power comes to those who combine new learning with:

- putting thoughts down on paper
- taking time to sit or walk alone and mull things over
- exploring your feelings at a pace you are comfortable with
- engaging in mindful physical movement and exercise (we'll explain what we mean by this in Chapters 6 and 8)
- meditation or prayer
- taking action

The exercises will help you to integrate four crucial realms—thought, feeling, intuition, and willpower—so that you can take courageous and effective steps in your life.

As you move through the book, you will develop greater and greater clarity about these central points:

1. What steps do I have to take to get my life fully on the course I choose?
2. What steps does my partner have to take in order to grow and change enough that our relationship can be satisfying and safe for me, and forward moving for both of us?
3. How do I decide how much energy and love I should invest in this relationship? When is it time to let go and move on, if the kinds of changes I desire aren't happening?

By the time you get to the last chapters, you will not only have made a clear plan of action for yourself, you will be following it. You will also have designed a clear plan of action with and for your partner. Whether he will be following that plan or not remains to be seen; but when we get there, you will know how to decide whether he is moving, and whether the speed of his development is good enough for you to make further investment in the relationship.

Here's the big picture of where we will be going together:

First Stop: We Sort Out What's Going On with Your Partner

When a man is behaving in ways that hurt you, the problem can be coming from a number of different sources, and it can be tricky to unravel the tangled threads. Maybe the main issue is that he grew up with men who taught him to control and use women instead of making genuine intimate connection. Or maybe he is more deeply attached to smoking weed than to being in a relationship that works. Perhaps he wants a mother to look after him, instead of a partner to share with. Or it could be that he has been badly hurt himself and is hostile with most people who try to get close.

So, in order to form a clear picture of where we're starting from, we will explore the following questions, and others like them:

- Is your partner immature and afraid of commitment? Does he still want to be a teenager, with his life revolving around having fun with his buddies, and just isn't ready for a mature and deep relationship with a woman?

- Does he have an addiction? Is he using alcohol or weed as a crutch, avoiding his problems and wasting time and money? Does his partying sometimes seem like it's more important to him than you are? Is he hooked on something other than drugs or drinking, like sex, pornography, or gambling?

- Are some of his behaviors quite strange or inexplicable? Does he forget important events from the past, such as blocking out times when he behaved in hurtful or twisted ways? Is he rigid and controlled most of the time? Have other people in his life noticed odd habits that tell you something isn't quite right with him?

- Does he get mean sometimes, call you insulting names, or make you look bad in front of other people? Does he ever get intimidating or frightening to you? Does he ever pressure you into having sex when you aren't in the mood, or make you feel bad sexually?

- Could it be that you are the problem more than he is? Are you overly critical of him or nasty to him? Do you blame him for all your problems? Does he act truly hurt and confused rather than very angry about why you are so upset with him? Is he trying hard to please you, but he just can't seem to get it right?

We will help you to make sense out of your answers to these questions and other related ones so that you can identify the key patterns than are emerging in your partner's behavior—and in your own, if that's an issue. Then we'll show you how to put these pieces together to form a plan to take charge of your relationship and your life.

Second Stop: We Guide You in Redefining Who You Are

When either partner in a relationship is behaving in unhealthy ways, both people go off-kilter. Women in particular tend to lose their centers while in relationships that aren't working because females are socialized to adapt themselves to what men want or need. Women also tend to find meaning in their lives through the bonds of relationship. As valuable a tendency as this is, it means that it gets very hard for most women to feel clear and strong in themselves when their romantic relationship gets rocky. So we are going to take you through some exercises that will help you find yourself—and, we hope, never get lost inside of a relationship again. We will be asking you to think about aspects of yourself such as:

Who were you before you met your current partner? What pieces of the person you used to be have you lost—or been required to give up—along the way? What are your favorite things about yourself? What is your favorite way to spend time with just yourself? If you were living true to the deepest aspects of who you are, how would you be spending your time each day?

Third Stop: We Help You Launch Yourself Toward Your Goals

We have known a great number of women who strike us as vibrant, capable, and talented. They seem filled with potential, poised to move into their happiness. It is obvious that they can succeed at whatever they choose. Yet they are inhibited. They don't act on their talents and dreams because they seem held back. Once we talk to them, it soon becomes obvious that great amounts of their creative thought, emotional focus, and time are spent on managing their relationship. Even with little information, we begin to see that the relationships that these women are in are keeping them from building the life they are capable of having.

Well, the best way to find out how much he's holding you back is this: Get up and walk, or even run, toward your dreams and goals. Take some action that fulfills your deeper needs—get your GED or start a class at a community college. Research what it takes to open the flower shop you have always wanted. Get a used guitar and see if you can trade lessons for some skill you have to offer. Join a dance class. If you do, you will stop wondering what's going on in your relationship, and it will come sharply clear. You will see whether:

- He tries to stop you from moving forward by sabotaging your efforts directly or indirectly.
- He doesn't stop you but he does nothing to keep growing himself.
- He shows no interest in your new passions.
- He complains that you are abandoning him.
- He gets up and gets moving himself toward his own dreams, and gives you wholehearted support toward pursuing yours.

One of our central messages throughout this book is that, when you are trying to grasp what is going on in an unhealthy relationship, "wait and see" won't work. We've watched women stay mired in confusion for years and years. Consider yourself a crime-scene investigator—a CSI—and your relationship is what you are studying; you are going to have to carry out a collection of experiments, and then you will see, with crystal clarity, what you are dealing with and where the problems lie.

Of course, if you make your own growth the top priority, you will run the risk of outgrowing your partner. You may shoot ahead so rapidly that the distance between you gets too great, and he can no longer catch up. As you work through the exercises in the chapters ahead, we believe you will come to understand why this is a chance you simply have to take; stunting your own development is just too high a price to pay.

Fourth Stop: We Launch Your Partner—If He's Willing to Step Up on the Launching Pad

Your partner does not have to sit by, staying stuck, while you race on into life. Materials that go with this book, designed for the male partner, are available for you to give him at ShouldIStayOrShouldIGo.net, giving him all the concepts, instructions, support, and resources that he needs to guide him if he is serious about changing and growing. Whenever he chooses to, he can stop kicking and screaming and get to work.

Part of why we have created the Web-based materials for him is that it isn't your job to spoon-feed it to him. You can get very involved with his change—if you find it rewarding and good for you—or have almost nothing to do with the process at all if that's better for you at this point in your life. We want you to do what best serves your own growth and well-being.

Fifth Stop: We Help You Prepare for Life Without Him—Just in Case—Even As You Keep Fighting to Make Life with Him Work

By moving forward decisively in life yourself, you will discover whether your partner can make the changes he needs to make or not. If you follow the process laid out in this book, doing your work while he does (or doesn't do) his, you will come to see very clearly whether your partner is up to the task. And if the results of your experiments start to show that he just isn't going to be willing to move far enough to make your relationship work, we will prepare you, despite the sadness, to take the leap necessary to build a wonderful life without him. And that life will be a dynamic and satisfying one into which a new partner, capable of meeting you at your level, will eventually step.

The process in this book asks for some hard work from you, not just from him. The work we give him is to help him change, and the work we give you is to help you move toward greater strength and clarity. You deserve that attention paid to yourself through the exercises, and without it the ideas in this book won't work nearly as well.

DO I SIMPLY EXPECT TOO MUCH FROM A RELATIONSHIP?

It's possible but, frankly, we doubt it. Women are more likely to demand too little than too much; as Nancy Kline, the author of *Women and Power,* has said, "Women are grateful for getting ten percent of what they deserve."

However, let's confront that question head-on, right now, because the voice in your head that puts down your wishes and dreams could get in your way as you work with this book.

What a Relationship Can't Be and Do

Popular movies and television entertainment, for all the enjoyment they bring us, are not a helpful source of information about real-life relationships and how they work. The messages from movie plots tend to go something like this:

"We were friends, and then figured out we were truly in love and lived happily ever after."

or

"We hated each other, but then figured out we were truly in love and lived happily ever after."

or

"We overcame dramatic obstacles (war, famine, social status, race, the Mafia, being from different planets, or possessing various negative personal qualities) and then figured out we were truly in love and lived happily ever after."

Once the couple enters the Romantic Stage, the credits roll and the show is over.

This style of storytelling, which we see hundreds of times each year, encourages us to believe in a mythical, magical love that doesn't exist. And that belief can keep us trapped in a relationship that is dragging us down—or can keep us dissatisfied in a relationship that's actually quite good. Falling in love is real, but an endless Romantic Stage, as we discussed earlier, is not. Living in real-life relationships teaches us that:

- **No one person can be everything you need.** Don't look to your partner to be your only friend or to fulfill you in every way—he can't do it, even if he does nothing else but try. You need good friends, meaningful work, enjoyable hobbies, and a sense that you contribute to making your world a better place. Even the best partner cannot substitute for these sources of satisfaction. A good relationship is one aspect—and just one—of what makes a happy, whole life.

- **No one can make you better than you were before.** While it's true that a loving, supportive partner can help you increase your strength, *you* are still the one doing the actual work of getting stronger, and *you* are the one building on good qualities that you already have. So he doesn't get the credit for ways that you have grown, and you wouldn't be less of a person without him. If he says, to choose one example, "I'm the one that got you sober, if it hadn't been for me you'd still be drunk on the street," he's a supporting actor claiming to be the star; if you got sober, you did it. (This also means that you can't look to your partner to solve your life's problems—though he shouldn't be making them worse.)

- **No one can be the person you spend all your time with.** People who spend too much time together tend to get irritable and annoyed with each other. You can't be together every second. It has to be okay for each of you to spend time with other people and engaging in other activities that are just yours.

- **No one can love absolutely everything about you.** Even on a day when you feel effective, happy, and divinely led, you are not going to love absolutely everything about yourself. Neither does your partner. Your partner is going to be bothered by the way you do certain things, and is going to want you to work on improving irritating habits or overcoming frustrating rigidities. And, in turn, you have the right to raise the subject of changes that you would like him to make. *This is a loaded area, however.* Grievances have to be raised in a respectful way, not in the form of insults or put-downs. And complaints should not be used as an excuse to control the other person about things that really are their own business.

- **No partner can do things for you that you need to do for yourself.** On the surface, this statement may appear to be untrue; you could certainly find someone to make all the money so you didn't have to work, cook all your meals for you, and handle your social calendar, right? Except that then you would have a father or a butler, not a partner. And being looked after in these ways won't actually make you happy; over time, you will just come to feel dependent and resentful, and you'll tend to blame your butler—oops, we mean partner—for not doing even more for you. You need the pride, satisfaction, and independence that come from running your own life.

If you are pursuing the unattainable fantasies above, you can make yourself miserable with a kind, decent partner. But what is more likely is that you will find, as you read the above list, that you are recognizing *your partner's* fantasies; part of his problem may be that he took those popular movies as his guide to relationships.

What a Relationship Can—and *Should*—Be and Do

If you expect to be well treated in a relationship, we're behind you 100 percent. Don't ever let anyone tell you that women have to settle for less. But good treatment doesn't mean being constantly catered to, and even the best relationship won't meet all of your needs. So what exactly is the bottom line? How much should you insist on? Here are the key elements:

- **You must be treated with respect.** No partner should call you names, make fun of you, roll his eyes at you in an argument, humiliate you, or mock you. Period. It doesn't matter if he's had a bad day or a bad decade, if he's drunk, if he's under tremendous financial stress, if he's furious at you, or if he feels that *you* were disrespecting *him*. There's simply no excuse for disrespect. There's always another option.
- **You must feel safe.** You should never have to worry that your partner will hurt you physically or sexually. If he behaves in ways that make you feel that an assault might be coming—even if it never actually does—or if he behaves in ways that lead you to have sexual contact with him that you don't want, you are not in a safe relationship. Safety can also disappear if you have to be concerned that he might cause you serious harm

in ways that are not physical or sexual, such as if he threatens to reveal important secrets, tries to deliberately cause you financial harm, says he will take custody of the children away from you, or exhibits other kinds of cruelty.

- **You should feel loved the great majority of the time.** Every relationship has its periods when everything seems to turn into a squabble, or where distance and disconnection take over and passion fades. But these times should be the exception, not the rule. And even during hard times, your partner should be capable of finding ways to get the message across to you that you are valued and appreciated. Although he might not be able to literally say, "I'm mad at you but I still love you," that message should come across. If the times when you feel loved are few and far between, and if your partner completely changes his attitude toward you anytime things aren't going his way, you deserve better.

- **Your relationship should create far more possibilities than it takes away.** Being involved in an intimate partnership requires some sacrifices on the part of both partners. (And even more so if you have children.) But the relationship should also open many doors. For example, your partner's love and support should make it easier for you to take on new challenges in your life. The two of you should be encouraging each other to pursue your deepest dreams. The sharing of financial resources should put you in a more solid position than you were as a single person. Being there for each other should make raising children more fun. You should each be a source of new acquaintances and social connections for the other. In short, ask yourself, "Is my relationship broadening my horizons, or is it narrowing them?" You have a right to expect it to be the former, not the latter.

- **You should have passion and intimacy.** Not everyone craves physical passion and sexuality, but most people do, and if these matter to you, you have the right to expect them to be a lively part of your primary relationship. Partners who care about each other and are committed to their connection can find ways to keep sexual energy and excitement kindled year after year. The notion that the passing of time inevitably makes a man lose his desire for a woman is false, a product of immature views of relationships and sexuality. Equally false is the view that monogamy deadens sexual energy and that infidelity is the only way to keep passion alive. If you want a sexy, faithful relationship, you are only asking for what you have every right to expect.

- **You should feel seen.** Consider these questions: Does your partner really know you? Does he like you? (It's possible to feel that your partner loves you but doesn't really like you.) Does he understand your dreams and ambitions? Does he grasp what your deepest loves are—whether those are people, or places, or hobbies? Do you feel that he's on your team in life, that he's got your back? Does he value what you give to the world? Is he a good friend to you?

As you read through this list, you may be thinking, "Oh, I couldn't possibly find a partner with whom I could have all that." But this list describes the *minimum* a relationship should have, not pie in the sky. Expecting too little can keep you trapped in an unhealthy relationship. You will tend to keep second-guessing yourself, feeling that you are to blame for having unreasonable desires.

Expecting the movie romance can also be a trap. It can lead you to under-value the decent, responsible guy, and overvalue the destructive one; ironically, the *least* healthy partners are often the ones who can be the most dazzling and charming early in a relationship, and who can best convince you that Prince Charming has come.

EXERCISE 1–1:

Take about ten minutes now—more if you want—to write in your journal or in the space below about the following questions:

1. What are ways in which your partner has unreasonable expectations for you or for your relationship? (As you write, check down the list on pages 21–23 of what a relationship *can't* be.)

2. Are there ways in which you expect too much of your partner or your relationship, going by that same list? If so, how?

3. How does your current relationship do at meeting the list of elements above that a relationship *can and should* have? (Check pages 23–25 as a guide before writing your answer.)

4. What was it like to answer question three? Were you relieved? Did you feel guilty or apprehensive? How did you feel?

We could say that we are now ready to begin our work together, but the truth is that you have already started. This introduction has presented you with some challenging pieces that you have begun to reflect on and digest. When you feel ready, turn to Chapter 2 and dive into sorting out what's going on. You are on the path to a better relationship—whether it ends up being this one or your next one—and a happier life.

TWO

Is the Problem Immaturity?

"I get so frustrated that he has to ask me how to do every little thing in taking care of our kids. Why can't he figure some of it out for himself? It's like he's helpless."

"Listening to him whine is starting to feel like fingernails on a chalk-board to me."

"I have places I want my life—our lives—to go. It feels like he just doesn't care, like he'd just be happy in this rut forever."

"He's so clueless sometimes. I try to point out to him that the way he did things just totally fouled up my day, and he just looks at me kind of baffled. What the hell was he thinking? Or was he even thinking at all?"

"Some days I'm not sure if he wants a partner or a mommy."

PICTURE THE FOLLOWING scene: About fifteen children, most of them nine or ten years old, are playing at a swimming pool. After an hour or so, the adults who are hosting the gathering put out refreshments on a picnic table, including twenty or thirty cookies. The children rush over to the table, with two boys leading the pack. When the front-runners arrive at the spread, they furiously begin grabbing cookies, holding about three in each hand and stuffing one in their mouths. So with this large group behind them, these two boys have just vacuumed up at least half of the cookies. What's going on? How come these boys, who are plenty old enough to figure out that there aren't nearly enough cookies for them to take so many, dive in and hoard them anyhow? And why do we so rarely see girls behave this way?

Is uncaring, self-centered behavior just "natural" in boys? Of course not. In most tribes—which is how human beings have lived through the great majority of their history—males were expected to always be thinking about how to make sure that everyone had enough, to be providing for their families and relatives, to be planning for what would make life work for the whole group. A male who was thinking exclusively of himself was severely reprimanded. And while some tribes permitted some degree of violent behavior from males, it was only allowed along strictly enforced lines and usually could not be expressed toward anyone inside of the tribe. There is nothing natural, or biological, about boys behaving against the needs of their communities. So what happened to these boys' sense of sharing and making sure everyone is included?

To put the answer simply: as a society, we allow boys way too much and we give them way too little. Hiding behind the unfortunate saying "Boys will be boys," adults wring their hands and stand passively by while boys behave selfishly, irresponsibly, or violently. Some adults, particularly some men, don't just tolerate antisocial behavior from boys but actually openly joke or wink about it, egging boys on. Then we act baffled and concerned when these boys grow up to become the men that adults have prepared them to be—competitive, selfish, and aggressive.

In the words of a wise bumper sticker that succinctly captures this problem, BOYS WILL BE MEN.

We said above that boys are not just allowed too much, but also given too little. What we mean by this is that while boys are granted too much room to be irresponsible or selfish, they simultaneously receive too little physical affection, too little support for their sadnesses and fears, too little chance to show who they really are. This lack of attention to their emotional needs can make them reluctant to mature; and the license they get to behave antisocially makes them conclude that maturity won't be demanded of them.

There are some additional wrinkles to the dynamic we're describing here. It's common for boys to receive a lot of catering as they grow up; depending on the family a boy is from, he may well have gotten more attention than his sisters did, bigger portions of food, more freedom to explore the world, more things brought to him so he didn't have to get up. You could look at a man like this and say, "His parents met his needs; in fact, they did so too much." But catering to children is only a superficial way to attend to them. What children crave much more than catering is genuine support, gentle touch, and attention to their feelings. And these forms of caring are often in short supply in the lives of boys.

Meddling and invasiveness are also no substitute for healthy caring. If your partner grew up with adults who watched his every move, constantly felt sorry for him, never let him have space in his body or in his thoughts, or ran his life for him, he won't know how to function as an adult in the world. He will expect you to do everything for him, and present himself as needy and helpless.

One of the results of this regrettable combination—too little healthy nurturing, too much permission to be self-centered or destructive—is that some boys just can't seem to grow up; they go into manhood still acting like those little boys at the picnic table. In this chapter we'll look at some of the signs that your partner's immaturity may be his main problem. Then we will guide you in how to evaluate his potential to step up and enter the adult world, and how to put your foot down so that he knows the time has come.

First Warning Signs of Immaturity

Begin by looking down the following list, checking off any items that ring a bell for you about your partner:

- ☐ He frequently leaves messes around and doesn't clean them up.
- ☐ He whines when you ask him to take care of things or meet his responsibilities.
- ☐ He still takes his laundry to his mother's house for her to wash.
- ☐ He keeps saying he isn't sure if he's ready to commit to a serious, monogamous relationship.
- ☐ He acts burdened if you express your needs or put demands on him.
- ☐ He seems to put more energy into his time with his buddies than into his relationship with you.

- ☐ He seems to put more energy into playing with his toys than into your relationship, whether it's working in his shop, tuning his car, mastering his new video game, learning to use his latest technological device, or pursuing his latest intellectual theory.
- ☐ He doesn't seem to be able to quite figure out how to interact with a female, as if you were a different species that he doesn't understand.
- ☐ He acts baffled when you point out to him the ways in which he has failed to take your feelings or wishes—or anyone else's for that matter—into account.
- ☐ He keeps falling apart—with a range of different excuses—when it's time for him to carry his weight.
- ☐ Whenever your life has a real difficulty or crisis, he comes up with an even bigger one, so that one way or another, you are never the center of attention for very long.
- ☐ He can't seem to manage the basics of adult life, such as handling his bank account, making dentist appointments, registering his car, or getting himself lunch. He acts helpless, and looks to you to do everything for him.
- ☐ He talks on and on about himself and doesn't listen very well to you.
- ☐ He has very little insight into himself, and he's quite closed about his inner world (although he may occasionally have big realizations about himself, which are actually things you've told him over and over).
- ☐ When you try to describe your feelings or experiences to him, he often responds by saying that you should feel what *he* would feel if he were in your position, as if for some reason you should have the same reactions. In other words, he keeps telling you that your feelings are wrong.
- ☐ He has curiously strong opinions on subjects that he actually knows very little about (and that sometimes are things that you, on the other hand, do know something about).
- ☐ He stays upset for an inordinately long time if he has to give up anything that matters to him, as if he should never have to make sacrifices.
- ☐ It's difficult to get him moving; he spends a lot of his time sitting around doing nothing, and complains about having to make any effort.
- ☐ He is flirtatious with other women, or even insists on keeping multiple relationships going at the same time, saying that he "just isn't ready to settle down."

Now, most any woman who goes through this list is going to find something on it that fits her partner; everybody, male or female, has ways in which they need to grow and develop. You quite likely struggle with a few of these issues yourself. So how do you determine if your partner has chronic issues with immaturity? How can you know if this is a primary cause of the frustrations you are feeling in your relationship?

Here are some ways to tell:

1. You didn't just check a couple of items on the lists above—you found yourself checking a lot of them.

   Your partner might have two or three issues on this list because he's "quirky" or "he has a couple of issues" or "certain subjects push his buttons." But if you're seeing a pattern where many of these characteristics seem to fit him, you're looking at immaturity.

2. You know what his parents' style was, or the other adults who were his key influences growing up, and it fits the picture.

   If he was overcatered to growing up, especially if it was combined with emotional harshness or lack of attention to his emotional needs, that's a good clue.

3. He keeps messing things up for himself.

   Notice whether his behavior seems to mostly cause problems just for you, or if he suffers a lot of negative consequences of his actions himself. If he is making himself miserable, that's likely to indicate immaturity. On the other hand, if things seem to work out okay for him, but you end up being harmed repeatedly by his behavior, that suggests that another problem is in play; you may, for example, be looking at the beginning stages of abusiveness, which we will discuss in Chapter 5.

4. His failure to take charge of his own life is driving you crazy.

   One way to discern the key problems in your relationship is to watch your own feelings. If you feel like you are living with a little child, and the frustration is starting to make you want to scream, your own reactions are a clue that your partner is refusing to grow up. If, on the other hand, there are other problems that feel much more pressing—let's say your partner behaves in ways that are bizarre or impossible to explain, or he puts a higher priority on partying than on being with you, or he calls you demeaning names and you feel intimidated by his anger—then you may find that the chapters ahead speak more directly to your primary concerns.

THE IMPACT ON YOUR LIFE

You need a partner who is just that: a partner. He should be an equal to you, sharing the planning and decision making, helping keep track of the many things that have to be taken care of in a couple's life, and carrying his weight. He should not be someone that you have to look after, harangue, and in other ways raise like a child. This becomes even more true if you have a family or are planning one; the presence of children in the home quadruples the workload and the number of details that have to be kept track of. If you are a mom or will be soon, you can't afford to have your partner hanging around expecting you to take care of *him*.

Living with an adult who refuses to grow up is exhausting. You may have days when you feel like he's just in the way of everything, like a child who has left toys strewn across the whole house. Do you want to go out? He's in the way because he's not ready to go, or because he's whining about the local restaurants, or because he's staying home but he can't figure out the basics of how to look after the children. Do you want to save up some money to get a reliable car? He's impeding progress because he refuses to spend responsibly and has to have his special (expensive) parts for his model-train collection. Do you want to get the house cleaned up? His stuff is all over place, and when you try to get him to help, he spends the next hour getting one sink meticulously clean, during which time you vacuum the entire house, pick up all of his crap, and make sandwiches.

This lifestyle is not likely to build your self-opinion. Do you find yourself wondering, "Why am I so crabby? Why do I get so impatient? Why do I feel some days like I want him to go live somewhere else, and we can get together on the weekends? Why are my nerves so frayed?" These are the predictable effects of living with a partner who is thinking primarily about himself and doesn't have the energy to share the meeting of your needs. There's a good chance the problem isn't you at all.

An immature partner has other predictable effects on a relationship. You are likely to find that you are constantly squabbling over little things, and that you find yourself saying, "I can't believe we're arguing about this. This is so stupid. Why does every little thing have to be a problem?" You may start to have trouble getting things done yourself, not because his issues are contagious but because your time is being eaten up with managing aspects of life and home that he should have attended to. It may be hard to get in the mood for lovemaking from the accumulation of irritations, and also because you are just plain tired out from doing everything.

CAN HE GROW UP?

Beginning in Chapter 7, we will be taking you through the steps for assessing what kind of growth your partner is capable of, and how to insist that he get down to business. There is no reliable way to figure out quickly whether he is going to mature or not. Maturing takes years, and in some ways it's harder to do it as an adult than as a child; development comes most easily when it is following the natural schedule. But here are some factors that can give you a very rough idea of how big a challenge you face in the time ahead, starting with the bad signs and then looking at the good.

He's less likely to mature if:

- His parents or other relatives are still running his life.
- He's older. (With each passing decade, the chances reduce that he'll ever step up.)
- He drinks or drugs.
- He has friends who are just as immature as he is.
- He is extremely self-centered (meaning that he interprets everything that goes on around him in terms of how it affects him, and refuses to consider how his behavior is contributing to his problems with people), or he has a personality disorder (explained in Chapter 4).
- He is verbally abusive or demeaning to you, or is sometimes intimidating.

He's more likely to mature if:

- He's younger.
- He is getting unhooked from a childlike relationship to his family of origin.

- He does not have an addiction.
- He's fundamentally kind.
- He's got some friends or relatives in his life who are better role models.
- You're not afraid to stand up to him and set clear limits, and it is safe to do so.

But as we will see in Part II of this book, the factor that will end up having a greater impact than any of these is his willingness to look honestly at himself, work hard to grow and change, and make it a top priority to build and keep a good, loving relationship with you. We believe you're worth it, and we hope he comes to see it that way, too. To bring him to the point of realizing your value, however, you are likely to have to start talking seriously about the possibility that your relationship may not work out; unfortunately, the chronically immature man tends to stay stuck unless the stakes are high.

IMMATURITY AS A SIGN OF DEEPER PROBLEMS

In the chapters ahead we will be looking at the other most common sources of unhealthy relationship behavior in men, including addiction, certain mental health problems, and abusiveness. A thorny issue, though, is that any of the problems we examine can also lead to immaturity and selfishness, though with different flavors.

So how do you know whether your partner's immaturity is just immaturity, or whether it's a symptom of one of these more challenging underlying problems?

The best way to answer this question for yourself is to take the time to read the next three chapters carefully, even if you don't believe your partner has these other problems. When you get to the end of Part I, you'll have all the information you need to figure out whether you have to worry about additional concerns or not.

In the meantime, here is a quick assessment you can take regarding your relationship to help you get an early read on the role that immaturity is playing.

For each of the items below (A–I) circle the choice that best describes your day-to-day experience in your relationship (leave the item blank if none of the answers is really a good fit):

(A) HE MAKES ME FEEL:
1. Torn down or intimidated.
2. Frustrated.
3. Like a low priority.

(B) WHEN I VOICE COMPLAINTS:
1. He's nasty or retaliatory, so I end up paying for having raised the grievance.
2. He seems to get it, but nothing changes. I'm wasting my breath. He makes lots of excuses in a whiny, victimized tone.
3. He has an endless series of excuses that he makes in a defensive, irritated tone.

(C) HE GREW UP IN A HOME WHERE:
1. His father or stepfather was abusive or demeaning to his mother.
2. His parents let him get away with too much or catered to him too much, or both.
3. One or more adults abused him.

(D) IF HE'S NOT THE CENTER OF ATTENTION:
1. He gets mad later.
2. He gets whiny later.
3. He does whatever it takes to make sure that he is always the center of attention.

(E) WHEN I ASK HIM TO MAKE CHANGES:
1. He makes me feel like I'm a bad person for needing him to make any changes.
2. He will eventually make small changes, but it's so much work.
3. He keeps appearing to make changes, but then things go back to exactly where they were before.

(F) WHEN I TALK TO HIM:
1. He doesn't listen to anything I say and doesn't respect my opinions.
2. He seems to hear me but then nothing ever really gets through.
3. He seems like he's in another world.

(G) HE USUALLY HANGS OUT WITH:

1. Guys who are disrespectful toward their own partners or speak in demeaning ways about women in general.
2. People who are all still into the same things they were into in high school.
3. People who seem to get him into trouble.

(H) WHEN IT COMES TO HIS PAST PARTNERS:

1. He tends to either disparage them or idolize them.
2. He was very dependent on them.
3. They were people who used to party with him.

(I) WHEN YOU THINK OF BREAKING UP WITH HIM YOU FEEL:

1. Afraid of what he might do to you.
2. Concerned that he won't be able to take care of himself.
3. Afraid that he might harm himself.

ANSWER KEY:

The number one answers are signs of abusiveness.

The number two answers are signs of immaturity.

The number three answers are signs of addiction (A, B, E, F, G, H, I) or of mental health problems (B, C, D, E, I).

What If He Seems to Be Somewhere in the Middle?

One of the central concepts of this book is that while some men who are exhibiting unhealthy behavior in relationships have one distinct problem at the root, others are operating from a mixture of overlapping issues. We don't recommend trying to stretch your partner's behavior to squeeze it into one category, like a doctor trying to come up with a diagnosis for a disease. Go with what your instincts are telling you, even if they tell you that he has "a little of everything."

One way to clarify your view of your partner is this: Take out a piece of paper. At the top center, write "Annoying/Looking for a mother/Irresponsible." About halfway down the right side, write "Addicted (to anything)." About halfway down the left side, write "Not emotionally well, does things that make no sense," and at the bottom center, "Disrespectful/Bullying/Intimidating/ Abusive." Then pick a point on that page to put a dot, wherever you feel is the closest to your partner's core issues as you see them now.

Your assessment of him may change as you read the coming chapters, which show you in detail how to assess how much each of these issues applies to him. But making this gut-level assessment now gives you a starting place to begin your mulling over of the questions we will be putting before you.

How Do the Solutions Differ?

In Part II, we will cover in detail the actions you can take to create the best likelihood that your partner will decide to deal with his issues. For now we will give just a preview of that discussion. Here are some examples of how the opening steps we recommend to you will differ based on the distinctions covered in the next few chapters:

WHERE THE PRIMARY PROBLEM IS HIS IMMATURITY:
- Set firm limits for his behavior.
- Be very forceful with him, with a no-nonsense tone (but not mean).
- Refuse to keep helping him do things he needs to do for himself; let him create his own messes and suffer his own consequences.
- Encourage him toward self-exploration through therapy, meditation, yoga, self-help books, men's groups, and other avenues to growth.
- Let him know that you are reaching your limit and that you are thinking about the possibility that you might have to break up.

WHERE THE PRIMARY PROBLEM IS HIS ADDICTION:
- Demand that he acknowledge that his addictive behavior is a problem.
- Tell him he needs to participate in an outpatient substance abuse program, go to a detox, or participate in peer-led groups such as a twelve-step program (the ones that end in "Anonymous").
- Refuse to have the substance in the house at all.
- Insist that he needs either to severely curtail or to completely give up his use of the substance (not just use "a little less" than he was doing before),

and that he needs to make a complete lifestyle change including a new social circle.

- Let him know that you are considering the possibility of breaking up, and tell him clearly what your conditions are for staying together.

WHERE THE PRIMARY PROBLEM IS HIS MENTAL HEALTH (INCLUDING TRAUMA, PERSONALITY DISORDER, AND DEPRESSION):

- Encourage or demand appropriate professional help, such as Trauma Focused Cognitive Behavioral Therapy (for trauma survivors), Dialectical Behavioral Therapy (for personality disorders), and other therapeutic modalities (for depression).
- Provide him with written resources (we will be suggesting books and Web sites that you can point him toward) that will help him understand his problems.
- Make it clear to him that you do not blame him for his mental health problems, but at the same time that he has to accept responsibility for how his behavior and extreme emotional states are affecting you.
- Tell him that he is going to have to get help and make changes for you to be able to stay in the relationship.

WHERE THE PRIMARY PROBLEM IS HIS ABUSIVENESS:

- Make your own safety, and the safety of your children, your highest priority, and reach out for support . Assess what level of danger you are in (see Chapter 18).
- Consider using the legal system, such as by calling the police or seeking a protective order.
- Look for ways to impose consequences on him for his actions.
- Encourage him to participate in a specialized abuser program (known as "Batterer Intervention") whether he is physically violent or not.
- Do all of the following that you believe you can try safely:
  - Demand respectful behavior from him, with no excuses.
  - Insist that he accept responsibility for his actions (and especially that he doesn't get to blame you for what he does).
  - Tell him you are considering ending the relationship.
- If the risk assessment in Chapter 18 leads you to conclude that you are in danger, call an abused women's hotline right away.

You will notice that each group of suggestions includes raising the possibility of ending your relationship. We want your relationship to work out for you. At the same time, our experience is that men who have these kinds of destructive issues don't tend to address their issues seriously until the relationship is on the line, though sometimes they will be motivated to look at their issues if they find themselves in severe financial or legal difficulties.

There are other common themes across the four categories listed above: your partner has to treat you with respect, he has to admit that he has issues and take charge of working on them, and he has to accept responsibility for his actions.

Finally, regardless of what your partner's primary issues are—or if he's got a mixture of all of them—you will need to make your own well-being a priority. We will be guiding you through many avenues to strengthening yourself, which will include the critical element of expanding your sources of emotional support.

The Risk of Mistaking Abusiveness for Immaturity

The successful approach to dealing with a man who has failed to grow up, as we will discuss in Part II, is for you to take on the mind-set of a parent. You will need to be firm with your partner, set limits, confront him forcefully at times, and "lay down the law." However, this same approach to dealing with a man who is abusive can be dangerous; in fact, if your partner's behavior includes any elements that frighten or intimidate you, or that involve hurting you or your children, we will be recommending that you exercise caution in how you challenge him on his abusiveness. Abusive men can become retaliatory and violent when challenged, and strategies for proceeding safely have to be considered carefully. We do not mean that you will automatically have less success with an abuser; a selfish, whiny, stuck man can be nearly as tough a nut to crack as an abuser. But the risk to you of taking him on is much less.

We therefore recommend strongly that you read Chapter 5 carefully before taking steps to confront your partner about his immature behavior. If after reading that chapter you determine that abusiveness is a significant contributor to your partner's behavior problems, you will want to draw in outside resources and follow our other recommendations carefully.

At the same time, most of the work we will be guiding you through in the chapters ahead *will apply to you equally regardless of the source of your partner's behavior.* A woman can underestimate the difficulty of her circumstances by thinking, "Oh, he's just immature, it's all going to be okay." The reality is that living with a chronically immature partner can take a great toll on you, and years can slip away as you try to get him to grow up. We want to see you in the life that you deserve, and don't want you to sell yourself short. You have just as much of a place with us in the process that this book teaches as the woman who is involved with an alcoholic, or a combat veteran, or a violent rager, and you will enjoy the benefits of the rewarding work that lies ahead.

Finish out this section by writing briefly in response to the following two exercises:

EXERCISE 2–1:

Describe your life as it would be if your partner could meet you as an equal. How would he support and encourage you? How would he challenge you? How would his life inspire and stimulate yours? In what ways would he be like a best friend to you (even if he wouldn't literally be your best friend)? How would you two be a team?

EXERCISE 2–2:

Write about yourself as a mature person. What choices or sacrifices have you made that demonstrate your process of growing up? What aspects of yourself feel the most adultlike to you? What areas are there where you feel you still need to mature further? Are there ways in which your partner is holding your growth back?

THREE

Is the Problem Addiction?

"I don't think he's alcoholic—I mean, he never even really gets drunk. He just has a couple of drinks in the evening to unwind."

"He gets really upset if I bring up his weed smoking. He says he's sick of me nagging him about it and it's not a problem for him."

"He doesn't drink that much unless he's around his relatives—then he gets hammered."

"I get scared when he's been drinking—he's like a different person sometimes."

"He says he's not using, but I don't get where all the money goes. And he's always complaining that he has a cold, like all through the year."

"How do I know when it's too much? I seem to be the only one that's bothered by his partying."

"Is his drinking going to affect our kids? I mean, so far I don't think they even notice anything, but will they later?"

"It turns out he's been cheating on me a lot. I feel horrible. And he's saying he can't control it because he's a sex addict."

ALCOHOL AND DRUG addiction affect many millions of people across the continent, tearing apart the lives of innumerable families. Yet substance abuse is still widely misunderstood, and myths and misconceptions abound about addiction in general. If you are wondering whether addiction is playing a role in the struggles you are having in your relationship, the pages ahead will help you to answer that question for yourself—and to start thinking about what action to take if the answer is "yes."

Other addictions besides substance abuse—gambling, overeating, pornography, for instance—can bring harm to relationships. Although we focus primarily on alcohol and drugs in this chapter, you can apply most of the principles to any addiction you suspect your partner may have. We need to express our reservations, however, about the claims by some men that they are "sex addicts." While there may be rare cases where this is true, we find that men who grab onto this label are usually attempting to escape responsibility for demeaning their partners by cheating on them, and have deep habits of using and manipulating women. These tend to be men who have trouble taking women seriously as human beings and as equal partners.

Before we try to nail down the question of whether or not your partner has an addiction, we need to look at some common beliefs about alcohol and drug abuse that aren't accurate. These misconceptions could throw you off the track, and leave you confused in thinking about your partner's partying habits.

MYTHS ABOUT ADDICTION

"The life of an alcoholic or drug addict completely falls apart."

The image of the drunk in the movies tends to be a man who loses his job, drinks away every penny he earns, and ends up sleeping in the bushes. But many addicts continue functioning pretty well on one or more fronts in their lives, including holding down positions of considerable responsibility. Some alcoholics never get drunk; they anesthetize themselves daily with a lower level of alcohol, say two or three drinks. Some cocaine addicts manage to conceal their drug dependency for years. The effects of addiction on this style of user isn't that he ends up on the street; his problem will tend to manifest itself more in avoiding close relationships, sleeping poorly (and other signs of deteriorating physical health), battling with depression, immaturity and selfishness, and avoiding responsibility.

If you can see that your partner's substance use is taking a toll on you and on your relationship, then he's got a problem even if he's managing to hold other aspects of his life together.

"Substance abusers are immoral lowlifes."

Addicts can be well-meaning people who have no interest in trying to hurt other people. Many alcoholic men, for example, are not vicious or violent to their wives or girlfriends; contrary to popular misconception, alcoholism and abusiveness are two separate problems, though they sometimes come together. Many addicts are law-abiding—except for violating laws against drug use—and believe in living ethical lives. Their ethics do tend to slip over time, as you might expect, with their dishonesty increasing to try to cover their drinking and drugging and cover their work or financial failings. But if we're expecting substance abusers to be bad people, most of them will succeed in flying under our radar.

"Substance abusers drink and drug constantly."

Patterns of use actually vary greatly among different addicts. Some alcoholics, for example, confine their drinking to weekends, but then drink a week's worth in a short time. There are binge addicts whose use may be even more spread out than that, perhaps going many weeks without the substance, and then using it nonstop for days at a time until they are completely depleted physically and unsure of where they have been. This style of person still has steady involvement with the substance, because he is fantasizing about his next party and planning for it all the time; but because he doesn't actually drink or drug every day, the depth of his psychological dependence on the substance is hidden.

"Alcoholic men are cruel and violent to their wives."

Alcoholism and abusiveness are two very separate problems. There are men with terrible drinking problems who don't threaten or hit or rape their wives, and who aren't even verbally abusive most of the time. And there are vicious abusers who never touch a drop of alcohol. Alcohol and family violence are so frequently linked in movies and television dramas that most people have been led to believe that they automatically go together. This misconception can leave a woman confused about what is going on in her relationship. In the words of a woman we spoke with just recently:

"I've been married for almost fifteen years, and my husband has never called me names, or torn me down, or even really tried to control me. And yet, I come out feeling so abused. I really do. His drinking has caused me so much pain. I feel invisible, like he just goes off to a world where I don't matter, or don't even exist. He stops caring at all about what this is doing to me, and to our family . . . And sometimes I feel invisible not just with him, but with other people, 'cause they're like, 'He's nice to you, so what's the big deal if he drinks?' I wish they had to live it for a while and see what it's like."

How Much Is Too Much?

People who are held in the grip of an addiction either insist that nothing is wrong, or they acknowledge the problem but minimize it, asserting that they just need to "slow down a bit" or "get it a little more under control." In the face of this denial, you may find yourself wondering, "Well, does he have a problem or doesn't he?"

To move toward finding an answer, spend a few minutes on the following exercise.

EXERCISE 3–1: EVALUATING WHETHER HE HAS AN ADDICTION PROBLEM

Answer the following questions about your partner's use of alcohol or drugs, or other behavior that makes you worry about addiction. Some of your answers may be more than just a few words, so we recommend writing in your journal if you have one.

1. Over time, have you noticed his use getting heavier (larger quantities), more frequent, or both?

2. Has he been in legal trouble because of his use anytime in the last several years?

3. Does he lie about his use or make it sound like less than it is? Is he secretive about his behavior or his whereabouts? Does he have certain "friends" that he doesn't seem to want you to meet or know about?

4. Does he seem to spend a lot of money on his habit? Has his use ever gotten him (or you, or your family) into a financial jam? Is financial planning for the future made harder by his habit?

5. Has his substance use put you at risk in any way? For example, have you ever been frightened by driving with him after he's been using?

6. Has he engaged in risky behavior or broken the law in order to continue his use?

7. Have you ever felt you had to lie for him about it?

8. Has his use had an impact on your own work or career? Have you had to change the way you live at all because of his drinking or drug use?

9. Have you ever felt embarrassed in front of other people because of his use? Have you had to make explanations or excuses for him, for example when he fails to show up somewhere because he's drinking?

10. Are his addictive habits affecting your children in any way? Has your life as a parent been made more difficult? Are your dreams for family life being altered?

11. Are his habits taking leisure time away from you (for example, because you always have to be the one to look after the children)? Are you spending leisure time differently than you would have otherwise?

12. Does he use his habit as an excuse for bad behavior?

13. How have you changed your life in order to cope with your partner's substance use?

14. Are there ways we haven't asked about in which your partner's use patterns have hurt you or been bad for you?

15. Have you increased your own use of substances now that you are with him? If yes, does this concern you at all? If you are in recovery from alcohol or drug addiction yourself, has your partner's use made it harder for you to stay clean and sober?

16. What do you imagine your life would be like if your partner didn't use alcohol or drugs, or used only occasionally and moderately? Do you ever find yourself wishing for that?

As you may be sensing from the process of answering the questions above, deciding whether your partner fits the accepted definitions of "alcoholic" or "addict" is not really what matters most; the critical issue is evaluating the toll his use is taking on you. If his drinking is causing problems in your life, then he's a problem drinker. If you have to worry about how much weed he's smoking, then he's smoking too much. If you are disturbed by his use of pornography, that probably means he's hooked on it.

At the same time, the list we have just taken you through does point to many of the established definitions of a substance abuser, as we will see.

The Key Characteristics of Addiction

Regardless of the particular "drug of choice" involved—which is likely to be alcohol, weed, or harder drugs, but sometimes is money (for those addicted to gambling), food (for those addicted to overeating), or pornography—addicted people tend to exhibit some consistent patterns and dynamics:

The Centrality of the Substance

As an addiction develops and advances, the pleasure that the addict associates with using the substance increasingly takes over and previous interests and ambitions fall away. Over time, he comes to a point where getting to his next "high" becomes his singular purpose; whatever other activities he engages in he sees either as means to get to the substance, or as obstacles, or as distractions to wait out.

Mounting Selfishness and Self-Centeredness

The addicted person starts to live in a dizzying cycle that goes:

Intense pleasure

The fading of that pleasure

Negative aftereffects

↓

Emotional distress (some of it from the effects of use and some of it from
other aspects of his life, including wounds from the past)

↓

Overwhelming longing to use the substance again

↓

Back to intense pleasure, and round and round

Picturing what it is like to live in this cycle, you can imagine that the addict is going to have less and less space to consider the needs and feelings of other people. His own needs grow in size and urgency, and other people's needs come to seem like annoyances to him, blocking his way from getting back to pleasure and staying there as long as possible. And in order to justify living this way, he is likely to develop more and more reasons why other people shouldn't be bothering him, and why he shouldn't be made answerable for the effects his behavior is having.

Over time, he comes more and more to simply define anyone who gets in his way as a jerk, and to completely deny responsibility for his choices. Everything becomes someone else's fault—and if he has a partner, she is a particularly likely place for him to lay the blame.

Changing Friendship Network

The addicted person gravitates, either gradually or rapidly, toward people who will laugh and joke with him about his drinking or drugging, who don't mind being around him when he is under the influence, and who won't bother him with reminders about reality. Who are these people going to be? As you can guess, the people most likely to fit the bill are other substance abusers. The next most likely are people whose personality style accommodates the addict, who gloss over obvious problems and avoid confrontation, no matter how necessary, and who are easy for him to manipulate.

Mounting Secrecy and Dishonesty

The more an addiction progresses, the more the addict tends to live a dual life: the one when he's using or procuring, and the one when he isn't. He strives to keep the people he knows in his "not-high life" from discovering the full extent of what he is doing in his "high life," including the disasters that are brewing. He has to cover up numerous facts, including the amount of money he is spending on his drug of choice, the time it is eating up in his life, the failure to come through for his children, or crimes that he is committing.

The addicted person orients his financial life more and more toward opportunities to procure and use his drug of choice. These poor decisions then lead him to have to hide from loved ones the economic mess he has created, and cause him to become slick at making up reasons for borrowing money from people and failing to pay them back.

The Downward Spiral

The pleasure that the addict gains from using tends to decrease over time, even as the addiction intensifies. One of the marks (and ironies) of addiction is that the person continues to have a powerful reluctance to give up the behavior even after it has started to make him feel terrible. In fact, the damage that the addict's behavior is doing to him, and to other people, intensifies his desire to use, as he scrambles to escape the pain and shame of it all. Recovered alcoholics often report that their sense of shame got worse and worse as the months and years passed, but the effect was just to tie them more tightly to the need to drink.

Damage to Health

Alcohol, drugs, and other addictions cause increasing risks to physical well-being the longer the addiction runs. Substance abusers develop weakened immune systems, making them vulnerable to frequent illness. Alcoholics can suffer liver damage and numerous other long-term deleterious effects. Some substances, including alcohol and many drugs (though not weed) are physically addictive, which means the body comes to depend on the presence of the substance and will fall ill if the substance is removed.

Tolerance

Typically, a substance abuser will go through a period during which his body appears to become inured to the substance, so that it takes more and more of it to make him "high"—and therefore his behavior can become more severely unhealthy as he becomes willing to go to greater and greater lengths to get his hands on his drug of choice. As the addiction progresses this tolerance can flip, so that an alcoholic, for example, may have a later phase where a very small amount of alcohol will intoxicate him.

EXERCISE 3–2:

Circle the headings of any of the sections above that seem to fit your partner. After doing that, give yourself ten or fifteen minutes to sit quietly, listen to music, or go outside for a walk. Allow your thoughts and feelings to be what they are.

WHAT IF ALL THIS INFORMATION IS POINTING TO "YES"?

If your process of digesting the concepts and questions in this chapter is leading you to conclude that your partner has an addiction, we are going to encourage you to take steps to address it. (However, if your reading of Chapter 5 indicates to you that he also has a problem with abusiveness, we want you to think carefully about your own safety as you decide when and how to confront him about his addictive behavior.)

You may read a book or peruse a Web site that tells you "not to try to control the alcoholic," and that you have to accept that he'll only stop drinking when he decides to himself. You may be told that he'll only deal with his addictions if he "hits bottom," meaning that his life falls apart so completely that his pain becomes too great for the substance to take away. According to these philosophies, if you get angry at the alcoholic or criticize him, you are just further harming his self-esteem, which in turn feeds his drinking problem.

In examining these kinds of advice, a great deal of sifting and selecting is necessary. Some of the commonly accepted "truisms" about substance abuse are actually harmful messages when given to the female partner of the addict.

So, let's begin with the accurate points in these frameworks. It is indeed true that in day-to-day life, you can't control how much your partner drinks (or drugs or gambles). If you try to hide his liquor, or throw beers in the trash, check his pockets to make sure he has no money to buy drinks with, or beg him not to go out, you will be hitting your head against a wall. He will find a way to get around you every time—nothing short of incarceration will stop an alcoholic who is determined to wrap his hands around his next drink, or the drug-dependent person pursuing his next high. You will trap yourself into hoping that your maneuvers can someday chase his problem away, and your frustration will grow.

But it isn't true that there is nothing you can do, and it's even less true that you should stuff away all of your natural reactions, including your anger and resentment.

Taking Action

According to a study discussed in the book *No More Letting Go* by Debra Jay, 73 percent of male substance abusers who got sober said that pressure they were under from friends and family was the main reason why they finally became motivated to deal with their addiction. If you have ever watched the A&E reality show *Intervention*, you've seen examples of loved ones of alcoholics taking dramatic action that combines bluntness with caring. In these kinds of interventions, friends and relatives of the substance abuser support one another, make a plan together, and coordinate efforts in finding a time and place to confront him. During the intervention the people present speak from the heart about their love for the addict and about what they see him doing to himself, and to them all, through his selfish and irresponsible behavior. Clearly, confrontation can sometimes work.

Because some alcoholics and drug addicts are also abusive or violent, either occasionally or often, we are not saying that confrontation is always a good idea; you need to decide for yourself whether you can challenge your partner safely, based on how he has reacted when you have attempted to call him to account (on any issue) in the past.

But if you do not have serious concerns about retaliation, letting your partner see what his behavior is doing to your life, and to your children, is likely to do more good than harm. And it could save you some of the negative effects of stuffing all your bad feelings away.

In the chapters ahead, we discuss many strategies for persuading a destructive partner to change, regardless of the specific source of his behavior, and for evaluating whether he is serious about taking meaningful steps or not. We recognize that there is a debate about whether alcoholism should be considered a "disease," but there is no need to resolve that question here; what matters is that the alcoholic plays a huge part in his own future and is not helpless. The same kinds of choices, habits, and values that propel the behavior of an abusive man, or a personality-disordered man (see Chapters 4 and 5), take a leading role with the addicted man as well.

ALCOHOL AND DRUGS IN COMBINATION WITH OTHER ISSUES

Alcoholism, drug abuse, and other addictions, in addition to being a source of unhealthy behavior in themselves, can feed other destructive issues that a man has. For example, an abusive man who also drinks and drugs tends to be even more verbally vicious and has a greater potential for becoming dangerously violent.

At the same time, getting an abuser clean and sober will *not* stop his abusiveness; at best it *may* lessen the extremes of his dangerousness and make him be mean a little less often, but it won't necessarily even do that. We have worked with many women who pinned their hopes on sobriety: "If I can just get him to stop drinking, then he won't be mean to me, he'll stop getting into his scary rages, he'll stop cheating on me."

The reality is that abusiveness and substance addiction are two separate issues, and some men have them both. If he gets clean and sober, that creates the *possibility* that he could also do the work of dealing with his other issues—which he certainly never would have done while actively abusing substances—but there is no guarantee that he will choose to do so. He will have to work as hard on his abusiveness, or on his personality disorder, as he does on his recovery from addiction. If he doesn't, his treatment of you will remain as destructive, or nearly as destructive, as it has been so far. We regret to say that we have worked with many men who were willing to face up to alcoholism, but then dug their heels in hard when it came time to admit that they were abusive or had a mental health disorder. They tended, in fact, to try to blame everything on the substance.

A SPECIAL NOTE ABOUT ADDICTION TO PORNOGRAPHY

We believe it is extremely difficult for a man who is a heavy user of pornography to have a healthy relationship with a woman, because the sexuality portrayed in pornography is so devoid of love and tenderness, and is so often disturbing and degrading to women. Pornography often portrays outright rape and other kinds of violence as sexy, feeding attitudes of contempt and aggression toward females. One study found a remarkably high percentage of women (around 25 percent) reporting that they had experienced some degree of pressure from their partners to carry out acts that the men had learned about from pornography, and that the women found distasteful or demeaning. Even if his use of videos, magazines, and Web sites does not directly lead to sexual mistreatment of you, it will condition him to have trouble taking you seriously as a person, and to be selfish and demanding of catering from you. And perhaps most important of all, his imaginary relationship with the women in the photographs is a form of constant mental cheating on you, and means that he is focused on what he wishes you were—more like the women in pornography—and not on who you really are.

EXERCISE 3–3:

We now would like you to reflect some on what it has been like to absorb the information we have covered so far. Here are some specific questions to help you do that.

1. Are you feeling upset by the number of signs you are seeing that your partner's substance use (or other addictive behavior) is at a problem level? Is part of you reluctant to accept that he could have an addiction problem? What are the implications for your life if he does have a problem?

2. Is part of you eager to believe that he *does* have an addiction, because it would explain certain aspects of his behavior? What mysteries would it solve for you? Do you feel any temptation to blame problems of his on substance use that may actually come from another source, such as abusiveness?

3. If your partner were sober and substance-free, are there other things you think would still be preventing him from being a safe, loving, and forward-moving partner?

OVERCOMING ADDICTION

Most of what we describe in the chapters ahead about how to motivate your partner to change, and what that change process will involve if he takes it on, applies to substance abuse as well as other addictions. There are numerous books and web sites listed in the "Resources" section of this book for overcoming alcoholism, drug addiction, compulsive gambling, overeating, and pornography addiction. As with all the sources of unhealthy behavior that we explain and discuss in this book, your partner will need to accept that he has a problem, and that you are not the cause of that problem, before he will be able to begin turning things around.

One key difference in the change process for substance abusers, compared to men struggling with the other issues we discuss in this book, is that they are dealing with some pronounced physical effects from the addiction. Therefore, for about the first six months of your partner's recovery, he will need to be focused on taking care of himself. As his brain chemistry works to normalize itself, he is likely to be struggling with a body and mind that don't feel right at all, and he may be just plain physically ill some of the time. Note also that his mood is likely to be the opposite of what it was when he was on his substance; if he was energized before, he may be depressed and lethargic. On the other hand, if he was mellow on his substance, he could get anxious, panicky, or even manic as he works to recover.

There are additional dynamics you are likely to observe if your partner gets serious about turning clean and sober:

- He will have to learn how to adequately make amends. Chances are he did not have the ability to be there for you about your negative feelings before he began to get sober. Once he has stopped using, he must learn to cope with his own shame so that he can focus on you and take it in while you feel and express your hurt and resentment over time.
- At first he may well connect more easily with people who are also in recovery than he will with you. It will be easier for him to feel close to people who are cheering for him and whom he has not repeatedly harmed (so he doesn't feel ashamed around them). Although this is a predictable dynamic, it may still feel unfair to you, and you have the right to be bothered by it and speak out about how it affects you.
- He may go through periods when he attempts to bargain with you about his use, in order to avoid the hard work of really dealing with his addiction. He may, for example, try to make deals with you about how much he can use, and refuse to get professional guidance.

With respect to the last point, we have worked with women who have confronted their partners on their addictions, and a common response from the man is to offer her a test, such as: "How about this? I'll stop drinking [or using drugs, etc.] anytime you and I are together. Then we'll see if things get better between us. If not, then we'll know the problem is *us,* not my using." There are a couple of reasons this kind of bargain won't reveal whether the addiction is truly a problem:

1. If he's using the rest of the time, then he's still keeping a close relationship with his addiction. That means that when he's with you, he will be thinking about and planning for his next use. This fantasy life in an addict can cause as many problems as actual use does.

2. Not using when he's around you can make him irritable and moody, because he has developed the habit of relying on his substance as his top coping skill. His addiction helps him tolerate the pressures of life and relationships; he may, for example, have deep shame, rage, or grief that he manages to just barely hold at bay through his addiction. When he forces himself to be sober around you, feelings will tend to come up for him that he has not yet learned how to deal with in any healthy way (the kinds of skills he would get in a substance abuse treatment program, for example). So, predictably, the relationship between the two of you will get worse. He then can blame you: "You see all the problems we have? And I'm not getting high/drinking around you! It's not me, it's us."

Remember, these are all distractions from the real problem—his addiction.

EXERCISE 3–4:

Complete your work for this chapter putting thoughts of your partner aside and writing for a few minutes about yourself, using these two questions as a guide:

1. Describe some of your strengths in staying away from addictive behaviors. What has given you strength in this area? What can you be proud of in the way you work to keep your life free from substance abuse? What are some good messages you have taught your children about this?

2. Are there points from this chapter that lead you to think that you might have your own issues of addictive behavior? If so, how could you get some support and assistance regarding this? Is there a friend you would trust enough to share your concerns with? (Refer also to the "Resources" section.)

FOUR

Is the Problem His Mental Health?

"I can see that Jake really suffers; he has a very hard life. He comes from a family that did really twisted stuff to him. But now I feel like I'm getting the brunt of it."

"Yeah, Sam is controlling. But I mean about everything. If you interrupt him before he stirs his coffee sixteen times counterclockwise—really, I'm not kidding—he just loses it."

"When Josh came back from Afghanistan, things got a little crazy. Sometimes he would seem like he was possessed, or like he thought he was back in the war zone. It got scary."

"Tom was caught stealing a ton of money from where he worked. He may end up spending some time in jail. But the weird thing is that he doesn't seem to feel bad about doing it at all—just about getting caught. He's kind of laughing about it, and saying what a jerk the owner was."

OUR DETECTIVE WORK continues, as we try to tease out what exactly is keeping the man in your life from being able to be a good partner to you. You may already have found your key answers in the earlier chapters; central pieces may be falling into place, giving you a feeling of "Aha—that's it!" But it's also possible that we haven't yet put our finger on your partner's pulse, and we'll need to do some more sifting to close in on his unique traits, the essential causes of his unhealthy patterns.

If the issues we've described so far in this book don't capture your partner well enough, reflect on your reactions to the following statements, and then circle "true" or "false" for each one:

My partner can get mean or intimidating sometimes, but in between those incidents he doesn't try to control my life; he doesn't interfere with my friendships, he's not extremely jealous, and he seems to want my life to go well. Most days he really doesn't seem to be trying to tear me down or criticize me. Then he'll just erupt out of nowhere, and it's hard to tell why.

TRUE   FALSE

My partner hurts me more by what he doesn't do than by what he does do. He sleeps a lot or zones out in front of the television. He used to like to do things, but now his motivation is gone. And he used to help with things, but now he expects me to do everything. He's not mean to me, but I come out feeling like he doesn't value me much.

TRUE   FALSE

My partner sometimes seems to relive happenings from his past in ways that are disturbing or even scary. He seems to be in the grip of old demons.

TRUE   FALSE

My partner seems pretty good as long as we don't get too close. But if we start to feel too much in love, or we start to be sexual often, he always pulls far away from me. Sometimes he's a little nasty about it and makes it my fault, like he's pulling away because of some shortcoming I have, and other times he just pulls away with no explanation. He doesn't seem to be able to handle emotional or physical intimacy for very long.

TRUE   FALSE

Sometimes he seems like he's controlled by his own patterns. The behaviors aren't usually directed at me, but if I get in the way of his doing what he feels he has to do, he'll get very angry with me. I feel like he's off in his own world a lot, like his life is a private conversation he's having with himself. Other people notice it sometimes, too. I'm not sure he's really okay.

TRUE   FALSE

He seems to have a distorted sense of who he is. He thinks he's always just about to have some great success, like he's going to write this great novel, or make this great invention, or make some huge financial deal. I think he really believes in his own powers, but nothing ever seems to come of it. On some level I sense that he dislikes himself, but he comes off like he thinks he's really great, and it's this exaggerated thing, kind of like a fantasy almost.

TRUE   FALSE

If you have answered "true" to any of the above questions, it's possible that your partner is struggling with mental health challenges. We will take a look at some of the more common emotional difficulties found in men who are unable to handle close relationships well, focusing particularly on:

- the effects of earlier traumatic experiences ("post-trauma")
- a group of problems known as "personality disorders"
- depression

Questions that we will explore include:

- how to recognize if your partner's behavior is rooted in severely psychologically damaging experiences he has suffered in his past
- how emotional disturbances can combine with abusive attitudes and values to make an especially thorny tangle
- your partner's level of responsibility for his behavior even if he does have mental health problems, and even if "it isn't his fault that he got that way"

SURVIVING TRAUMA

"He doesn't talk about it much at all, but once he told me what he went through. When he's so explosive, I just keep wishing he'd have dealt with all of that in therapy or something. Then maybe he wouldn't be that way to me."

Does your partner have a background in which he has suffered severe violence or abuse, or shocking losses? Is he a combat veteran, for example? Did he grow up in a family where he was beaten, or where his mother was beaten? Did he grow up exposed to frightening and dangerous situations in his neighborhood? Has he ever been sexually assaulted, or have other severe emotional injuries in his past that you know about? If so, there's a good chance that he is suffering from the unhealed effects of trauma.

Psychological trauma is a severe emotional wound that is more than a person can tolerate, so it leaves him shaken to the core. A single traumatic event could be a time when he was badly frightened and physically harmed; it could be an experience of sexual violation; it could be the death of a parent when he was a child; it could be a time when he was left alone for a long time at a young age in a way that terrified him. Most adults who are suffering the effects of trauma have many such events in their histories, though, so the effects become compounded.

People can also suffer trauma from tragedies or outrages that they witness happening to someone else, especially if the person being harmed is a person they care about. This form of trauma is often less understood; yet research has found that witnesses to an assault, for example, can be as traumatized as the person who was the direct target.

Whatever the terrible events are, they reach a level that causes the person intense and lasting fear, helplessness, or horror in response. At the heart of trauma is a sense of complete helplessness combined with feeling abandoned by those who could or should have protected him or her.

Modern research has shown that the impact of trauma includes physical changes inside the brain and to brain chemistry. These changes can cause a lasting increase in the person's sensitivity to certain kinds of stress while simultaneously taking away some of the person's ability to handle that increase. He becomes overwhelmed by these emotional disruptions

"Uh-Oh: I Think *I* Have This."

As we look at some of the signs of psychological trauma in your partner, you may feel anxious because you recognize many or all of these symptoms in yourself. It may be true that you *and* your partner suffer from symptoms of trauma, or that he is not particularly traumatized but you are. If either of these scenarios is true, there is no need to panic; you will find extensive assistance in the chapters to come for examining and planning your own healing.

Discovering that you have some post-trauma effects does not mean that you are the primary cause of the problems in your relationship.

We want to underline this point because so many women who are in unhealthy relationships get accused by their partners of having mental health problems, typically accompanied by the man blaming his behavior on the woman's psychological issues. But in reality:

1. He is still responsible for his own behavior, regardless of what your issues may be, and
2. Your symptoms may well be in great part a result of your partner's treatment of you, especially if he has been demeaning or bullying (as we discuss in Chapter 5).

In other words, when you are trying to let him know how much his actions have harmed you, he has no right to come back with something like "Well, you are pretty messed up yourself, just look at you!" (which is a type of painful and confusing attack that some destructive partners tend to launch). We are keenly aware that by doing so he is reversing cause and effect, telling you that your wounds are the cause of his attacking behaviors, when in fact, your wounds are probably largely the *result* of his attacking behavior.

Even if you have been carrying some vulnerabilities from before you knew him, his attacks have undoubtedly had the effect of making your earlier wounds deeper, which we will say more about in a moment.

We do not believe that your partner has the right to refer to your wounds in this blaming and disparaging way. We will look in detail at what we believe are respectful and supportive ways your partner can express his awareness of the injuries you carry.

How your wounds are handled by him is one significant way of determining if your relationship is destructive.

We are not saying that you can avoid responsibility for dealing with your own emotional symptoms and your own behavior, or that he has caused all of your difficulties in life. We do mean, however, that it is important for you to deal with these challenges in a safe and supportive environment. This could also mean that you might need to take time away from your current relationship if you keep getting new emotional injuries, or keep having to focus on your partner rather than on your own healing needs. Severe stresses in your current life can trigger and worsen the effects of old wounds. This effect can be even greater if the new hurt takes a similar form to the old one; in other words, new violations can be potent triggers for past violations, intimidating behavior can reopen wounds from past terrors, and a partner's alcohol or drug abuse could feel like a stab into memories you have of growing up in an alcoholic home. Finding current peace and safety is crucial to getting the chance to heal from the past.

in a way that makes it hard to respond to the reasonable needs and expectations of others—which naturally will make intimate partnership extremely difficult.

COMMON AFTEREFFECTS OF PSYCHOLOGICAL TRAUMA

Let's reflect on your partner's emotional habits and his behaviors as we look at some of the common aftereffects of severe psychological injuries. After examining these questions, you will have a better sense of whether your partner needs to get help from a therapist or a program that specializes in healing from trauma.

Hyperarousal

Hyperarousal refers to an emotional condition where the person experiences his emotions at a high pitch, and where he is on almost constant alert against possible dangers or threats. Some questions you could think about in this category include:

- Does your partner usually seem wound up or tense rather than living in a normal state of relaxed attention?
- Does he seem to have rapid and exaggerated reactions to what goes on around him?
- Does his wound-up state cause you uneasiness?
- Does he take a long time to fall asleep, is he more sensitive to noise, and does he awaken more frequently during the night than most people do?
- Does he seem to be in a constant state of being on alert?
- Do his emotions seem to be unusually raw?

Intrusion

Intrusion refers to ways in which the person gets flooded with memories, images, or emotions that appear to come from earlier bad experiences. These waves can come at most any time, like a kind of invasion from the inside. Here are some points to consider:

- Does your partner awaken with nightmares that seem completely real to him, as if he were reliving some intense memory?
- Does he often awaken from nightmarish dreams that have a very negative emotional impact for him? Does he begin crying intensely when he attempts to describe them to you? Does he awaken flailing or yelling from vivid dreams?
- Does your partner relive intensely negative situations in the past as though they are occurring in the present?
- Does he react to current situations that seem harmless to you as though they are intensely negative situations?
- Do you often feel that your partner is not responding to what you actually have said or done, but instead he has instantaneously reinterpreted your actions and turned them into something extreme, way beyond what you actually said or did (or would even remotely have intended)?
- Is he unusually impulsive and irritable?
- Does your partner swing between extremes of needing absolute acceptance and then rejecting you as untrustworthy?

Constriction

Constriction refers to a sense that the person's energy and emotions are profoundly bound up and can't get free. Some questions to look at include:

- At times does your partner act with a profound passivity?
- Can he be so totally inhibited that he does not act, react, or respond to you at all?
- At times does your partner have a detached sense of calm that creates a buffer that is impossible to reach, as though he lives behind a Plexiglas wall or is made of Teflon—where nothing you say or do sticks?
- Does he tend to view himself as being somehow defiled or broken by something he has gone through? Does he, at the same time, consider himself superior to you because he has had such deeply awful experiences and he believes that you could not possibly understand what he has been through?
- Does he seem to be much more involved with his inner life than with the outside world? It's normal for introverts to like to spend time around only a few special people they choose, but do you get the sense that your partner is actually far more internally focused even than this? Do you notice that most of his strong opinions about your life together are drawn from his ongoing internal reflections, and you have the feeling that lengthy conversations are occurring internally, silently, and without you?
- Does your partner have a narrow emotional life—a life whose inner expressions seem confined to just a couple of feelings, and whose outer connection to others is similarly limited in range?

Disconnection

Disconnection, as you may have guessed, refers to problems that the person has maintaining a normal level of interaction with the social world. Here are some points you might reflect on:

- Is your partner isolated so that he has no connection to a surrounding community of people, or his connection is so limited and fragile that he would be alone without you?
- Does he speak of or act as though he cannot trust others?

- Does your partner see all relationships through the lens of extremes—
  is there an "all or nothing" quality to them, where there is no moderate
  engagement or moderate risk? Does he, for example, seem to view people through a lens of "You are one of us or not one of us" or "You are in
  the inner circle or you are out"? Does he switch back and forth between
  intense attachment to you and intense withdrawal from you? You may
  also notice this occurs with his friends.
- Is your partner often joyless?

Adolescence Again

The next set of questions looks at whether your partner's trauma history may
be making it hard for him to fully grow up. It could also be that recent trauma
has caused him to have to relearn many of the things he learned during his
adolescence. A once-confident man may be emotionally overwhelmed by the
demands of even the smallest social gatherings. A formerly successful worker
can become too anxious to apply for entry-level jobs. Following traumatic
events, once-effective, engaged people now enter into the social and working
worlds filled with insecurities and a shaken sense of confidence that the
trauma has left behind. They feel as though they are experiencing adolescence
all over again.

- Do you feel your partner is having struggles that he should have overcome at a younger age—struggles with being independent, taking initiative, finding a sense of competence, knowing who he is, and learning
  how to reach out to you?
- Do you sense he is overwhelmed with these difficulties?
- Is he competent and capable with you in some areas of the relationship
  and then completely adolescent or infantile, dependent, and vulnerable
  in others?
- Do you notice that your partner seems attentive and flattering to others
  in a way that does not strike you as genuine? Your partner may be acting from a post-trauma belief that he can't successfully navigate normal
  social engagement and differences without becoming someone he is not.

(Some of these concerns can also simply be signs of immaturity, as we discussed earlier, but if you are finding that they come along with quite a number

of the other indications of trauma that we are examining, then they fit in here.)

Memory and Being Present

A trauma history can interfere with a person's recall of the past and cause him to "zone out" in the present. He can't keep track of his own train of thoughts and feelings and so his opinions may change drastically depending on how he is responding to his environment in the moment. It becomes too challenging to remain present with and aware of his own experiences as they occur because the way he receives and processes information has been changed by the trauma. This makes him appear to be constantly distracted.

- Do you notice that your partner has significant gaps in memory?
- Do you hear him claiming contradictory beliefs, holding no awareness of his contradiction?
- Does your partner make commitments he cannot recall, or make absolute statements and plans that seemingly disappear?
- Does he "check out" from time to time—where you notice he is robotically, even dutifully, going through the motions, but you sense he's not really aware of what he's doing?

Trying to Manage the Pain

Trauma survivors sometimes develop some unhealthy behavioral patterns in an effort to escape the sharp or overwhelming pain they are carrying from their emotional injuries.

During periods where you notice your partner is acting particularly joyless or irritable, do you also notice any of the following:

- that your partner overeats or goes long periods without food?
- that your partner is using substances?
- that he deprives himself of sleep?
- that he plays video games or watches television, sports, or movies to the exclusion of other responsibilities, even when they interfere with his relationships or with accomplishing his goals?
- that he's masturbating or using pornography compulsively instead of having a sexual relationship with you? Or he may still have sex with

you, but his use of pornography is changing how he relates with you sexually in a way that makes you feel disrespected, unseen, or demeaned?

Physical Manifestations

People suffering from the effects of trauma experience a host of physical complaints that may include chronic fatigue, stomach and digestive complaints, headaches, muscle pain, and more. Every person has a "body signature"—a unique way that his or her body has responded to the stress of trauma, depending on the individual's history.

- Does he have stomach complaints, or other complaints of the body that you feel are related to his difficulties?
- Do you notice that he falls ill when he is being challenged in many of the ways we explored above? For example, does his body respond with illness when he is forced to socialize with people for an extended period of time?
- Does his health fail if he is unable to turn to the strategies he has to manage his pain, such as using substances, video games, or gambling?
- If he is put in the position of being responsible and having others depend upon him, does he fall ill quickly?

If you answered "yes" to many of the above questions, and especially if you also are aware that your partner has a history of severely destructive experiences, you can safely conclude that the unhealed, unresolved effects of trauma are an important factor in his inability to have a successful relationship with you. We will be looking at various ways that he can address the effects he is struggling with—if he's ready to take that leap. But he will have to be willing to get help, and will have to work with a professional who has been trained in healing from trauma.

COULD MY PARTNER HAVE A PERSONALITY DISORDER?

Now let's look at a rather different set of questions from the ones we examined in thinking about trauma.

- Do you repeatedly feel that you have made significant progress with your partner, only to find that you are right back where you started?
- Do you find that he suddenly switches to denying that there is any problem at all with his behavior, even though you had previous conversations with him where the two of you had discussed his unhealthy patterns in detail, he had completely agreed at that time that he had to make changes, and he had even said what kind of work he was going to do on himself?
- When you bring up your concerns, do you always (or almost always) find that they do not get addressed, and instead you end up arguing about *his* outrage at *you* for even bringing these things up at all?
- Does he seem completely unable to see or acknowledge how you are affected by things that he does?
- Alternatively, do you notice that he does apologize, but he later retracts it or makes statements that effectively retract the apology, such as, "Well, when you *made me* apologize . . ."
- With respect to what makes him attractive, do you notice that he's unusually exciting and fun?
- Do your complaints frequently get turned against you, with him saying, "Well, I feel the same way," or "You do the same thing"?
- Is he high functioning—even extremely successful in one area of his life, such as his career—but can't maintain any close personal relationships? (This can make things difficult, as it is hard to see clearly just how bad things have gotten when he's managing brilliantly elsewhere—and he can point to how well he handles other aspects of his life as "proof" that you shouldn't be saying that he has serious issues.)
- Do some other people (at least a few) notice that something is wrong with him?
- When you call him on his bad behavior, does he say he can't help it, and you start to get the sense that it's really true? Do you start to sense that he truly is not in control of his emotional state? (As we discuss at various points, he is still responsible for his actions even if he has this level of mental health problem.)
- Do you notice that he doesn't just have different moods, but that he seems to become almost a different person, including perhaps making statements that are completely opposite to things he has said at other

points? (This is not just the distinction between the angry partner and the partner who is no longer upset. A partner with these kinds of mental health issues can espouse a whole set of beliefs, make serious decisions, and make emotional statements that later he has no recollection about whatsoever, is dismissive of, or comes up with explanations for them that are not believable.)

- Do you notice that your partner acts as though *you* have harmed *him* when he has been rude or cruel to you? Do you engage in conversation or argument about this where your partner cannot acknowledge any facts that don't support his intense upset at his perceived victimization at your hands ?

- Do you notice that your partner will pull you closer emotionally, then push you away vehemently once you've established emotional intimacy? Does this seem to be a recurring pattern? Does he always seem to come up with some reason to have a fight if you two are starting to get really close?

- Do you notice that your partner sometimes sows seeds of tension between you and someone you care about while perhaps at the same time talking with you about how this other person is really the cause of so many problems?

- Is your partner very perceptive, able to see all of these kinds of things in other people, but not in himself? Does he seem to have a distorted self-image, exaggerating his own skills and abilities?

- Does he seem oddly lacking in guilt after he has engaged in a behavior that harmed another person, caused pain to an animal, or polluted the environment?

If you are answering an emphatic "yes!" to many of these questions, explore the section below carefully with your partner in mind; he may have a type of mental health problem known as a personality disorder.

When you are in a relationship with someone with a personality disorder, the patterns described above don't just happen on sporadic occasions, but tend to happen consistently, especially when a stressful situation arises. The collection of behaviors that makes up a personality disorder can take a huge toll on the man's partner. The patterns are so stubborn that outsiders cannot help but think you are exaggerating when you try to explain, for example, that you have repeatedly come to honest agreements or shared understandings—which seemed to be real breakthroughs at the time, and which took a lot of work to bring about—and still wound up right back where you started. Would-be helpers prefer to believe that if you just did or said the perfect series of things, these patterns could not occur, certainly not for years on end. They are, of course, dead wrong, as you know if you have lived with a partner with these issues.

We are not attempting to diagnose your partner for you. But we do hope to support your coming to a more accurate understanding of what is going on with your partner and what you might expect in your relationship with him.

The Nature of a Personality Disorder

The central elements of the mental health conditions known as "personality disorders" include:

- The person has recurring patterns of behaving in ways that are harmful to others, to himself, or both. (And these problems appear on various fronts in his life, not just with his partner, though they may take their worst form with her. If his destructive behaviors are limited almost entirely to his intimate partner relationships, then he is abusive, not someone suffering from a personality disorder—see Chapter 5.)
- He perceives those problems as being located in other people, not in himself. In other words, in his mind he is constantly having to deal with other people who are messed up, and that is why he is having all these problems.
- The different aspects of his character are not integrated, by which we mean that the different pieces of who he is don't fit together well and he doesn't recognize the contradictions. (For example, he might be an animal rights' activist who is cruel to his own pets, or he might lie and cheat chronically while often speaking about how he prizes honesty and integrity above all.)
- He can become irrationally angry at people who call him on his behaviors, and may simply erase those people from his life or label them "bad." He tends to get very wounded when he's criticized, even when those criticisms are entirely appropriate.

- He lacks perspective-taking skills with respect to himself; what we mean by this is that, while he may be good at imagining other people's experiences and may be supportive and generous toward people in many ways, he can't wrap his head around people's experiences *of him*. As a result, he is frequently feeling misunderstood and unfairly criticized, and feels like people just don't get how loving, generous, and honest he is. He can feel this way even (or perhaps especially) when someone is pointing out something obviously selfish, irresponsible, or mean that he has done.

- He has developed a fairly (or very) high level of skill at covering up and rationalizing these issues. As a result, arguing with him about his conduct can be extraordinarily frustrating or can even make you start to feel that you are the one that is crazy. Heated arguments are virtually impossible for you to win because he is so good at twisting things around, and he always has a comeback for everything, no matter how undeniable your point really is.

- Most people who know him will find him quite charming, and they usually will need extensive involvement with him over time to discover how much trouble he can cause. You may get tired of having everyone tell you how wonderful he is (though this can happen with an abusive partner also, as we will see).

- On some level he seems to really want to be freer, well adjusted, and meaningfully connected to others (with the possible exception of the antisocial personality disorder, which we discuss later), but he can't face the harm he has done in the past, nor can he face the crippling sense of shame that distorts his own awareness of himself; and these in turn make it impossible for him to make the kinds of changes that would allow him to stop doing harm in the future.

Where Do Personality Disorders Come From?

It is our belief that personality disorders are heavily rooted in early experiences of abuse, neglect, or profound invalidation. One could reasonably see these conditions as simply another shape that post-trauma effects take in certain people, perhaps in combination with biological predispositions that the abuse brings out. There are psychologists who agree with us and others who don't—the cause of personality disorders is a hotly debated topic—but there is a broad agreement on one critical point:

> **The personality disorder creates a kind of "locked-in-place" condition, so that even if the person gets considerable help healing from early trauma, the behavioral problems and distorted perceptions don't tend to go away. In other words, a trauma survivor who does not have a personality disorder will often get great relief from his symptoms if he finds a skilled, trauma-informed therapist; whereas even the most highly accomplished therapists don't tend to make much progress in helping clients overcome personality disorders.**

Does this mean that nothing can be done? Fortunately not; but a highly specialized kind of assistance is needed, as we will discuss.

How Much of This Is True About Your Partner?

When thinking about your partner's behavior, let's think in terms of degree. As you read through the list of traits below, ask yourself how often these problems arise, and how severe they are. Use your instincts.

Ask yourself to rate how much these characteristics are present in your partner's personality and behavior on a scale from one to ten, with one being "rarely" and ten being "all the time."

- Not seeing he has a problem _____
- Being resistant to going to therapy or getting any form of help _____
- Having insights that are short-lived _____
- Overestimating his own recovery from his destructive behaviors, for example speaking of recent horrible things he did as though they existed in the deep past _____
- Having genuine forgetfulness about significant events, agreements, and conversations _____
- Engaging you in arguments where you must reestablish patterns of fact and events that should have been clear and obvious, or that you have already gone over and he had agreed to what he did _____

- Reinterpreting what you actually say into something different (twisting your words), then arguing against what you never said _____
- Refuting your statements about his behaviors that you bring to his attention, and/or accusing you of doing the same things he does _____
- Being unwilling to be held accountable for wrongs that he has done, and exhibiting extreme reactions to your efforts to get him to address his actions _____
- The above issues come up over and over again _____

If you are finding that you gave high scores to several items on the list above, that gives you an additional indication that your partner's difficulties may fit the personality disorder category.

The Different Kinds of Personality Disorder

Psychologists break personality disorders down into specific types, and looking at these may sharpen your sense of what shape your partner's issues take. However, be aware that a majority of people with a personality disorder do not fit perfectly into any one of these types, as they have aspects of more than one; so don't try to squeeze one of these onto him if it doesn't really fit. The general principles that we have discussed above are more important than the specifics.

Obsessive/Compulsive Traits—*"Everything Has to Be Just This Exact Way."*

Maya was getting a lot out of her support group at the battered women's program. She could really identify with the kinds of controlling, intimidating, and selfish behaviors the other women described going on in their homes. But no one else had a partner who had to pet the back left leg of their cat before leaving his chair. No one else had a partner who had to rub the doorknobs ritually and who freaked out and yelled if you interrupted him.

Maya's partner had a particular kind of personality disorder that features obsessive/compulsive traits, where the person feels that he has to engage in certain ritualistic movements, place items in oddly specific spots, or repeat certain behaviors a specific number of times.

Narcissistic Traits—*"I'm Special."*

Your partner may have a grandiose self-regard, exaggerate his achievements and his talents (even if hasn't really accomplished much of anything), and be deeply wounded by any criticism. His expectation of being seen as extraordinary can be exhausting and irritating, and can make it so that he is always the center of any positive attention and you rarely are. The person with narcissistic traits manages to make everything be about him. When you visit your relatives, for example, which can be stressful for you, he demands you attend to his needs that result from his strong feelings of being inadequately appreciated by them. However, if you are visiting *his* family, the same attention by you to him will be required.

Even further, the person who experiences the world narcissistically has a kind of genuinely selective recall. Information that doesn't fit with his feelings and assumptions simply doesn't register with him. He is isolated within his narrow world, often feeling resentful because the world fails to serve him above others. The person who remains trapped in this narcissistic prison often expresses a sense of outrage that his (unspoken) feelings, needs, wants, and assumptions have not been met, as though they should have been known, anticipated, and met without his having to ask .

Paranoid Traits—*"They're Out to Get Me."*

Your partner may not trust you or anyone else and believe that people are conniving to harm him. He may not believe in the loyalty of his own friends, and think that everyone wants to take advantage of him. He is always on the lookout for insults, and when he finds one, he holds a grudge about it for life. These fears aren't based on any real reason to fear or mistrust the people around him.

Antisocial Traits—*"Trust Me/Hey, What'd You Expect Anyway?"*

You may find that you are in a relationship with the "Bad Boy" who doesn't want to follow any of society's rules and seems to be focused on manipulating people and taking advantage of them. This style of person is also known as a "sociopath"; despite the image of a murderer that the term may conjure, it more often describes a person who commits less serious but chronic crimes, violence, and using of people for selfish ends. The person with antisocial traits is most often quite charming or even disarming. Even if you see obvious signs of danger, you will find it hard to reconcile these aspects of him with his skills at getting people to like him and be impressed by him. He may have a keen ear for what needs to be said to please the other person or win someone over, and can anticipate people's needs and expectations and give them what they want—or at least appear to do so. If you have an antisocial partner, he may sense your deepest needs and hopes, telling you things that will move you or touch the core of your being; which then can make you feel confused or betrayed when he acts in ways that are deeply hurtful to you or violates solemn promises.

At the core of the antisocial personality disorder is the experience of the *absence of a conscience;* the person just doesn't feel guilty about violating trust, or using other people, or causing harm. But his viciousness is hidden under a thick cover of friendliness and charm, so he can be hard to make sense of.

Borderline Traits—*"Everything Is Black or White."*
If your partner has a set of patterns known as borderline traits, you might notice that he:

- has intense relationships with people where he very quickly decides that the person is just wonderful and amazing and comes to feel rapidly close, but then at some point down the road a conflict happens and he swings to the other extreme, completely devaluing the person and declaring that he or she is terrible.
- behaves impulsively—and ends up hurting himself as a result. Perhaps he makes huge life decisions such as quitting a job without considering the consequences; spends money excessively; goes on eating binges; has irresponsible and indiscriminate sex, and similar out-of-control behaviors.
- has marked mood shifts lasting hours or even a few days, where he goes from a normal, even-keeled state to intense irritability, anxiety, or depression.
- gets angry in ways that seem way out of proportion to the issue, gets overdramatic when he's angry, or is angry constantly.
- has a history of feeling suicidal, perhaps with a number of times when he actually threatened to kill himself or made suicidal gestures.
- can't seem to handle gray areas in life—everything is either great or terrible, good or bad, delightful or worthless; and this means he can't deal

with the fact that you love him but also have deep resentments about how he has treated you, so he'll insist that you must not really love him.

- craves emotional closeness, but then hates it when a relationship gets really close and is afraid that he will be either engulfed or abandoned.

People with these qualities sometimes are known to struggle with a sense that they are masquerading as a "normal" person. They describe not having the spontaneous joy, compassion, or deep feelings of connection that they see others experiencing. They have difficulty recognizing their own authentic thoughts or feelings, They vacillate between blaming others for their unhappiness and feeling profound shame and powerlessness, all the while feeling so isolated that they may claim that other people treat them as if they don't exist.

(By the way, the term "borderline" is more or less meaningless, dating back to a time when it was believed that this particular collection of mental health symptoms meant that the person was right on the brink of a major mental illness, such as multiple personality disorder. This belief went out long ago, but the term remains for now.)

Can a Personality Disorder Be Overcome?

Personality disorders are notoriously difficult to heal, largely due to the fact that the person's perceptions are highly distorted but he believes he is seeing things clearly. The one therapeutic approach that has been found to be effective is "**dialectical behavioral therapy (DBT).**" DBT is an intensive program that combines specific behavioral and emotional skill training through intensive group work, one-on-one psychotherapy, and aftercare. Participants learn first to "stop making things worse" in their lives and in the lives of those trying to love them. DBT skills help people regulate their own emotions and manage distressing periods of life. The skills work culminates in the repair and care of relationships through mastery of a set of interpersonal effectiveness skills. You can call social service programs or mental health clinics in your area to find a DBT program near you.

Depression

Since the subject of depression has been covered so well in other books (see "Resources"), we will address it only briefly here. Depression is actually a fairly common cause of men's inability to be good relationship partners, but is less recognized than it is in women and so can go undetected. Also, symptoms may not appear the same in men as they do in women. Some indications that you might notice in your partner include:

- He has lost much of his motivation, so that he seems to have less and less energy and initiative as time goes by. He might, for example, drift off and spend increasing amounts of time watching television, sleeping, mindlessly surfing the Web, or doing nothing at all.
- He used to contribute more to what needs to be done, but now just seems to expect you to take care of everything, and he responds as though anything you ask him to do involves a huge and overwhelming effort.
- He complains about various problems, but feels he can't take any steps to do anything about any of them.
- His drinking or marijuana smoking is increasing.
- He's putting in a mediocre effort at his job, or isn't working at all and isn't making meaningful efforts to find a job.
- He often seems sad but he rarely cries, and his emotions seem somewhat numbed rather than sharp and painful; in other words, he seems stuck in a sort of low-level misery.

Depression can sometimes be relieved quite successfully through psychotherapy, sometimes including some period of using antidepressant medication. Blocked, unprocessed grief and anger are often at the root, combined with isolation.

Do you recognize your partner in these descriptions? Recognizing these challenges can explain so much about your experience. Mental health challenges are so prevalent, and with approximately one in five veterans returning from Iraq and Afghanistan developing post-traumatic stress disorder and/or addiction problems, if you are in partnership with a veteran, these descriptions may hit home particularly hard.

If any of the issues we described are untreated, or if the mental health challenges are managed without fundamental respect for you, you are probably already feeling depleted and hurt. And very often, these issues combine in a powerful and negative way with abusive ideas, so that recognizing the mental health challenges still may be only part of the answer for you. Together, we will continue our investigation of these questions in the next chapter.

Give yourself some time to digest and consider what you discover. We don't expect that you will like all of the answers you uncover, but we promise that the clarity you gain from this work will help ease your anxiety. Take heart; we have prepared a way that will help you move forward, no matter what you find.

EXERCISE 4–1:

Spend fifteen or twenty minutes (more if you want) writing about your strengths. Some questions you might reflect on include: What have been some of your successful relationships with friends, relatives, or other people you care about? What are some ways in which you have shown that you have good judgment? How have you avoided some of the less healthy aspects of the family you grew up in? What are some ways you have come through for people who needed you? What are some ways in which you have taken good care of yourself?

Then write a couple of sentences about how this exercise went for you. Was it hard to write about yourself as a well person? If so, why?

FIVE

Is the Problem Abuse or Control?

E MILY LOOKED DOWNHEARTED as she spoke to us during a break at a conference:

> *"I feel like I'm working so hard trying to make my partner happy, but it doesn't seem to be working. He's dissatisfied with me so much of the time. He says that I've changed, and . . . I guess I have. But he says really cutting things to me, things that make me feel terrible. And he's so angry sometimes that I feel kind of scared."* She paused, taking in how her words sounded. *"I don't mean to make him sound like a bad person. He was so nice at the beginning. And I would really like to make it work with him, but nothing I try seems to get us to a better place . . . I just don't know what to do."*

You may be feeling some trepidation as you begin this chapter. "Abuse" is a powerful buzzword, and though it means different things to different people, the connotations are almost always loaded. You may be afraid that this chapter will inform you that your partner is an abuser, which might feel something like receiving a cancer diagnosis.

So let us begin by saying that we are going to be examining a *spectrum* of behaviors, very few of which will look anything like the batterers in *The*

Burning Bed or *What's Love Got to Do with It?* Most of what we will be talking about is verbal abuse, not physical violence or sexual assault, though we will touch on those also. And some of the central principles we discuss apply to *all* relationships, and concern questions that every couple needs to spend time meditating on separately and hashing out together.

Before we wade into these waters, we want to step back and ask you to reflect on a set of principles for any healthy relationship. Pause after reading each one and take a few breaths, noticing what you are feeling. Then read the prompt that follows and write your answers in your journal. (If you find you don't have much to say in response to the prompts, that's fine.)

Principle 1: In a relationship, each partner is responsible for his or her own actions. You don't cause what your partner does, and he doesn't cause what you do. Neither of you gets to blame his or her behavior on the other.

Prompt 1: Here are some of the ways that my partner says I have caused him to do bad things that he has done:

Principle 2: Feelings are not an excuse for destructive or unfair behavior. "I was angry," "I was frustrated," "I was hurt," "I was disappointed"—these are all valid feelings, but they don't justify insulting a partner, giving her the silent treatment, or frightening her (even by accident).

Prompt 2: Here are some ways that my partner has used his feelings as an excuse for saying or doing things to me that hurt me:

Principle 3: Behavior in a relationship cannot be justified by what the other person did. Two wrongs do not make a right, and one injury can't excuse another.

Prompt 3: Here are some ways that my partner says that, because I did something that he doesn't like, it's okay for him to do something that he knows hurts me:

Principle 4: A healthy relationship involves roughly equal exchange. Each partner has to do his or her share of the listening, the generous giving, the showing of kindness, the forgiving, the child care, the giving of sexual pleasure, the showing of affection, the making of sacrifices. Within reason, things should come out even.

Prompt 4: Here are some ways that my partner takes more (perhaps a lot more) than he gives:

Principle 5: For a relationship to be healthy, a comfortable balance has to be found between holding on to the things that matter to us the most, and making some sacrifices and adjustments so that the other person can get what he or she wants and needs. Neither person should have to give up too much.

Prompt 5A: Here are some ways that my partner has been inflexible about making reasonable adjustments or sacrifices so that my needs can be met and so that I can have the things that are most important to me:

Prompt 5B: Here are some ways that my partner expects me to give up too much so that he can have exactly what he wants:

Principle 6: The two members of a couple are equally valuable human beings with equally important thoughts, opinions, and strengths, and equally valuable judgment. Both partners have a right to equal say over all decisions that affect both people or affect the family.

Prompt 6A: Here are some ways in which my partner makes me feel as though I am less than he is:

Prompt 6B: Here are some ways in which my partner takes away my say over certain issues, by silencing me, overruling me, getting nasty, or going ballistic:

Now go back over the principles above and pick out the two that feel the most important to you. Write a note to yourself explaining why you chose the ones you did.

Are you finding that you feel a little stirred up inside? These principles cut to the core of many of the more difficult dynamics in relationships. Underneath most of the fighting that goes on between couples are these questions:

Who gets to have the final say when we disagree?

Who is giving what in our relationship, and who is receiving what, and is the exchange a fair one?

What kinds of sacrifices can we each reasonably expect the other to make?

POWER AND CONTROL

Now we'll take the leap and begin looking directly at the subject of abuse. Since, as we said before, the term is used in such varying ways (including by an abusive man himself, who often ends up telling the woman that *she* is the abusive one), we want to lay out our way of defining the key behaviors of an abusive man and the characteristics of the relationship that he creates:

- Give-and-take in the relationship goes grossly out of whack. You end up giving way more than your share, while your partner is taking way more than his.
- You pay a high price for bringing up certain subjects, so that you start to feel, "I just can't talk to him about that."
- He tells you that things he has done to you are your own fault.
- You get punished for standing up to him about certain things. If you don't back down when he reaches his limit, he will get you back for it by ripping you apart verbally, threatening you, scaring you, hurting you physically, or taking steps to intentionally ruin your day. The bottom line is, if he doesn't get his way about something that's important to him, he makes sure to make you miserable.
- You feel more and more controlled and devalued by him over time.
- He hurts you for being hurt by him. In other words, if you tell him how you have been affected by his destructive behavior, or he notices those effects himself, he uses those effects to ridicule you or to do you more harm in other ways. (As in, for example, a client from one of our cases who said to his partner, after she flinched during an argument, "You're afraid of me? You're *afraid* of me? That's the most pathetic, hysterical thing I've ever heard!")
- He refuses to accept responsibility for his own actions.

Although books have been filled with information—most of it valuable—about abusive partners, in many ways it can be distilled down to the points above. Give yourself a minute to look back over the list and take it in, along with a couple of good breaths.

There are additional elements that are often present in the behavior of an abusive partner that we will list below to help you put your finger on the specifics of how you are being harmed.

———————

Check off the ones that your partner has exhibited:

- ☐ Calling you offensive, degrading, or antifemale names (such as "bitch," "whore," etc.)
- ☐ Cheating on you
- ☐ Accusing you of cheating on him, or of wanting to
- ☐ Belittling your dreams or ambitions
- ☐ Making it hard for you to see or talk to friends or relatives, damaging your relationships, isolating you
- ☐ Putting you down about your weight, trying to control what you eat
- ☐ Controlling what you wear or where you go
- ☐ Controlling you in other ways
- ☐ Ignoring you, punishing you with silent treatment
- ☐ Hurting you through your children
- ☐ Demanding constant attention and catering from you
- ☐ Checking up on you frequently, such as calling you repeatedly at work, requiring you to carry a cell phone and always answer his calls, or reading your e-mail/regular mail
- ☐ Interfering with your work life, making it hard for you to keep a job
- ☐ Pressuring you for sex or for specific sexual acts
- ☐ Touching or grabbing you sexually in ways that are demeaning or that are unwanted
- ☐ Forcing you to have sex, raping you
- ☐ Scaring or intimidating you, whether intentional or not
- ☐ Shoving you, slapping you, or pinning you
- ☐ Blocking your way
- ☐ Hitting you or physically hurting you in other ways

SHOULD I CALL IT ABUSE?

Putting a name such as "abuse" on systematic mistreatment sometimes helps a woman to feel stronger. Labeling his behavior "abuse" helps you remember that you aren't crazy, and that his behavior is not your fault. And your ability to reach out and find support can increase from knowing what to call your experience.

On the other hand, what matters most is to do what works for you, and not to get hung up on terminology. If using the term "abuse" makes you feel more victimized, or if you don't feel that it captures well what your partner's behavior problems are like, leave it aside. But either way, reflect carefully on the material in this chapter, and then address—in the ways we will recommend—any of your partner's behaviors that do fit the pattern.

Finally, you may find that the first thing that comes to mind about this subject is an image of how ferocious your partner's response would be if you referred to his behavior as abusive. And that in itself is a clue that abuse may be at play.

THE ABUSIVE MENTALITY

If your partner is showing patterns of using abusive behaviors—whether or not you feel the label "abuser" properly fits him—take a moment to absorb the following critical understanding:

> **Despite how angry, hurt, insecure, or unhappy your partner may appear to be, his abusive behavior is rooted far more in how he *thinks* than in how he *feels*. The answer to what has gone wrong lies primarily not in his *heart*—except for its lack of compassion toward you—but rather in his *mind*.**

Believe it or not, research using psychological testing has shown that even physically violent abusers are usually psychologically normal, and that their behavior problems come primarily from their attitudes and values, not their emotions.

As we examine some of the common beliefs that drive abusive behavior, consider whether they fit your partner's way of approaching you. Bear in mind that these qualities usually don't appear during the early months of a relationship, and can take two years or more to come to fully manifest themselves; if you find yourself thinking, "Well, he's this way now, but he didn't *used* to be," we regret to say this is typical of men with abuse problems.

He Believes He Has the Right to Control You

The abusive man thinks that he can take power over your decisions and your life when he decides that it's necessary to do so. If you don't like it, he'll let you know it's your own fault. He has his justifications ready, such as:

"It's for your own good." The message is that you are so incompetent, or stupid, or reckless that if he didn't take control, you would make a terrible mess of everything.

"There's a right way to do things and a wrong way." And the right way is his way. Sometimes this will be connected to saying that his way will save money, but that's no excuse for taking away your right to share the decisions and have your full say.

"That's just the way men and women are." By claiming that biology has determined roles for men and women, or that his religious scriptures make the rules (whether Christian, Jewish, or Muslim), or that "everyone knows" what's appropriate—everyone except you, of course—he'll defend his right to control what you wear, how late you can be out, where you can take the kids, or what happens in your sexual relationship.

"I'm defending my rights." This rationalization is an especially common one among abusive men. Your partner might tell you, for example, that he gets to forbid you to go to certain places "because how am I going to look in town if people know my wife is hanging out in that kind of joint?" He's claiming that his *preference* is actually his *right*—a typical twist for an abusive man to make. What is really happening is that he is taking *your* rights away.

"Because I said so." This last one amounts to admitting that he has no right to be controlling you, but is a way of announcing that he is going to do it anyway, making his abusiveness barefaced and overt.

EXERCISE 5–1:

Jot down a few responses to these questions:

1. What are some ways in which your partner has taken your freedoms away?

2. How does he justify doing so?

3. Which of his justifications get you the most unsure or confused?

One way to summarize the central point of this sections is to say:

You have the right to do things that make your partner uncomfortable, or that he disagrees with, or that he thinks are not good for you. He can ask you to do things the way he wishes you would do them, but he has no right to *make* you. Your life belongs to you, from little things like how much hot water to use to big things like which friends and relatives you can love and spend time with.

Start noticing *payback*. If you refuse to do things his way, do you end up paying a price for it? If you resist his control, does he retaliate against you through put-downs, silent treatment, wrecking the rest of the day, or intimidating you? Payback is one of the surest signs of an unacceptable level of control. Make a note in your journal each time you get punished—overtly or subtly—for going ahead and doing something that you had every right to do.

Finally, ask yourself, "Does he ever act like he *owns* me?" A mentality of ownership is a sure sign of an abuser.

He Believes His Needs and Desires Come First

The second guiding principle of abusive behavior, following control, is **entitlement**. What we mean by the term "entitlement" is your partner's attitude that his desires come ahead of yours, and that therefore it is your job to keep doing more and more for him. In his mind, the relationship stops being about "give-and-take" and becomes simply "take."

Among the most visible results of an entitled outlook are *double standards*. Does your partner have a very different set of rules for you than for himself? Here are some examples:

- He jumps all over you if he thinks you are checking out another guy, but he looks at women long and hard, perhaps even commenting on their looks to you, and says that he's just doing what's "natural" for a man.
- He criticizes you harshly, but you can't raise a grievance about his behavior, no matter how carefully and tactfully you bring it up.
- He keeps saying "we can't afford it" to things that matter to you, but there seems to be money available for his favorite activities or purchases.
- He tells you that you are too sensitive and that you shouldn't be bothered by the things he does, but when he's the one whose feelings are hurt, he yells that you should care about him more and should know not to do things that he dislikes so much.

This list could go on, but rather than giving you more of our examples, let's collect some of yours. In your journal write some of the ways in which your partner enforces double standards.

Double standards are, in a word, selfish, and if your partner has a collection of entitled attitudes, you will keep hitting up against times when he acts infuriatingly selfish and self-centered. Other people—meaning people who aren't involved in a serious relationship with him—may think he is the most generous, giving, supportive guy in the world, but your experience will be that he keeps coldly or angrily pushing your needs into the background. He believes that coming first is his due.

Here are some typical entitled attitudes that an abusive man might have, though he won't necessarily ever say them aloud:

- *"If you bring up complaints about how I treat you, you are wronging me and hurting me."*
- *"I have a right to expect sex from you whether you are in the mood or not, and even if I haven't been nice to you lately."*
- *"You should be prepared to deal with my relatives and spend time with them even though they are difficult people, but I'm not going to put any effort into dealing with your relatives."*
- *"You should be able to tell what I want even if I haven't expressed it, and it's your job to anticipate my needs."*
- *"You should be grateful for whatever I contribute and not bug me to actually carry my weight in this family."*

Abusive men frequently make reference to their wives and girlfriends "nagging" them, which you can translate as "she presses me to meet my responsibilities"—something an abuser believes his partner has no right to do.

EXERCISE 5–2:

A woman who is living with an abusive partner can increase her mental clarity by learning to identify and name (to herself) his entitled attitudes. Look over the list above, and mark any of the attitudes that you have seen your partner exhibit.

Then take a moment to reflect on any other ways that he exhibits a "You owe me" or "It's your job to do things for me" kind of mentality, and write down a few examples.

He Believes He's Better Than You Are

We're going to ask you now to work on forming a mental image of *dignity*. You can picture someone you know who seems particularly self-possessed—but not arrogant—or a character in a movie or book, or yourself on a good day. What is the person wearing? How does she move and walk? How does she interact with other people? What is it about her that makes you think of dignity?

Close your eyes for a few moments and let this image develop in your mind, and then spend a brief time making some notes about what you saw.

You have the right to move through the world with your dignity intact. An abusive man keeps making cracks in his partner's dignity, and he widens them over time. Typically, the first assault he makes in that direction is to let you know, through his insulting words, demeaning facial expression, and superior know-it-all tone of voice, that he believes you are *less* than he is, that you are beneath him. He may think of you as less intelligent, less logical, less competent, less insightful, less caring (how ironic!), less aware of how to raise children, or all of these combined.

To spend hours of your life around someone who thinks in these ways about you eats away at your self-confidence and your pride. It can start to erode your ability to think clearly. And then your partner jumps all over your mental errors, saying that those mistakes prove that he's been right about you all along. In other words, *he uses the harm that he has done to you as a way to justify doing more harm!*

His attitude of superiority has nothing to do with who you really are, or who he really is. He carries this attitude through all of his intimate relationships. (When he is with a new partner, he might consider the woman bright and capable, but only for a while. For example, if you break up and he gets with someone else, he may rub it in your face how much smarter and more together she supposedly is than you are. But before too long, he will be looking down at her also.)

So if you are involved with a destructive partner, one of the most important points to reflect on and digest is:

You will not be able to change his negative view of you by doing better, working harder, giving more, and making bigger sacrifices. His negative attitude toward you will stay the same regardless. It's about *him*, not about you.

To put matters starkly: it is impossible to have a healthy and satisfying relationship with a person who talks or looks down at you. He will have to either learn equality and respect or lose his place in your life.

Get in the habit of viewing all of your partner's behaviors, even during periods when he is being nice to you, through a lens of *respect*. Ask yourself:

- Is he talking to me in a way that shows he values my thinking?
- Is he respecting my opinions even when he disagrees with them?
- Are his "good periods" respectful, or even then is he just treating me like a prized doll on his shelf?
- Is he taking me seriously?
- Can he show anger without turning contemptuous or disgusted?

What tends to happen when you start to apply this lens is that many of his behaviors that you used to have other names for—"insecurity," "stress," "frustration," "anger," "getting triggered," and other terms along these lines—suddenly reveal themselves as *disrespect*, plain and simple.

"I was angry," by the way, is an excuse that abusive men use ad nauseam for all manner of selfish, destructive, or even violent behaviors. Anger is an emotion, and it does not require the person who is feeling it to take a certain course of action. No matter how angry he is, he still makes choices about his behavior. Notice that in his eyes *your* anger doesn't justify *your* behavior; in fact, your anger, to his mind-set, just shows what an angry, unreasonable, out-of-control person you are. But *his* anger gives him license to unleash his verbally abusive or violent urges.

Anger does not cause disrespect, and anger does not cause violence. Keeping these categories from getting blended together in your mind will make it harder for your partner to confuse you about what has gone wrong in your relationship.

He Believes That You Do Not Have the Right to Stand Up to Him

Did your partner seem like a great catch in the early months of your relationship? Did you feel crazy about him? Believe it or not, that is actually the typical experience that women have when they first get involved with an abusive or destructive partner.

So now see if you can trace back to the time when he first started to show signs of behaviors that were hurtful, demeaning, or scary to you. What was going on in your lives and in your relationship at that point? What you are quite likely to discover, upon reflection, is that his treatment of you changed around the same time that you started to *challenge* him significantly; you stood up to him about an issue that was important to you or called him on something he was doing. It is common for abusive and controlling men not to show their true colors until the first time that they are confronted.

Confrontation and conflict are part of all relationships, as we saw in Chapter 1. The needs of relationship partners collide. One person gets frustrated or offended by how the other is behaving. A partner challenges the other one about responsibilities that he or she is not coming through on. Someone behaves in a way that hurts the other one's feelings, perhaps through insensitivity or perhaps just by accident. *These dynamics of tension, arguing, and working toward resolution are normal and are present even in the best of relationships.*

However, when you are involved with an abusive partner, confrontation and conflict become a nightmare because he doesn't believe you have the right to stand up to him, and so he decides to punish you for doing so. Conflicts don't work toward resolution, they just escalate and become more and more hurtful, especially to the nonabusive partner.

Nothing else of any significance can change or improve in your relationship until he accepts that you have the right to disagree with him, call him on attitudes or behaviors that you don't like, and demand changes. Until he's ready to be answerable to you, progress can't happen.

Note here that the abusive man's outlook on relationships is that there are two choices: you can either be the person who is *controlling* or the person who is *controlled*. So when you refuse to be controlled by him anymore, he is going to insist angrily that *you* are trying to control *him*. For example, if he is required to deal respectfully with your disagreements, he will claim that now you aren't allowing him to disagree. Do your best not to fall for this turning of the tables. He still has the right to disagree with you—he just doesn't get to insult you and intimidate you, and he has to take your opinions seriously. If he is going to choose to act victimized about having to live within these entirely reasonable guidelines, that further reveals his attitude.

He Views a Relationship As a Power Struggle

What's the difference between an intimate partnership and a football game? Everything. What happens if a man has trouble telling those two things apart? He's hell to be involved with.

The abusive man typically thinks of a relationship as involving aspects such as *winning, planning maneuvers, maintaining the upper hand, avoiding being snagged,* and *keeping the other side guessing about what you are planning.* When speaking to friends about his wife or girlfriend, for example, he may ponder what would put him in a "stronger or weaker position," what kinds of mistakes he might make that could "give her the idea that she is the one in charge," or how best to make sure to "keep her off balance." His view is that if she becomes more self-confident, better connected socially, more successful, and generally stronger, it will make things *worse* for him!

In short, he sees a relationship as a seesaw; you can't both be up at the same time. If you want to avoid being on the bottom, it's very important to remain on top.

We will look at just three examples, out of many we could choose from, illustrating the direction this mentality will take him in. First, he is likely to put on a dramatically different face for the outside world than he shows in private, giving outsiders the impression that he is generous, funny, and sensitive. Some days you may wonder why he can be so charming to everyone else and so mean to you. The answer is that having these two faces increases his power, and power is what he's after; as long as the public thinks he's a great guy, it's harder for you to get people to understand what you are dealing with.

Second, he's likely to be manipulative. He may make secret maneuvers regarding money that end up ruining your credit or that allow him to get away with a bunch of your money. (We've been involved in a number of cases, for example, where the abusive man kept saying that he was "coming into a big settlement soon," and borrowed more and more money from his partner on that basis, and then never repaid her.) He may be misleading about important issues but avoid telling outright falsehoods, so that when his dishonesty comes out, he can just say, "You misinterpreted what I said—I didn't lie to you." He is likely to have times when he pretends to be watching out for your interests, when he's actually trying to promote what he wants; for example, he might pressure you to quit a small business you are running by saying that he thinks you will be happier without the pressure, when the real reason is that the independence that your business brings you is a threat to his control.

Third, he may try to turn you against friends or relatives, or even against your own children. We've worked with many cases where the man bullied the woman or her friends so badly each time they got together that she gradually gave up trying to see people (and then felt like it was her own fault that she didn't have friends). Divide and conquer is a classic tactic of those who seek to expand their power. On some level he is aware that the more connected you are to loved ones, the more likely you are to stay strong. He's also afraid that someone might tell you that you aren't to blame for his actions, or you might find out about support groups for abused women, or someone might tell you how to get a protective order against him.

If your relationship feels like a constant struggle for who is on top, and if you feel that you are kept on the defensive, then you aren't involved in intimacy, you're involved in a battle. You deserve better than a partner who thinks the goal of a relationship is for him to tackle you.

These ideas may be quite new; you may never before have thought of your partner's behavior as coming from his attitudes; most of our society assumes that a destructive partner gets "that way" because of his emotional problems and insecurities. Now that you have this information, you'll be surprised how often you notice that selfish and disrespectful thinking is underlying his destructive actions.

The Perfect Storm of the Destructive Relationship

"I think he's got it all: mental health issues, definitely trauma, and he's using drugs for sure. And he definitely doesn't treat me with respect."

As you might have noticed, it is possible that your partner is destructive in more than one way. He might have abusive values that combine with his immaturity and mental health problems. And he may have addiction problems on top of it all. Each of these destructive forces might be colliding into you all at once in your relationship.

For many women, it is a combination of these thorny problems that together make up "what is really going on with him". If he is in therapy or substance abuse treatment, his values, attitudes, and beliefs about relationships and about women typically won't receive any attention from the professionals who are helping him. **And if your partner resolves his trauma or addiction without addressing his destructive or entitled values, then he will continue to be a destructive partner.**

If your partner considers bullying you a reasonable approach to enforce what he wants, and if he believes that his needs and desires matter much more than yours, these attitudes will worsen the effects that his addiction or trauma have on his behavior. Addictions and deep emotional disturbances are hard enough to overcome even *without* an abusive or violent mentality; when you add those aggressive attitudes into the mix, they can create a virulence and overt oppression that are hard for people outside of the relationship to fully imagine.

Let's look at how abusive behavior can mix with the other kinds of problems we've been examining.

Personality Disorders Combined with Abusive Values

Below is a list of traits that are common in people who have personality disorders, drawing from what we covered in Chapter 4. Following each trait, in italics, is an abusive attitude that can get linked to that trait if the man is also abusive. Put a check mark next to any combination that you see happening in your relationship.

- ☐ Not seeing that he has a disorder and *believing that he is inherently superior and that men are inherently superior.*
- ☐ Being resistant to going to therapy and *believing that it is a woman's job to accept a man as he is.*
- ☐ Having insights that appear important but then vanish soon and *believing that he has the right to tear you down if you point something out about him and it threatens his self-concept.*

☐ Overestimating how much he has recovered from his destructive behaviors, and/or speaking of recent horrible behaviors as though they took place in the deep past and *believing that it is your job to celebrate his recovery and not mention how little he has actually changed.*

☐ Having genuine memory problems about significant events, agreements, and conversations involving the two of you while *believing that he gets to act disgusted or insulting if you point out the important things he has forgotten.*

☐ Engaging you in arguments where he is suddenly changing his version of what happened in past events (which forces you to go back over it all again) while *believing that he has the right to establish reality to his liking.*

☐ Twisting your words into something different from what you said while *believing he has the right to use contempt and intimidation to sidetrack you from your complaints.*

☐ Denying the behaviors you bring to his attention, and throwing back at you that you supposedly do the same thing to him, while *believing that you don't have the right to bring complaints to him.*

☐ Having extreme emotional reactions when you bring up his wrongdoing while *believing that contemptuous or violent expressions of those extreme reactions are justified because he should never have to be answerable to you.*

Going over the above list can draw your attention to how much more tightly knotted these personality disorder traits become when interwoven with abusive beliefs, though even separately they are highly stressful to deal with.

Anxiety Combined with Abusive Values

Your partner may be unusually *anxious* about change in his environment because of his addiction or mental health problems. However, if this anxiety combines with beliefs of his to the effect that:

- it is your job to accept how inflexible or irrational he gets when he has to deal with change . . .

- it is your job to create a world around him that protects him from having to deal with change at all (for example, if he acts like you should have been able to foresee all possibilities and keep anything from happening that would make him uncomfortable) . . .

. . . then his emotional wounds are not the whole problem. His anxiety is real, but he is also using it as an excuse to not look at his disrespect toward you, which is just as crucial.

Low Frustration Tolerance Combined with Abusive Values

Your partner may be easily *frustrated* and upset when things don't go the way he wants them to, some of which involve you and some that don't. He may get more profoundly upset and stay that way for longer periods than people who don't have his kind of deeper emotional struggles. However, if he also carries entitled or disrespectful *values* about what you owe him as his female partner, that mentality will shape *when, how,* and *over what issues* he becomes frustrated, and will make him feel justified in taking those frustrations out on you. For example, if he believes that you should always put aside your feelings and needs in order to focus exclusively on keeping him happy, that attitude is what is causing him to become frustrated in the first place. And it is his destructive values that determine **what degree of bullying or mental cruelty he finds acceptable** when he's blaming you for his frustration.

Addiction Combined with Abusive Values

When an addict is under the influence of alcohol or drugs, he might go on a more severe verbal tirade against you than he would do when sober. The chemicals in his system can disinhibit him, so that he lets everything that he is thinking come pouring out uncensored. But the substance didn't put that thinking inside of him; it was already there. The content of his tirades reveal his values about your role as a partner, your worth as a human being, and the purpose of a woman's body.

We've also dealt with several cases where the man went out drinking or drugging to rev himself up for verbal or physical abuse of his partner that he had already decided she deserved, knowing that later he could blame his behavior on the substance. (Abusive clients of ours have admitted to doing just this.)

Here are some other ways these two dynamics can combine, with the addictive trait given first, followed by the abusive trait (in italics):

He often makes excuses to evade responsibility for his actions, and *he particularly tends to blame his behavior on you.*

His addiction keeps him locked into being an angry person, and *he believes he has the right to be a bully when he's mad.*

His finances tend to be in a mess, and *he acts like you're being a bad person when you try to complain about all the stress that his financial irresponsibility is causing you.*

He can't connect in a meaningful and intimate way emotionally or physically—because he's really not himself in the grip of the addiction, and *he calls you a "demanding bitch" or other degrading names when you express how bad it feels to be involved with a partner who is not really there.*

Hoping He's "Just Sick"

It can be tempting to see your partner as having psychological problems, rather than seeing him as choosing the way he is treating you. It may feel better, for example, to conclude that your partner's history of trauma is the reason why he is so controlling, so that the issue has to do with how he interacts with everybody, not just you. Perhaps it is easier to stand by him and struggle for change if you see him as having a "disease" or a "sickness," and you can feel less personally wounded by the way he treats you. It can be harder to consider, for example, that you partner's controlling behavior might be coming from his belief that a man has the right to make all the key decisions in a relationship, and that your opinions are less valuable than his.

We have two concerns, though, that we would like you to consider. First, a personality disorder is actually no less difficult to overcome than a problem with abusiveness; in fact, there are indications that it may be *more* resistant to change. Post-trauma reactions show better rates of healing than personality disorders do, but the path is still a difficult and uncertain one. So determining that your partner's core problems have primarily to do with his mental health, not his attitudes, can give you a clearer path but not an easier one.

Second, we want you to listen closely to your own inner voices and intuition. If you are recognizing abusiveness in your partner's attitudes and behavior, it's important not to overlook that; as we will explain in detail in the pages ahead, your well-being, and perhaps even your safety, depend on looking squarely at his issues.

Hiding Behind the Hurt

Destructive people often hide behind their history of injuries as a way of not taking full responsibility for their choices or their selfish intentions. This can be confusing, as their injuries *do* play some role in their destructiveness; however, whatever the root cause of destructiveness, be it emotional disturbance, specifically traumatic disturbances, addiction, or abusive values, your partner is exercising a greater range of choice in how he acts than he is admitting.

We recognize that your partner's mental health problems can make it hard for you to tell just how much *choice* he really has over his actions. Our years of experience working with people with traumatic pasts who have gone on to mistreat others persuade us that the most helpful stance for you to take is:

Regardless of the damage your partner has sustained emotionally, he is responsible for his behavior and his thinking.

It is a reasonable expectation on your part that your partner both attend to you *and* take responsibility for himself, even as he heals or goes through a process of recovery. There are large numbers of people who have been terribly hurt yet do not go on to hurt others, and who in fact become loving and giving people. They are able to make meaning in their lives that builds on the strengths and resilience that they salvage from the emotional wreckage they have endured. They do not escape unscathed; no one does. But they also are not human wrecking balls, despite their horrific pasts. People can and do heal, becoming strong in the broken places. However, changing violent and disrespectful attitudes about relationships, especially when those beliefs are reinforced by friends, family, media, and key role models (including some celebrities), can actually be a harder task for the destructive partner than healing from what has been done to him.

What If My Partner Fits Some (or Many) of These Abusive Characteristics?

No woman wants to live with the discovery that she is involved with a destructive individual—especially when she has seen that person's better aspects, and loves him. The following set of steps will help you digest the information you've just worked through, and to sort out some sticky questions. In addition to doing some writing about each point, look for a supportive person in your life who could listen well to you as you think out loud about your reactions to these exercises.

EXERCISE 5–3:

Reflect some on who you are now compared with who you were when you met your partner. Are you happier or less happy? Has your self-confidence gone up, or has it decreased? How have your connections with friends and relatives gone during this period? Are you becoming isolated? Is confusion a more common part of your life than it used to be? Do you feel more attractive, or less so? How has your energy level changed?

EXERCISE 5–4:

Think about how people you care about view you, and view your relationship, at this point. If you have been dismissing other people's concerns, work now to make more space inside yourself to take their perspective in. Has anyone expressed being worried about you? Are people saying that they see your well-being declining? Has anyone said that they are not sure you are being treated well? Have any friends or relatives let you know that they don't like your partner? Do you find yourself repeatedly having to make excuses for him? Are you keeping secrets about him because you don't want people to think badly about him?

Note that we are not asking you to believe what everyone else says; you should continue to form your own conclusions. But we would like you to let your guard down enough to take in what they are seeing and understand where it is coming from.

EXERCISE 5–5:

Let's look now at your own internal dialogue. What explanations do you give yourself for his behavior to make it feel okay? What are the messages you give yourself about why, and how, his behavior is going to improve in the future? Are these messages realistic, given your experience with him so far? Are you running away from signs that his behavior is not going to change? What are your own intuitions telling you? Are you avoiding hearing things that your own inner voices are saying?

As you do this exercise, avoid self-criticism as much as you possibly can. Just notice what is going on with you. Clarity will come to you over time if you just keep observing your own thoughts and feelings, and writing about them.

EXERCISE 5–6:

This one might take some time. Write down everything you can think of that you have avoided saying to your partner, and all the aspects of who you are that you have avoided letting him see. Are there subjects that you don't dare bring up because of how strongly he will react? Are their parts of you that you know he won't like, so you keep them hidden? Have you given up activities, or attachments, or even things you used to enjoy thinking or dreaming about, because you know he doesn't approve of those things? (Really think about this. You may have made sacrifices without even realizing it, to keep the peace and avoid his criticism.)

Next, consider what you would say to your partner if you felt safe to tell him exactly what you think and feel—about him, about yourself, about your relationship, about your opinions on life and the world. Let it all out on paper now. Then keep that piece of paper in a very safe place, or even ask a friend to hang on to it for you so it isn't in the house where he might find it.

If many of the ideas in this chapter have been new to you, you may find your-self feeling stirred up, or downhearted, or even a little freaked out. Many women have reported similar reactions when they begin reading Lundy's book *Why Does He Do That?* We understand that this is a hard process. Try to reach out to anyone you can think of whom you trust, and open up about what is going on for you. Or if no one comes to mind who could fill that role, call an abused women's hotline anonymously and pour out some of what you have been holding in. Hotlines are not just for women who have faced physical vio-lence or sexual assault from their partners; any woman who is feeling hurt or confused about the way her partner is treating her is free to call. (And the partner need not be a man; if your relationship is with a woman, the hotline has an ear for you, too. As we mentioned in the preface, women can be abusive and destructive to other women.)

If you are coming to the conclusion that your partner is abusive, it does not mean that he is a bad person, or that you need to stop feeling love for him. It does mean that you will need to face up to the fact that he is not good for you, that he is a toxic force in your life. He will either have to give up his abusive-ness or learn to live without you. You may reach the point where you decide you have to stay away from him permanently, for the sake of your own mental health; but even then you are likely to continue having caring and loving feel-ings for him—from a safe distance.

Awareness Can Be Painful—but It's Worth It

Anyone in a destructive relationship has asked herself, "What is going on with my partner?" If you are like other women in this position, you ask yourself this question and spend hours piecing together the evidence with whoever will listen. The search for the answer is also a search for hope. You hope that if we could understand what is going on, then you would feel a sense of relief from the tensions you face and you would know what to do.

However, even when you *are* successful, when you find answers that pro-vide you with a fairly accurate map of the patterns of behaviors that have dis-appointed you, you may remain troubled. One reason is that the clearer you become, the more you experience a sense of loneliness and growing distance from your partner, as you come to realizations about him that he is not ready to face up to yet, or has only begun to look at. Your awareness is way ahead of his, and as a result you can see how much work it's going to take for him to fix it. You wonder anxiously, "Can he do it? Will he?"

Your awareness also tends to bring you a sense of loneliness.

Still, hang in there. Finding clear patterns is validating and reassuring of your sanity. This work of clarifying what is going on with him is for *you*. It is intended to help you see better what is happening with your partner so that you can make your decision about going or staying with more certainty about what exactly you are keeping and what you are leaving behind.

Whether the root problem is emotional disturbance, trauma, addiction, abusive values, or a combination of them all, staying in a relationship where any of these is present—even if progress is being made—will come at a cost to you emotionally, physically, and spiritually, and likely financially as well. Whether you leave or stay, we want to provide you with a way to honor the struggling human being for whom you obviously care while honoring yourself at least that much. As you sort out what you believe to be the root problem, know that whichever it is, the road to his recovery is multilayered, will move with fits and starts, and ultimately is not about you, even after all the life and energy you have given. For even if your partner does engage in all the hard work to maintain a life of healing and recovery, even if your partner is able to live in a way that makes amends to you, your life will not be made anew by his healing and recovery. *Your* healing will still need to take place—from the pain that he has caused you—and your relationship will need to be rebuilt in a new way.

The freedom he may earn through his efforts toward recovery and healing certainly can bring you some relief. But mostly what his progress will do is to provide an *opportunity* to build a new phase in your relationship; it will take time to see how successful that work is going to be, and how much it will lead to your feeling better. In short, even if you stay to see his freedom begin to blossom, this will only mark a new state, a delicate beginning that rests on tender new connections. Beneath these are losses that can never be undone, though their effects can heal over time. For these reasons, much of the work ahead in this book will be asking you to make yourself and your children your highest priority, guiding you in assessing what your own needs are for healing and rejuvenation, and leading you into that renewal process.

KNOWLEDGE LEADS TO POWER

We have taken you through an exploration of how emotional disturbances, trauma, and addiction combine with abusive values to create a destructive force that can exhaust you and confuse you. Despite the complicated feelings all this information may bring up for you, the good news is that you are on the path to clarity.

Regardless of what you find is the root of destructiveness in your relationship, throughout this book we will ask you to:

- define what you expect
- take stock of what the relationship gives you
- insist on what you want (as safety permits)
- assess progress forward

You have the right to expect:

- that your partner will trust what you tell him about the problems in his behavior and the toll it all has taken on you, and will not keep fighting you over the facts to avoid dealing with his issues
- that your partner will commit to ongoing and appropriate help if he wants to be in a relationship with you
- that your partner will attend to you, your life, and your needs while getting his ongoing help, rather than claiming that he can't be sensitive or attentive to you "because I'm working on myself right now"

You are brave. We know that we are looking with you at some painful patterns that are not what anyone hopes for when they start a relationship. We have a vision for you. We can see your courage. We write this thinking about your finding your way, and getting the clarity and freedom and love that you deserve. We believe in you.

SIX

Am I the Problem?

"Maybe I'm the problem. I get so angry."

"I've got a lot of baggage from before him. I'm no picnic."

"He tells me all the time that I've changed, and you know, it is true; I really have changed."

"Do you think I'm just taking my frustrations out on him that are really about other things?"

I WAS A HOT mess," Kim tells us. "My husband had all of these PTSD symptoms, like sometimes waking up in cold sweats and trying to choke me. Then he'd come at me with these abusive ideas about how I was supposed to just handle all the extreme stuff he was doing. In this whirlwind, I hadn't even begun to realize I had my *own* trauma to deal with. But the way he was toward me just set me off deep into my own heavy stuff. Then he turned that on me, of course, said that I was crazy, told me that he had gotten sober and he had done all the changing he was going to do, and goddammit the rest was on me. From here on I was the problem as far as he was concerned."

Kim's situation illustrates how confusing it can be to sort out when you are having natural reactions to unhealthy conditions, and when, on the other hand, you are seeing signs of things in yourself that you do need to work on changing.

In this chapter, we will:

- examine your partner's effects on you, so you can stop blaming yourself for the things that he's responsible for
- introduce the importance of seeing *context* in understanding the kinds of powerful feelings that come up for you, and the reactions you have to events in your relationship
- look closely at your beliefs about what it means to be a loving woman in a relationship
- help you distinguish between extreme emotional states (which other people can cause you to have) and inappropriate *behavior* (which you need to take responsibility for yourself)
- look with you at any destructive tendencies or attitudes that might be creeping into your own actions

DOES IT ALWAYS TAKE TWO TO TANGO?

You may have friends, relatives, or professionals (such as a therapist) who respond to what has happened to you by expressing some of the following mistaken philosophies:

- "All relationship struggles are made up of two people who are equally responsible for the bad chemistry."
- "You sought out and found a destructive partner in order to fulfill some deep need you have to be treated badly, probably rooted in the dynamics of the family you were raised in."
- "No shame, no blame. It doesn't help to call him out strongly on what he's done, or tell him the kind of harm his actions have caused, because he can't really help his destructiveness, given how wounded he is himself."

Our work has taught us that these outlooks are actually part of the problem, not part of the solution. First, these people are taking principles that go with healthy relationships and applying them to a destructive partner; it's like telling someone who has been bitten by a charging dog, "Oh, here, next time just use this command to tell the dog to sit; everything will be okay."

In a healthy relationship, for example, we can look at the "Conflict Stage" and find ways to reach compromises, or create a new vision that meets both partners' needs, or help people manage their emotional reactions to intimacy. *That* you could legitimately think of as a dance. But dealing with an unhealthy or destructive partner is completely different. **It's not a tango, it's a train wreck.** The destructive partner's issues cannot be improved by trying to fix the "chemistry" of the relationship, and his style will keep preventing compromises and solutions from emerging—except for ones that only work for him, not for you.

Can both people in a relationship be destructive? Sure. But we find that it's far more common that the destructive behaviors and unhealthy ways of thinking are coming primarily from one partner. And in the process, the other partner is getting all twisted up from trying to figure out how to manage the results.

The women we have worked with do not seek out a destructive partner to fulfill some mad inner drive toward destruction. They fall for partners who are charming, who seem loving at the beginning, and who are exciting; the problems come later.

Whatever the dynamics of your relationship may be, there is no excuse for anyone mistreating you. Declaring to yourself, and to whoever else will listen, that you will not be responsible for your partner's behavior, only for your own, is part of what begins the healing process. And for him to change, he will need to accept that he owns his actions 100 percent, and other people will need to help hold him accountable.

"He Says I'm the One Who Changed and Ruined Everything."

If you have changed after being treated poorly, that would be normal. We are going to take a careful look at the impact this relationship has had on you so that you can see where the changes in you have come from. Do you have some problems? Of course you do—*everybody does*. And now, because of having lived in an unhealthy relationship, you may well have a few additional problems that weren't there before; but that doesn't make you the problem in your relationship.

So if each partner says the other one is responsible for bringing in the unhealthy element, how do you know which one is true? The simplest answer is to look back at the principles of healthy relationships that we outlined early in Chapter 1; if one partner is violating those principles over and over again, he or she is the source.

In the next series of pages, we are going to explore concepts, questions, and exercises that will help you zero in on the main issues you are struggling with emotionally, and help you assess how serious they may have become. We'll also help you understand where those difficulties come from, including what role addiction may be playing for you.

LOOKING AT THE EFFECTS OF TRAUMA ON YOU

In Chapter 4, we looked at some of the effects that trauma may have had on your partner. Now let's look at how similar experiences, including traumatic events that may have occurred in your current relationship, have affected you.

This chapter contains reflections that may be painful. We encourage you, if at all possible, to work on this chapter with a trusted friend, therapist, or support group, in order to strengthen your sense of connection to others while moving through your reflections. If you choose to reflect alone, we have included short interludes or breaks from some of the heavier reflective work. During these breaks, we ask you to commit, as part of the workbook, to putting down the book and engaging in the short rituals or moments of awareness that we provide to help you reaffirm your sense of strength and wholeness.

Let's begin together.

EXERCISE 6–1: BODY SCAN

Sit comfortably in a place where you feel at ease. Take a moment and scan your body, paying attention to where you feel a sense of softness in your body and where you feel tension. Start at the toes and move your attention upward, checking in with each part of your body. Don't try to relax, or try to change what you notice; simply notice. When you are done, write what you noticed about the ease and tension as it exists in your body at this time. This is a practice we will return to periodically. We want you to get familiar with paying attention, without judgment, to the sensations in your body. We will practice simply noticing, without rushing to understand, what it is that you are physically sensing. This kind of awareness in the present moment is called being mindful of your body experience. This kind of slowed attention can quicken your healing process. Remember: the slower you go, the faster you heal.

EXERCISE 6–2: TAKING STOCK

Now let's take time to reflect on these questions about how you are doing.

YOUR SENSE OF EASE

1. Do you think you feel wound up, edgy, or tense in reaction to your partner's behavior?

2. Do people you trust tell you that you seem that way?

3. Did you feel this way before you met him and feel it more now? Or has this begun only since you started the relationship?

FINDING SLEEP

1. Do you awaken with nightmares that seem completely real to you, as though they are an exact filming of some intense memory?

2. Do you awaken flailing or yelling from vivid dreams?

3. Do you take a long time to fall asleep?

4. Are you sensitive to noise, awakening frequently throughout the night?

INTENSITY

1. Do you relive negative situations in the past as though they are occurring in the present?

2. Do you react to stressful situations as though they are intensely negative situations—later to look back and see that they are not so negative—or later to get feedback from those you trust that the situation was not as profoundly negative as you had perceived it to be?

If you find that you are resonating with these questions, we want to assure you that the effects we are describing are natural reactions, and you can heal. Continuing with the process of this book and working the exercises will be a healing process in itself. We will also be discussing various options you can pursue to take charge of your own emotional well-being; Chapter 21, "Growing a New Heart," is particularly devoted to this topic.

We do recommend that you begin thinking now, while you are still early in this process, about where you might find additional supports for your healing, whether through support groups in your town, sharing more deeply with friends and relatives, or using professional therapy. (The "Resources" section in the back of the book also offers additional healing ideas that you can pursue.)

THE IMPORTANCE OF CONTEXT

This next question is a tricky contemplation. A partner who is trying to avoid looking at himself will typically claim that your reaction to his treatment of you is inappropriate and overblown. By doing so, he is negating **context**, meaning the history of his behavior over time and how the effects of mistreatment have *accumulated*. All the unfair or mean things that your partner has done in the past *shape how you experience what is happening* now—and they should! Context is everything when sorting out what something means to you.

For example, think of Joanne. Joanne has lived with Josh for five years. Josh struggles with severe depression, has used substances on a daily basis, and has been unable to hold on to steady employment. Joanne is profoundly relieved that Josh has begun taking medication, going to therapy regularly, and getting work through a temp agency. Then one day Joanne arrives at home to find evidence of his substance of choice in the living room and that he's obviously been sleeping all day and missed work; she is panicked, understandably, and feels irate, seriously questioning her ability to stay in this relationship. She wakes Josh up and speaks furiously to him. But his response is to wave his hand dismissively at her, and he says with disgust in his voice, "I called in sick *one* day and caught up on sleep—what is your problem? I can't believe you're making such a big deal about it."

Joanne fears she is witnessing the crumbling of the foundation on which she had based her hopes that the relationship would survive. She is looking back, questioning the wisdom of giving the support, love, and time that she has already given. At the same time, she is trying to figure out whether there is hope for a future, and whether she has the energy or desire to work with Josh through a relapse into depression and substance use.

Is Joanne's reaction controlling, overblown, unstable, or unfairly demanding? Not at all; she is actually being entirely reasonable when the *context* is kept in mind.

Men who are stuck in destructive patterns erase, dismiss, or trivialize the context of their actions. In other words, you can't determine whether your reactions to him are appropriate or not by what *he* says about it; he's ignoring how the history of hurt and broken promises adds up. The additional challenge for you, though, is that he points at the intensity of your agitation and says that it proves that something is wrong with you, or even shows that you're crazy. (And you may start to feel crazy.)

EXERCISE 6-3: LOOKING AT YOUR FEELINGS IN CONTEXT

Are there things that happen in your relationship to which you find yourself reacting very strongly, with a "heat" and upset that you did not always have in the past? If so, what are the things that happen *now* that trigger such a strong reaction in you?

EXERCISE 6-4: PREPARING YOUR VISION

We are going to ask you soon to write some about the history, or context, that makes your reactions feel so strong, including things that have occurred in your past before this relationship. Since this can be intense, we'd like you to first try an exercise that prepares you with a positive vision of yourself and your future.

This exercise works best if you can go out into a pleasant outdoor, natural spot; if this is not an option for you, use what you can find around you indoors. Search around and find two objects, natural ones if possible, that represent the following to you:

1. Where you are now when you think about your sense of healing and your relationship

2. Where you picture yourself being when you've reached your healing goals and feel clear about your relationship. Choose something that represents how you imagine you will feel once you are truly satisfied with your decision. It may be a flower fully in bloom, or a beautifully woven tapestry that speaks to you, reminding you that this is the kind of complete and flourishing feeling you will be experiencing once you know what to do about your relationship.

Once you return from out-of-doors, you can place the objects you've chosen on a simple altar. An altar can be a small space that is invested with meaning for you; it might be a little table, or a spot next to your toothbrush, or where you keep your shoes. Try to find a place that you will see often. If your partner is disrespectful of your space and your beliefs, it might be more important to you to find a space to keep your altar that is not noticeable to him, or to use a shared space, but to keep your altar unobtrusive. The dried sticks and the seashells (for example) may look like nothing more than decorating choices to others, but to you they will be invested with the recognition and honoring of important parts of yourself.

Take a few minutes to consider what exactly these things mean to you, reaching for the truth of the feeling, the core of it. Then, when you feel ready, put some of these thoughts into writing.

EXERCISE 6–5: ANOTHER BODY SCAN

As you complete the exercise above, and especially thinking back on the question "Where will you be when your healing goals are fulfilled and you are clear about your relationship?" notice any sensations in your body that come to your attention. How are your head and shoulders positioned? What is the feeling in your belly, or your legs, when you consider where you will be when your healing goals are fulfilled and you are clear about your relationship?

Write your answers in your journal.

PREPARING TO "WALK ON COALS"

Just as a woman would not walk on coals without adequate mental and physical preparation, we do not want you to run headlong into upsetting material. We are going to ask you soon to write about the things that have happened to you that you feel are the cause of *why* you react so strongly, so powerfully negatively, and so deeply in response to certain events, either within or outside your relationship. (Some of the thoughts you have may feel too big or too disturbing for you to write about them, and that's okay. Do what feels right for you.)

- Before you write, we ask that you think about anyone with whom you have shared your story, or significant parts of it. If it was a positive connection, is it possible to arrange to speak with that person after you write? Do you have someone you can talk with about what you are exploring for yourself?
- Notice how you are feeling when you consider writing about your story. How do you usually handle your upset related to these things? Do you feel a sense of relief accompanied with crying or do you feel something closer to bereft and stuck?
- Do you feel you have at least a few reliable ways of bringing yourself to a place that feels good and healthy after you have been upset? For example, some women get very cold when dealing with deeply upsetting feel-

ings. They know this, so they plan to take a hot bath or shower after this kind of work. Or they plan to gather warm blankets around themselves. Some women turn their attention to noticing what they hear, physically sense, or see around them to help reorient them to the present. A swim in cold water might be just the thing you turn to, or a long run. If taking in beautiful surroundings, listening to music, or watching a funny movie are things you know work for you, take the time to nurture yourself with these things when you need a break.

If you know enough about how you handle these kinds of reflections, and feel confidence going forward, we encourage you to proceed with the exercise below with all the caring and skill you already possess.

However, if the event(s) that come to mind are things that you haven't told anyone about before, and you

- feel overwhelmed
- feel like hurting yourself just by thinking about doing this exercise
- feel that you don't know how to, or can't, take care of your own upset feelings

we ask that you only proceed with this exercise with the support of a hotline advocate, a positive supportive group, a skilled friend, or a therapist with a good background in trauma. If you choose a friend, be sure it is one who knows how to truly focus on you in a way that feels supportive and loving.

(There are several therapeutic approaches that can be very effective for dealing with trauma. We will list these in "Resources." One form, Trauma Focused Cognitive Behavioral Therapy, has a clinician work with a woman to write what is called her "Trauma Narrative." Other body-based interventions help you thoughtfully experience the gestures or movements that your body needed to make in response to past emotional distress but that you were not able to let out in the moment of the traumatic event so they remained incomplete. These interventions help you process the feelings, memories, and sensations that are trapped in your body as you work through your story. Over time, you work with the story of what has happened so thoroughly that you can refer to it or think about it without the same devastating impact.)

Now, if you are ready to proceed . . .

EXERCISE 6–6: WHAT HAPPENED

If you notice that you react with great upset or heat to what is happening in your relationship now, we want you to write about the things that have happened to you in your life that have hurt you the most deeply. If something prior to this relationship comes to mind, write that down; you may be thinking of events from your childhood, or from other times in life. Writing events in their chronological order might help you organize your thoughts.

Write until you feel you have told your truth about what happened to you. Write until your truth leads you to the present, wherever it is you feel you are now in your life's story of prevailing over hurt. Take plenty of breaks as needed. Use the framework provided below if it helps you. Address these prompts with the slow, unrushed attention that we know speeds along healing.

> *It began when . . .*
> *The next thing I remember happening that stands out is . . .*
> *The following three things stand out as most significant after that . . .*
> *Now I . . .*

What was writing that like for you? Write what it feels like to have traced the context of where you are now in your relationship.

EXERCISE 6–7: BODY SCAN AND SELF-CARE

Hold or gaze upon the object you chose to symbolize where you will be when your healing goals are fulfilled. Take deep breaths as you gently bring your attention to this image and notice the sensations in your body. It may help, after reflecting, to move, get up, and notice the different objects that are in the space where you are: trees, plants, the sky, or if you're indoors, paintings, plants, furniture, colors. Take note of the things you hear, the sensations under your foot or hand, and what you see around you. You might put cool water on your face. Allow water to run through your hands, all the while congratulating yourself for the work you are doing to gain clarity.

EXERCISE 6–8: BEHIND GLASS

What if you don't experience great upset and emotional heat as a result of your experiences? What if you feel a sense of numbness instead? Do you feel sometimes as though you exist behind a glass wall, feeling removed, watching events that you know should matter, but not feeling them? If so, can you describe briefly a time when this has occurred?

Do you often feel that no one really "gets" you? Are you feeling isolated? Is it often exhausting to be around others?

Think about your friendships. Do you think you tend to see any of these relationships through a lens of extremes, such that your friends are in the inner circle, unconditionally, or else they are out of the circle for good? Do you notice that you feel an intense desire to attach, but then you withdraw from the friendship once the attachment happens?

If these questions resonate with you at all, take time to write some of your thoughts and feelings.

EXERCISE 6–9: BROKEN CIRCLE

Do you feel you cannot generally trust in others? If so, was there a time earlier in life when you remember being able to trust people? Was there a turning point where you lost trust? If so, in your journal create a symbol, a picture, or a word that symbolizes this event to you. When you are finished, put a circle around what you have drawn.

If you are not someone who draws, you can instead add to your small altar, choosing an object that represents and honors the loss of your sense of trust.

EXERCISE 6–10: THE CONTEXT OF YOUR SPIRIT

Knowing we will return to these things, let's take a look at this symbol of your broken trust in other people in another context. The larger context this time is not the history of loss, but is *you*, your spirit, and the things that strengthen the spirit of you. Take a moment to think of the things that bring you hope, that remind you of a deep, abiding sense of love. Is there a song that stirs this in you? Is there a spiritual teacher or being whom you love and honor? Is there a person, a thought, a prayer, poem, or an idea that stirs in you the expansive place of wellness? Of goodness?

Go back to your symbol of loss of trust. Next to it, or surrounding it, draw an image or write some words that represent your sense of wellness and goodness. Surround the symbol of loss of trust with a drawing that represents hope. If you have chosen to add to your altar instead of drawing, place your symbol of hope beside what honors your losses. By now, your altar might feature:

- something that honors your loss of trust

- something that represents where you are now when you think about your sense of healing and your relationship

- something that represents where you will be when you feel you've reached your healing goals and feel clear about your relationship

- something that represents your sense of love, wellness, and goodness

EXERCISE 6–11: TIME AGAIN FOR BODY SCANNING

When you are done representing your symbol for hope, love, and goodness, take a moment to notice what is happening in your body. Scan again, from the toes to the backs of your knees, through to your hip bones, through your belly, up to your chest, your shoulders, the throat, the feeling around the eyes, and the top of your head. Make a note of anything that comes to mind.

EXERCISE 6–12: TRYING TO MAKE IT GO AWAY

Let's take stock of how you are managing your stronger feelings. After each question below, there will be a series of statements in italics. Please read them and circle any that resonate with you. There is also a place for you to write your own statement.

Do you try to manage overwhelming feelings or numbness by eating too much?

> *"I am always rummaging for food, silently asking, 'What can I have now? What can I have that's special for me?'"*
>
> *"I can have more, so I will."*
>
> *"I'm always hungry."*

Yours:

Do you use substances to manage your feelings?

> *"I deserve a break."*
>
> *"What I'm doing is not as bad as what he does."*
>
> *"I'll stop when things get better."*

Yours:

Do you compulsively play video games or watch television, sports, or movies to the exclusion of your natural sleep and rest rhythms, or so that they interfere with your responsibilities and possible connection to others?

> *"I'll just watch/read/do one more thing."*
>
> *"I don't get any time for myself. I'll just stay up."*
>
> *"I can't sleep anyway with all this on my mind."*

Yours:

Do you compulsively spend money you can't afford in order to feel good?

> *"I deserve something special."*
>
> *"No one else is going to take care of me."*

"This will make me feel better."

Yours:

Do you use masturbation or pornography to a degree that you notice keeps you from ever dealing with parts of your life that are painful for you?
   "I deserve this."
   "It doesn't hurt anyone and it's nobody's business."
   "Leave me alone."

Yours:

NOT AS FLEXIBLE AS YOU WERE

There are various changes that happen to the internal world of people who have been in unhealthy relationships, leading them to have a harder time than they did before responding to people and events with a sense of openness or ease. It wouldn't be surprising, then, for you to find that you have lost some of your flexibility. As you read, notice which of these difficulties seem to be challenges for you.

- Handling Change and Transitions
   Your partner's unpredictable changes and explosions may have had the effect of leading you to feel anxious or off balance regarding change

in general. He also may have put you down about how unskilled and unintelligent you supposedly are; these kinds of verbal assaults can make you lose your sense of being competent to face the unknown.

- Losing Your Sense of Humor

   "I used to be funny" is one of the most common laments we hear from women in destructive relationships. If your partner takes no joy in your intelligence and puts no value on your point of view, he is not likely going to find you amusing either. Without a good audience, or with a toxic one, you are not going to be funny. The ability to be humorous also represents the resilience of the spirit, an ability at least for the moment to stay alive and fighting; and it's no surprise if you aren't feeling all that springy these days. Don't worry. You will see your capacity for creating laughter come back to life.

- Problem Solving and Planning

   If your partner has been unreliable (or reliably destructive), it makes it hard to plan for the future. How can you figure out what you have to work with if the rules keep changing? Not only that, but your partner may have taken over most of the decision making, leaving you without a say. So now you may feel uncomfortable and at a loss when you're faced with making a plan.

- Anticipating Outcomes

   Destructive partners are notoriously fickle. What pleases them one day will make them irate the next. Long exposure to this trait in your partner makes it hard for you to guess how other people will react to you in daily situations.

- Listening Deeply to Opposing Points of View

   In a destructive relationship, communication is like learning the signals at the train crossing so that you don't get caught on the tracks when the train is coming. You are listening for signs of reproach and blame, ready to evade the ongoing wreck when necessary, particularly if your partner has been controlling or abusive. This history with him can make it hard for you to adjust to communication with people who want you to fully engage with their opposing point of view; conflictive interactions may feel quite unsafe to you for a while. It might also be hard to sort out the "gray areas" in new situations after years of having to deal with the rigid, black-and-white rules of your partner's approach to things.

- Expressing Concerns, Needs, or Thoughts Directly

  You are out of practice. You may have found that expressing yourself directly with your partner led often to ugly scenes, or at least led to him dismissing you with a laugh or other put-down. So you've had to learn to be indirect, or simply to keep everything to yourself.

- Managing Emotional Responses

  You might feel upset by a wide range of events, feel deeply upset when triggered, and have a hard time returning to a baseline of well-being. Being with a partner who does not recognize and validate your feelings and your point of view, or who has hurt you deeply emotionally or physically, has lasting effects. It can feel almost crippling to accept any negative feedback, no matter how gently given.

- Accepting Authority or Direction in a Group Setting

  One's partner's refusal to participate in fair decision making is one of the most common characteristics of a destructive relationship. To function well in a group of people now, you need to be able to speak up, take a different point of view, and accept new ideas, while letting go of the urge to rally teammates to fortify your point of view. In your relationship, you've probably paid a high price for communicating in these healthy ways. It takes some healing work to accede to ethical leadership after an unhealthy relationship. When you've been in a relationship where your partner has abused authority, you are likely to need to do some healing work before you will feel comfortable trusting other people to use authority appropriately, and trusting yourself not to give over too much of your own power.

- Recognizing Internalized Abuse Distortions

  You might be certain that "nobody likes me." You might feel the need to hide the "fact" that "I'm stupid," and you may find all efforts for change useless because "things will never change." These distortions imposed by your partner (if he behaved abusively) can become so familiar that they just don't seem like distortions. It takes work to recognize when they are at play, restricting your horizons.

- Hard to Be Alone

    It can be excruciating to be alone when you have a huge well of unmet need for intimacy. Spending time by yourself can be frightening when you don't know how to process your grief or deep upset in a safe way. Chapter 8 is devoted to helping you learn to come back to your center, and to discover that your center can be a good place to be again.

EXERCISE 6–13: BELIEFS ABOUT YOUR ROLE IN A RELATIONSHIP

Let's examine some of the beliefs that you may have about intimate relationships. Below you will find statements. Please read them and their accompanying comments, and then write down your thoughts in response to the questions that follow:

YOU CAN BE A SUCCESS BY "COMPLETING" A RELATIONSHIP.
Women are under great pressure to be in a relationship and to stay in a relationship. But when a relationship or commitment ends, you have the choice to consider it a "completed relationship" rather than a "failed relationship."

What do you find most challenging about this thought?

How is it different from related ideas you may have heard or have?

LOVING WOMEN LEAVE RELATIONSHIPS.

Women are rarely supported in the notion that it can be a loving decision to detach oneself from a relationship even when her partner really doesn't want to say good-bye. But you can be a loving person and still decide to leave a relationship.

What do you find most challenging about this thought?

How is it different from related ideas you may have heard or have?

IT IS COMMON TO FEEL INTENSE ATTACHMENT TO AN UNHEALTHY RELATIONSHIP.

It can be incredibly confusing to feel a deep attachment to someone that you have left or are going to leave. Attachment to destructive relationships can be very powerful. Men, women, children, prostitutes, even prisoners of war, all experience a greater bond to the person who hurt and scared them if that person was also occasionally caring or kind, or provided necessities of life such as food or shelter.

What do you find most challenging about this thought?

How is it different from related ideas you may have heard or have?

IT IS NORMAL TO FEEL GRIEF OVER LEAVING A RELATIONSHIP WHERE YOU HAVE BEEN HURT.

When you are leaving a destructive relationship, there are many things to grieve. You need to grieve:

the loss of what you might have had, or wanted to have.

the loss of all that you had given.

the loss of whatever good you were getting.

the loss of the chance of repair. You want the person who has caused the harm to repair it, and if you leave him, you are accepting that he never will.

Once you have told your friends or family about the bad side of your relationship, you often lose any support from them for grieving your losses, because people don't understand how much we can love people who have harmed us.

Some women choose to wait to leave until the sense of attachment and hope has withered or frayed nearly completely, in the hopes that it will spare them some of the grief of choosing to go. If you choose this route, pay attention to the cost: your inner resources are also withering and fraying. Your grief will be there, but do not be afraid. Your grief can, and will, heal.

When you are sorting through the pain, the events, and the moments of decision in your relationship, you will likely return again and again to the same stories. Think of your process as a spiral, with you moving up toward a greater perspective, even as you circle over the same events.

Yet sometimes you can find yourself telling your story repetitively without gaining any further perspective or benefit to yourself. It can be tempting to think that if you just keep retelling your story, it will somehow relieve your pain. If you notice that you are doing this, *slow down*. When you talk, talk more slowly. Listen deeply to your own truths held within your stories. There could be any number of things for you to notice about your own story, but sometimes the deep truth you are conveying is simply your pain and grief.

What are your thoughts about the grief you have?

SPIRITUAL WOMEN HOLD THEIR PARTNERS ACCOUNTABLE AND LEAVE RELATIONSHIPS.

For women who live a life of spiritual worship, it is important to find a way to honor your partner as a spiritual being. You need to do this while considering:

his level of destructiveness

what it takes for him to change, and

whether he can honor you spiritually enough to deserve your partnership

It is true that love works miracles of healing, but that healing still can only come if there is also hard work and devotion on his part. If you do decide to leave, *it can be a path of love and wisdom that leads you there.*

What do you find most challenging about this thought?

GOOD MOTHERS IN DESTRUCTIVE RELATIONSHIPS HAVE PERIODS WHEN THEIR CHILDREN BLAME THEM FOR THE DAMAGE.

Unfortunately, this is very common. If you are less scary as a parent than your partner is, if you are more consistent and more reliable toward the children than he is, one difficult outcome can be that your children find it safer to vent their feelings of rage and impotence toward you. It's good that you have made it possible for them to express themselves with you in a way they can't with him, but the results can be stressful for you.

If your partner is overbearing, always "right," and attempting to assert control over what happens in the family (and all the while not taking responsibility for keeping it functioning), your children may identify with his position rather than yours—being on the "winning" side looks more bearable to them. Older children might long for you to simply accept that they feel they must attend to the destructive parent's needs, perhaps spending more time with him than with you. Older children might pull away from you for a while. Sadly, they might even let you know that they can truly be themselves only with you, while still spending their precious time, energies, and holidays appeasing the destructive parent. At these times you can see that your children are also managing a destructive relationship, and perhaps with significantly more vulnerability than you.

What do you think of the idea that a good mother in a destructive relationship can have periods where her children blame her for the destruction?

WOMEN WHO ARE IN DESTRUCTIVE RELATIONSHIPS CAN HAVE GREAT FRIENDSHIPS.

We think of a woman we have worked with named Rachel, who, while navigating her way through a couple of destructive relationships, has been able to successfully keep a circle of supportive confidantes by adopting guidelines that she has shared with them:

TIME LIMITS

Rachel will call a friend and say with humor, "I'd like twenty minutes to go on and on about my thing. I know I've said it all before, but I need to do it again. Can you do twenty minutes?" And then Rachel, against every intense pull to the contrary, will stick to the twenty-minute limit.

RECIPROCITY

Rachel will call the friend back the next day and devote her attention entirely to the friend's cares and concerns, and not mention the relationship issue with which she is still obviously struggling. This way, Rachel is able to take advantage of a wide network of friends who do not get burned out by the intensity and circular nature of sorting through the relationship issues.

REGULATING EMOTIONS

By naming what she is going through and what she needs specifically from her friends, Rachel is managing the often intense pressure and ongoing urgency she feels to figure out this painful situation. Rachel is:

observing her emotions

naming them, and

accepting them with humor and love

Rachel is doing this rather than being swallowed up or consumed by her emotions. Her approach goes a long way toward preserving her friendships because her friends have a sense that Rachel exists outside the relationship struggle, and is connected to them in other areas of their lives. Perhaps more importantly, so does Rachel.

Are there any of Rachel's approaches that you think you might try?

YOUR PARTNER IS RESPONSIBLE FOR HIS OWN WELL-BEING.
Deeply loving women struggle with caring profoundly for partners who are not good for them. They care for them with a love and a sensitivity to their spirits that their partners are not giving themselves—and certainly are not offering in return. It is a challenge to find a way to fully honor a partner who is embroiled in addiction, or who is suffering emotionally in other ways, but who periodically is cruel to you. And it can be unimaginably painful to leave a partner you love who is self-destructing.

Your partner's relationships with others, his spiritual path, and his inner life are his own. If he grows and changes, it will not be because you repaired his relationships, found a spiritual path for him, or learned the inner workings of his psyche. When—if—he changes, it will be because he did these things himself. You can lay out your requirements or even outline resources for him, but then you must step away.

What do you find most challenging about this thought?

HAVE YOU BEEN DESTRUCTIVE?

Since you have been in this relationship, you have likely not conducted yourself perfectly. And, if it has been destructive to you, you have probably heard yourself say and do things that you never thought you would. As we established in our discussion of context, your *feelings* of outrage or exhaustion may be completely justified. But you do not want to allow the abuser's *behaviors* to creep into yours. This risk increases if you are feeling absolutely worn down to the threads, and feeling the fury of not having been seen, heard, or understood regarding what you have endured. Let's recall **Healthy Relationship Principle 3** from Chapter 5: Behavior in a relationship cannot be justified by what the other person did. Two wrongs do not make a right, and one injury can't excuse another. This is true for you.

Places Where It Is Easy to Become Destructive Following Bad Treatment

Aside from becoming destructive to oneself, there are a couple of places where it is most common to become destructive following bad treatment:

- with family members who frustrate your wishes or around whom you feel humiliated by your situation
- with children who are acting out their own anger, presenting behavioral challenges, or simply expressing their own deep and ongoing needs

If you see yourself becoming abusive or destructive in your own behavior, it can be very confusing. Your partner may have been telling you all along that you are the one with the problem; this is how he avoided his own responsibility. *We are not joining his voice.* Your partner is responsible for his own choices. He is responsible for the impact his actions have had on you over time. You need to take responsibility for your own behavior, but not for his.

Your Issues in Your Own Space

If you have done some things that you feel bad about, that doesn't mean that the mistreatment you've endured from your partner is somehow canceled out by your own behavior. Yes, if you have made abusive choices, we want you to stop and get support and help to change; and we do support your committing to your own work and getting help regarding any area in which you have become destructive. But we do not support a counseling strategy for working together as a couple that includes looking at your own possible destructiveness side by side with your partner's, as might happen in couple's counseling. An addicted, personality-disordered, or abusive partner finds addressing his own behaviors intolerable; if his work is done in the same context as yours, he will use that platform to stay focused on what you are doing wrong, and escape looking at himself. Your healing work in this regard is most safely done individually.

You are responsible for your acts. We have deep compassion for those who are severely wounded and wound others, and the terrible pain that causes you and others. You can and must take steps to see, name, and commit to stopping any destructive behaviors that have crept into your own choices—whether they come from mistreatment you have been subjected to or are emerging from other unhealthy role models you have had or values you've been taught.

EXERCISE 6–14:

We ask that you refer to your altar as you prepare for this exercise. We also recommend that, if possible, you work with a friend, support group, or therapist for this part of your reflections.

Read the sentence below and consider if the descriptions fit. Write in the spaces given (or in your journal) examples of what comes to mind.

If I look at my behavior with my children, my family, my friends, my coworkers, and with strangers I meet, I can see that there have been ways in which I have been:

Humiliating
Disrespectful
Aggressive
Contemptuous

EXERCISE 6–15: STATEMENT OF COMMITMENT

Next, write a statement of commitment to yourself that answers whatever it is you found in your reflections above. As you strive to fill yourself with the healing attentions you deserve, we are asking you to make guiding commitments to refrain from taking on destructive choices yourself. This statement should be one that you read aloud, perhaps at a regular interval such as during your morning drive or walking the dog.

For example, you might have found that you are satisfied with how hard you work to protect your children in so many ways from your partner's behavior, and you don't hit your children. However, you also notice that you are extremely impatient with them. You haven't been able to attend to their negative emotions because of how exhausted you've been by this relationship. Your commitment might look like this:

- *I will not hit my children. I protect them.*

- *I also can accept their deep frustration and upset and talk to them about ways to show it.*

- *I will commit time to validating their feelings, even when those feelings are about me.*

- *I can hold my ground with them and still maintain a connection to their point of view.*

- *I will choose consequences for their negative behaviors that do not break the bonds between us.*

Refer to the "Resources" section to find supports that will help you uphold your statement of commitment.

(If your partner has shown any signs of abusiveness—even in subtler ways—it's highly important that he not get hold of anything you've written where you own up to your own behavior problems, as he could use what you admit to against you in the legal system. Make sure to keep these writings in a safe place.)

AM I THE PROBLEM?

This chapter has given you a number of ways to look at the question of whether you are the main source of destructiveness in your relationship. To summarize these in a succinct way, we can say that you are the one who really needs to change if:

- You frequently violate the Relationship Principles we taught in Chapter 5.

AND

- Your partner rarely violates those principles.

AND

- You have at least as much say and power over what happens in your relationship as your partner does—in other words, he has to worry as much about keeping you happy as you have to worry about keeping him happy.

Unless all three of the above points are true, your partner is almost surely the source of the problem, even if he insists that it's you. If you have worked carefully through the previous chapters, trust the conclusions you have come to about whether your partner is abusive, has a mental health problem, struggles with addiction, or is chronically immature. Then focus on doing the work you need to do for yourself, important pieces of which you have already begun in this chapter. We are here to help you face the challenges that lie ahead in your own growth and development, and in seeking to discover what kind of change your partner is capable of. We are confident that you can find your flexibility, power, and humor once more, in safety.

The first six chapters of this book have equipped you with the information you need to sort out what is going on in your relationship. With these insights, you can not only stop blaming yourself, but you can avoid pouring energy into projects that are unlikely to help. In the chapters ahead, we will support you as you turn these understandings into *action,* taking concrete steps that are right for you, that give your partner a clear plan *if he's willing to do the work,* and that will give you back control of your life.

PART II

MOTIVATING FOR CHANGE— HIS AND YOURS

SEVEN

What Makes a Man (Finally) Look at Himself

WHERE WOULD YOU place your partner, based on your current understanding of him, on the following spectrum?

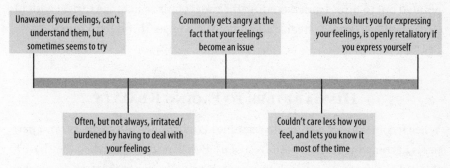

And now find where he goes on this spectrum:

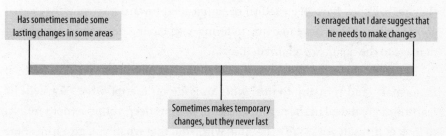

A few weeks or months from now, as you start to see what results you are getting from applying the steps in this book, your assessment of where your partner stands in these areas may change—for the better or the worse. But your initial take gives you a starting point to reflect on. You know your partner well enough to have some intuitive sense of what could get him to move, overcoming the ways in which he is invested in staying stuck. In this chapter, we will look at the kinds of challenges and interventions in a man's life that can motivate him to change. We will then ask you to reflect on which areas you have control over and which ones you don't; for example, you can separate from him, which sometimes spurs a man to look at himself, but you can't get him a better set of friends, which may be crucial to his progress. Finally, you will explore the pros and cons of using those interventions that are available to you, to exert the maximum influence on your partner that you can.

Before we pursue these important areas, we first have to take a step back and look at why he *doesn't* change, or at least why he hasn't wanted to so far. Why does he avoid growth and development? Why doesn't he want to face his problems? Why does he react so strongly when his negative attitudes are pointed out to him? Understanding the roots of his reluctance to deal with his issues will help you strategize about how best to get through to him.

His Barriers to Facing Reality

When it comes to not wanting to examine his more unhealthy aspects, your partner is in company with all of the rest of us. Everyone feels bad when they have to think about the ways in which they are taking poor care of themselves; or when they start to wonder if there are significant distortions in their memory or in their perceptions and sense that their mind isn't working quite right; or when they realize they have been selfish or bullheaded toward someone they cared about; or when they have to come to terms with having done some significant damage to the quality of a human life.

However, there is a difference between being somewhat avoidant—which is normal—and refusing to deal with an issue no matter what. You will be learning a great deal in the period ahead about how deep your partner's refusal to look at himself goes. We're hoping, with you, that when you give him some stiff prods, he's going to decide to grow rather than stay stuck. But you may find out that he is committed to avoiding growth and to blaming it all on you, no matter what the cost. The steps in the chapters ahead will help you to know which way things are going to go.

- **Guilt:** A first barrier to progress for him is guilt. He can't change what he does in the future unless he's willing to face the harm he has done in the past, and in order to do that, he is going to have to accept a time of going through guilt feelings. But what if he can't handle those feelings? This inability can turn up in people who grew up being so severely shamed by their families that they are cast into depression and self-hatred anytime they are challenged about their actions. It also appears in men who are highly selfish, or who consider themselves above "having to go through all that".

- **Absence of Guilt:** An equally problematic barrier is the *absence* of guilt. In truth, too little guilt is even harder to overcome than too much; if he doesn't care how he has hurt you, what could motivate him to make changes? He might make superficial adjustments out of a desire not to lose you, but they won't last long if keeping you is his only motivation.

- **Fear:** His fear of what he may learn about himself, and of what feelings may come up for him if he delves down, can be part of why he keeps coming up with excuses to sweep problems under the rug. He's unlikely to admit that fear has anything to do with it, but trust your own intuitions about the role that it plays.

- **Laziness:** Facing his issues and overcoming them would be a lot of work; one side of him would rather just read the paper or watch the ball game, and pretend that the problems will go away.

- **Disrespect for You:** If he has developed a mental system that gives him elaborate reasons for why your opinions do not need to be taken seriously, you will find it challenging to get him to look at himself through your eyes, and see what you see. You may have already found yourself in a frustrating circle where, for example, you say to your partner, "You are disrespectful to me," and he answers, in a voice that is superior and demeaning, "I'm not *disrespectful* to you—you're disrespectful to *me*." This is the kind of crazy-making interaction that can leave you screaming—or at least wanting to.

- **Escaping uncomfortable feelings through addiction**. If he anaesthetizes himself, that will keep him from seeing what he does. What we mean by this is that growth requires some ability to sit with uncomfortable feelings. If he chases his feelings away with alcohol or drugs, pornography, gambling, or some other addiction, the things you are challenging him about won't sink down to a deep enough level to make a difference. Think of it as a situation where you are successfully pouring medicine into his cup, but he keeps quickly emptying his cup onto the floor before actually drinking it. The result is he doesn't grow.

- **Viewing women as second-class citizens.** He may have the attitude, "She's not supposed to be telling me what I need to work on; she's supposed to be taking care of me and making me happy. Whatever her complaints are, she should take them somewhere else." He's not looking at himself because he doesn't believe he should have to.

- **People in his life who want him to stay stuck.** Friends and relatives sometimes don't want the man to grow. His drinking buddies fear they'll lose him if he faces his alcoholism. His siblings may be invested in blaming his cheating or his abusiveness on you, because they don't want to have to think about what *their* father did to their mother. People who hear only his side of the story, such as his therapist if he sees one, may think that they need to protect him from *your* unfairness. In other words, these people won't believe that they are trying to keep him stuck—they may even believe that they are trying to get him free, because they have heard the whole story backward. In addition to stunting his growth, those outsiders who collude with him can take quite a toll on you; you can end up feeling ganged up on, or even start to doubt your own perceptions of what is real, especially if the people siding with him are admired in your social circle.

The experience of Stacey captures this last point. Her husband, J.D., came from a home where his father was a violent abuser and his mother a chronic alcoholic. When J.D. finally got serious about changing, he found his friends and relatives to be among his greatest obstacles.

"My husband had a friend, Brian, who was like a brother to him, he was even best man at Brian's wedding. But when J.D. started to get serious about admitting how controlling and degrading he had been toward me, and changing his behavior, Brian would make fun of him and be a jerk about it. Like Brian would call our house and I would answer the phone and then go tell J.D. that the call was for him, and when J.D. got on the phone, Brian would go into his sarcastic bullshit, '*Oh*, the wife let you come to the phone, did she? She let you out of your cage? Why is she always the one answering the phone?' And then the worst one: 'Why do you always pick those feminist bitches?'—which meant any woman that didn't want to be walked on.

"Well, J.D. did the right thing. He told Brian that if he couldn't speak respectfully about me—and to me—he wasn't going to be able to be friends with him. Brian went out of his mind, saying he couldn't believe J.D. would put a woman before a 'brother.' J.D. eventually realized that he just had to cut contact with him."

Think of your partner as having surrounded himself with piles made up of some combination of the dynamics described here. If you can zero in on which ones you think are playing the biggest roles in your relationship, it will help you clarify the kinds of tools you will need to get him dug out.

EXERCISE 7–1:

> From the list of obstacles we just covered, circle the ones that your partner seems to be hiding behind the most. Then write some thoughts about what it was like to read about these.

WHEN WILL HE DECIDE THAT GROWING IS WORTH THE WORK?

One way of answering this question is quite simple:

> **He will get down to business when the discomfort of staying the same becomes greater than the discomfort of changing.**

Your job, then, is to be a creator of discomfort, to persuade him that facing up to his issues is worth it. In this section, we will look at a range of ways in which you can do this. These are presented as steps, from the least drastic to the most; if one level of intervention proves ineffective, it's time to move on to the next. You can skip any that don't fit who you are, that feel potentially dangerous, or that you know you have tried enough already.

LEVEL ONE: CONNECTING TO HIS EMPATHY

Intervention begins with testing how much your partner is capable of caring about how bad you are feeling. This level begins with a series of talks where you tell him fully, no holds barred, how much you are being hurt by the way he is behaving. You stop trying to protect his feelings, which means you don't sugarcoat anything; you pour your heart out about the kinds of sadness, anger, frustration, loneliness, and other kinds of pain you are going through. You ask him if he cares about what a hard time you are having. You ask him if he is willing to take steps to stop hurting you in these ways. You ask him if he is prepared to actually put some serious time, energy, and self-reflection into working on the issues, not just into saying, "Yes, I'll deal with it," and then going back to life as usual.

After opening up the truth of your experience in this way, the next step is to keep returning to the subject over a period of weeks. You don't have to be a broken record about it, nor do you have to be mean or harsh with him; but you do need to put steady pressure on him.He needs to get the message that you are done pretending that everything is okay, and that you are not willing to go on endlessly having his needs always coming ahead of yours—including his "need" to sit and do nothing, refusing to take responsibility for his life.

If you have children, and you are concerned that his behavior is also harming them, he needs to hear about that crucial issue as well. You might want to set up a separate time just for talking about the kids; if you pack too many issues into one conversation you are less likely to get a constructive response from your partner, and people in general tend to be at their most defensive when being criticized about their impact on children.

You might tell him that you are working from a book and that it has a bunch of exercises that are for you and a bunch that are for him, and ask him whether he would be willing to start reading the sections that are for him and doing the exercises. (You can print out the pieces to give to him at ShouldI StayOrShouldIGo.net.)

Next, put your thoughts and feelings into writing. The things you write can essentially be a restating of what you said to him directly, but if you choose to, you can also include points you didn't feel able to express in person. When you are ready, give it to him to read, keeping a copy for yourself.

Then, *ask him for a written response to your letter.* It's fine if he wants to talk to you about it in person, but it's very important that he also take time to put his reactions and ideas down on paper and *give those to you*—we will explain later why this matters so much.

Take the actions above if: (1) your partner has never physically or sexually assaulted you or threatened to do so; (2) you are not particularly afraid of him; (3) he seems, at least some of the time, to have a capacity to care how you feel and to take it seriously when you are in pain.

Skip this step, or use it only after careful thought about the potential risks, if: (1) you are afraid of your partner, or he has assaulted you or threatened to before; or (2) he seems highly or completely lacking in compassion for your distress or pain most of the time. (If he is not capable of any empathy, this level isn't going to work now anyhow.)

When we refer to "threats," we are including nonverbal threats such as raising a fist to you or punching a hole in a wall when he's mad at you. We are also including veiled threats, such as "You'd better watch it," or "You don't know who you're messing with."

We don't recommend handing this book to your partner; as we will explain later, it's best not to give him too much information about *your* process, for several reasons, and to keep him focused on his own. That's why we've put his pieces on the Web site for you to download and print out for him.

Finally, we recommend that you prepare yourself emotionally for the possibility that you may not get very far with this approach. A relationship partner who is repeatedly behaving in unhealthy ways has often fallen into a place of selfishness and self-centeredness, and it is challenging to penetrate that wall. Appealing to your partner's compassion, even if you work at it long and hard, may not be enough to motivate him.

EXERCISE 7–2:

Write a letter—to keep for yourself, not to actually show your partner—that is addressed to him, and in which you tell him, holding nothing back, what his behavior has been like, how it has made you feel, and how it has affected your life. Put the letter away in a safe hiding place or have a trusted friend keep it. (If you decide to write a letter that is really to give to him, write a second version; you will notice that you express yourself differently when you are writing a piece that he will actually see.)

LEVEL TWO: GETTING OTHER PEOPLE TO CHALLENGE HIM

When you and your partner first got together, he had a strong set of positive feelings for you, right? Perhaps he was even crazy about you, enthralled by you. You no doubt spend a certain amount of your time now wondering, "Where did his feelings for me go? Now he seems to find so much wrong with me." The sad reality is that a partner who has deep issues of his own sometimes chooses to run away from himself by focusing on what is supposedly wrong with you. Over time, he collects these "faults" to the point where he has trouble focusing on what he originally liked about you. (The reason we put the word "faults" in quotes is that he may not just criticize your weaknesses; he may define some of your greatest strengths, ambitions, and passions as things that are wrong with you—anything to avoid confronting himself.)

Some men begin this process of finding things to complain about quite early in the relationship. Others stay positive early on, but later they rewrite the history to make it sound like your relationship was never that great. Has your partner, for example, ever surprised you by talking about an earlier period in your relationship as if it had been a really difficult or just plain bad time, when you have a clear memory that things were good then? Obviously he was happy then; you weren't imagining it. But he was also beginning to make his negative observations about you, and now that he has a big pile, he's hurling them at you.

A slightly different way in which this dynamic can play out is that he may acknowledge that there was an extended good period when you were first together but insist that you are the one who changed, not him.

To top it all off, some men with destructive issues make opposite state-ments on different days; for example, he might tell you on Saturday that you're a great person and that everything that has gone wrong between the two of you has to do with his own issues about intimacy, and then on Wednesday he may be growling that you're just incapable of being happy and you insist on finding something wrong where everything is good.

The key point is that over time your partner builds a wall around his heart that keeps him from feeling deep love for you and blocks his compassion for your pains or distresses in life, especially the ones that he himself has caused.

But, oddly enough, this wall doesn't necessarily keep people in his life other than you out. So mutual friends of yours, or relatives that you both care about, might have a shot at getting through to him. If his own sister tells him that she is bothered by the disrespectful way he speaks to you, it's not so easy for him to just dismiss her. If a friend he has cared about for years tells him his drinking is destroying your family, he won't find it as easy to say, "Fuck you," and walk off to the comfort of his bottle. If a colleague from his work calls him on the fact that he's going out to strip clubs, he has to face that per-son every day, so he can't run quite as easily.

Persuading people to firmly call him on the carpet about his treatment of you is a challenge, but it's worth working on. Our culture has a strong message that says, "You should stand by your family and friends, right or wrong." When a man is mistreating or devaluing his partner, people in his life tend to back him up and bad-mouth the woman for calling him on what he's doing. We also have societal messages that say that it's better to remain neutral in a conflict between relationship partners, which people use as an excuse to avoid taking a stand.

However, public understanding about addiction, mental health problems, and abuse (including infidelity) has grown over the past twenty years. We hear many accounts nowadays where the man's parents or siblings are supportive to his partner and agree with her that he needs to deal with his issues. Mutual friends, or sometimes even people who are primarily friends of the man's, take the woman aside and express their concern for her safety and well-being, and try to figure out how to help. We hope that some of these trends have found their way into the culture of the community you live in.

Of course, it's much easier for people to quietly and privately express their support to the woman than it is for them to bravely speak up to the destructive man and hold him accountable. You are likely to find that you have to cajole people quite a bit before they will gather the nerve to challenge him.

Here are some factors to think about in deciding how and whether to have other people talk to him:

- Choose someone whom he respects. If he looks down upon his own sister the way he looks down on you (because he's antiwoman, for example), then he isn't going to listen to her either. The person doesn't necessarily have to be a man (though there are some advantages if it is), but it does have to be someone he listens to.

- Choose someone who won't be nasty or insulting to him. First, he's not going to take in anything someone says to him if it isn't presented decently. Second, and perhaps more important, if the person gets him really pissed off and inflamed, he will run off and do something even more unhealthy than he usually does. The trick is to find a friend, relative, or colleague who will speak to him firmly and directly, without letting him off the hook and not allowing him to blame you or minimize the problem. At the same time, the person needs to speak calmly and respectfully, and express caring for him while confronting him.

- Try to impress upon the person the importance of calling him on his attitudes, not just his behavior.

- The person should express to your partner how bad he or she feels about the pain your partner is putting you through. Your partner needs models of people being compassionate and caring toward you, and he needs to hear that regardless of what his complaints about you may be, he has no excuse for hardening his heart.

- Make sure the person is not invested in fighting your fight for you. We have observed that well-meaning people, in their anger at a man's irresponsibility or selfishness, sometimes jump in and tell the woman what she should do about it and making their anger take up more space than hers does. Loved ones need to focus on helping you get stronger to fight your own fight while they remain mostly in the background; this is about you, not about them.

    If there are people in your life who want to be there for you, but their assistance is ending up being somewhat unhelpful or is even making things worse for you, give them a copy of *Helping Her Get Free* by Susan

Brewster, a book that guides the reader on what kinds of help really help—and what kinds just add to the problem—for a woman who has a destructive partner.

- Ask the person to keep hammering on the core issue of *respect* when they talk to him. Their conversation may include trying to get through his denial about his drinking, his mental health issues, or his abusive behavior, but all roads should keep leading back to this question: What would he be doing differently if he were viewing his partner as an equal, a valuable person whose distress matters and to whom he owes it to be answerable?

- If your partner has a history with you of being violent or threatening, or if you have reason to be concerned about his stability—if he has threatened suicide, for example—weigh carefully the risks and benefits of having people speak to him. Confrontations with destructive men who have been intimidating in the past sometimes backfire against the woman or against her children. Although you can't perfectly anticipate how he will react, your inner voices and intuitions are important to take seriously. If other people are overeager to challenge him, insist that they wait until *you* are ready; their frustration and impatience will not lead to safely handling this important but risky step. Only move forward on having someone confront him when—and if—you feel sure that taking those chances is worth it to you.

Should I Have Multiple People Talk to Him?

You may find it challenging to find even one person who is willing to "get in the middle," but if you can get more people involved, you increase the chance that he'll decide to stop running away from his problems. But the trick is they have to be people who mean something to him because he cares about them, respects them, has to deal with them constantly (e.g., at work), or sees them as having authority of some kind. Otherwise, he'll just claim that "everyone" is ganging up on him and he'll play the role of the victim. (He may do this anyway, but it's harder for him to get away with if the ones who are challenging him are important in his life.)

If a number of people are going to talk to him, our experience suggests that it is more effective for them to challenge him one at a time over days or weeks, not all at once in a group; a group confrontation can freak out the person with mental health problems—we've seen it happen—could stimulate nasty retaliation from an abuser, and has been shown to sometimes backfire with a substance abuser. We have seen examples where sequential challenges—meaning spread out and one at a time—from multiple people have contributed to a man deciding to take a look at himself, and we believe this approach is a better bet.

Involving Your Spiritual Community

If your church, temple, mosque, or other spiritual community is an important source of strength for you, consider whether it may be able to support you regarding your relationship—including whether it could play a role in challenging your partner about his actions. Start by having a confidential conversation with your clergyperson, and explore his or her openness to hearing and grasping what you are going through. Be a little guarded at first, as you may find that you receive responses that minimize the problem or that reinjure you, such as "We need to understand what is bothering him," or "Love and forgiveness can heal all relationships." Some clergypeople focus primarily on keeping the couple or the family unit intact, rather than making the woman's rights and safety—and the needs of her children—the priority. However, in many cases, the faith community is prepared to take a stand that demands that the man stop harming his partner and children, or himself, and that offers support to the woman.

There are a number of advantages to involving your place of worship. One is that it carries moral weight; faith communities are seen as carriers of ethics, as having some authority to determine what is right and what is wrong. If your partner cares about his spirituality, he might be shaken up—in a positive way—by having members of his community telling him that his behavior is not responsible. Another advantage is that, since men with destructive issues tend to dismiss anything inconvenient that an individual says to them, a faith community can challenge him in significant numbers, making it harder for him to brush them off. Finally, your community can help you deal with the concrete needs of life by offering you places to stay when you need them, helping you with emergency food or transportation, and giving you emotional support when you feel your strength getting sapped.

There are risks to consider as well, however. If your partner is a slick manipulator, he may be able to turn people against you in order to defend his position within the community; some alcoholic or abusive men get mileage out of playing the role of victim, insisting that they are being falsely accused of harmful behaviors. Easily influenced people can end up feeling sorry for him and angry at you. Involving your faith community also sacrifices your privacy somewhat.

In our experience, the benefits outweigh the risks for women *if most of the spiritual community stays solidly behind the woman.* So start by telling only a couple of people, including the clergyperson or leader; if you meet with insensitive reactions, stop there. Avoid letting the issue become public in your community until you find a way to develop some solid allies, including at least one person who is respected and influential in the larger group.

EXERCISE 7–3:

1. Make a list of any people you can think of who might be willing to talk to your partner and press him to change his behavior and attitudes. Circle those who you think would do the best job communicating with him.

2. Make a separate list of people you would definitely *not* want to have speak with him. Then cross off every name on the list. (You'll enjoy this.)

LEVEL THREE: STOP PROTECTING HIM FROM THE CONSEQUENCES OF HIS ACTIONS

We understand that your partner is someone you love and feel attached to. We also recognize your need to take steps to keep the peace in order to make daily life bearable for you and for your children. So you probably feel that you have to shield your partner from the effects of his own behavior. We're not saying that protecting him is a bad idea; it's a natural human reaction, and in many cases can be the right choice—especially if your partner is a risk to turn cruel or violent if you don't. But it also may be time to consider stopping. Mark items on the following list that feel familiar:

❑ I have to give him money sometimes to help him pay debts or meet his basic needs, because he hasn't handled his money responsibly or isn't working.

❑ I make excuses for him to other people, and they aren't always entirely true (such as covering for him for missing work or for skipping important social occasions, explaining away his behavior when other people are upset with him, dealing with people he owes money to).

❑ I cover up for ways he has mistreated or harmed me, so that other people won't know.

❑ I soothe him and try to make him feel better when his own selfish or irresponsible behaviors are the cause of his unhappiness.

❑ I always take his side in his conflicts with other people, even though I'm starting to suspect that he's not necessarily in the right.

❑ When he makes excuses or blames other people for his problems, I pretend to agree with him.

❑ I don't talk to him about how his behavior is affecting me (and my children) because I don't want to upset him and add to his burdens.

One of the ways you can motivate a man to change is to leave him stuck in his own messes, using a kind of "tough love" approach to him. You don't have to be nasty and insulting to him about it. If possible, use the same patient but firm tone you might use with an irresponsible child: "I love you and care about you, honey, but you have to learn to take care of yourself"—or—"I've been trying to help you, but I don't think my help is good for you anymore"—or—"I love you but I love myself, too, and I'm not going to put myself through the pain of cleaning up your messes anymore."

Again, if your partner has tendencies toward violence or cruelty, he could erupt when you refuse to keep bailing him out. We want you to stand up to him if you are ready to take that leap, but we also want you to anticipate his reactions, and have strategies ready for how to keep yourself and your children safe. (See resources on, "Safety Planning," in the back of this book.)

EXERCISE 7–4:

> Write down a few examples of ways in which you have helped your partner
> escape the consequences of his actions. Then put down some reflections on
> why you have chosen to do this. Last, write about what you think would
> happen if you withdrew your rescuing, and where you think you might
> safely begin.

LEVEL FOUR: TAKING SOME TIME APART

We arrive now at a difficult truth: in our experience, the unfortunate reality
is that many men—perhaps most—who are behaving selfishly or destructively
won't change unless the relationship is on the line. The three levels we have
taken you through above can lay some important groundwork and increase
your chances of success in the long term. But to make it all take hold you may
well have to show your partner that you are ready to start moving away from
him—both emotionally and physically.

You don't have to begin by talking breakup; you may not be ready to think
in such drastic terms yourself, and you may be worried that his reactions will
be volatile if you suddenly start preparing to end the relationship. Instead, use
expressions such as "I need some distance because of what is happening," or
"I need time to myself to clear my head and figure out how to make things
work between us." Then raise the possibility of sleeping in separate beds or in
different rooms, or of staying in separate places for a few weeks or months.

To speak bluntly, there are some men who will step into reality a little if
they lose their access to sex. Shutting him off from intimacy is a first way of
communicating that you mean business, and that your insistence on change
has moved to a higher level. How much have you really been in the mood for
sex with him anyhow? A man who is drinking or high all the time, or who
makes you the lowest priority in his life, or who snarls whenever he talks to
you is not exactly a turn-on. There may already have been times when you
have slept with him to keep him from straying, or to keep him from getting
angry and nasty, or to give yourself some semblance of closeness in a relationship where genuine closeness just isn't happening. Stepping out of sexual
intimacy in these conditions can mean being truer to yourself—and might
wake your partner up to the fact that there are limits to what he can get away with.

Women in this type of situation sometimes ask, "Well, if I stop sleeping with him, isn't he just going to go 'get it' somewhere else?" Yes, he might—and then you will know that a relationship with him cannot succeed. The kind of man whose response when the woman stands up to him is to go out and cheat on her is the kind who is so attached to bullying her that positive change is next to impossible for him. Seeing how he reacts when you refuse to have sex with him is a good way to start assessing his potential for mature growth.

Taking a Break from Seeing Him

If you've tried everything we've talked about, and you can see that he is still not taking action to deal with his issues, it's time to be staying in separate places for a while. We can't predict how long you will need to spend apart, but we recommend that you plan for not less than two months.

And here is the most critical—and most challenging—point in how you take this step: *you have to cut all contact with him during this period,* except for necessary communications about your children. We have observed that if a couple is kind-of-apart-but-kind-of-still-seeing-each-other, the man makes some halfhearted efforts to impress the woman but doesn't take any meaningful steps. You don't have to be officially broken up; in fact, we have seen couples make an agreement that they are still together and that they will not sleep with other people during this period. But it has to be a true break. If you continue talking on the phone, and writing e-mails, and maybe meeting once a week just for dinner, and then deciding well, we'll have sex just this once, the whole purpose of taking time apart crumbles.

(And, in fact, we have seen in many cases that the man uses sex as a test; to his mind, if he can get her into bed, she's not serious about the separation, and he doesn't have to be serious about changing his ways. Often, making love to her takes her strength away—because she's feeling tender during the intimate contact, and she's been hungry for it herself—so she gives in and goes back to living with him the next day, or even that very night. Don't, don't, don't sleep with him during a separation.)

At the end of the first period you set for yourself—let's say it's two months—meet with your partner in a public place, say for a dinner or a coffee. The focus of that conversation is *what he has been doing to work on himself.* You will learn in the pages ahead, particularly in Chapters 9 and 11, what kind of work he should be doing, and what kinds of questions to ask him about it. Don't go off into chatting in detail about news from your lives; you can plan another time to get together to share all that *after* you feel adequately persuaded that he has actually begun doing some serious confronting of his issues.

If your intuition tells you that he has decided to face up, go back to seeing him if you want to, or even move back in together if you feel ready. Don't ignore your own warning voices, though; if you have a nagging sense that he's just putting on a show for you, you are probably right. And if he isn't making progress at the level that you need him to be, set another period when you won't see him, at least as long as the first one. And you may need to ratchet the pressure up now, which means taking the leap of saying, "I think we should see other people during this next break."

EXERCISE 7–5:

Write about how you would like to spend the extra time you would have if you spent a period not seeing your partner. Are there friends or family you would like to spend more time with? Is there an exercise or yoga class you'd like to take? Would you like to join a book-reading club? Would you like to take walks alone, or spend more time writing in your journal? Get more sleep? Whatever your wishes might be, put a few of them down on paper. Then write some thoughts about how you might feel during that break, in both the good aspects and the hard ones.

LEVEL FIVE: BREAKING UP

We bet you don't even want to start thinking about this yet, and we aren't going to ask you to. We hope you never have to take this leap.

However, as we take you through various pieces of inner exploration in the chapters ahead, you will actually be preparing yourself for the possibility of moving into a life without your partner—just in case. And if you get there, it won't end up being as hard as it seems it would be, thinking about it now. Have faith.

For this chapter, though, there is just one point we want to make about breaking up: you can go ahead and end your relationship without being 100 percent sure that you are ready. In fact, 100 percent certainty may never come. If your partner turns up months, or a year, down the line, and you are single when he comes along, you always have the option to start up with him again. We've known a few men who didn't decide to face the pain of growing up until their partners broke up with them for real and stayed away. So it's okay if you are still holding a little reserve in your heart in case he comes around. The critical point, as we guide you through the coming chapters, is to move ahead with your life, and don't waste another minute waiting around for him; if he decides to catch up later, and you're still interested at that point, that's great.

Ironically, the more you live your life assuming that he won't change, the better the chances that he will—because your growing strength, and your independence, are the biggest motivators for him. In short, destructive men generally change only when they have to.

A LITTLE REMINDER ABOUT WHAT THESE LEVELS *DON'T* INCLUDE

You can probably tell by now that we are strong adherents of the following two perspectives:

1. If you want to give your current relationship a serious try and see if it can be made to work, you deserve the chance to make that effort.
2. We don't want to see you pour years of your life, sacrificing yourself and your children in the process, waiting for your partner to make changes that he is clearly not going to make.

These two views can go together—we wouldn't espouse them if we thought they contradicted each other—but it is easy to get lost in number one and thereby lose sight of number two. Another way to state our message is that we don't want you to give up hope prematurely, but we also don't want you to place your hopes on impossibilities. So since this chapter has taken you through a long list of approaches that sometimes work to motivate a man to change, we now need to look at ones that never, or almost never, lead anywhere.

Don't dump on yourself about the fact that you have been trying to use the mistaken strategies we describe below. *Everybody* makes these kinds of attempts in their relationships when they are hoping to bring about improvements. And the trap is that, for ordinary relationship struggles and dissatisfactions, people sometimes find some success down these paths. But they will not work for the woman whose partner has an addiction, has an active untreated mental health problem, or is chronically cold, selfish, or mean (even if he has good periods in between).

You are likely to feel some grief as you stop making these attempts, because you have been pinning your hopes on them. But you will also feel expanded energy for your own life and goals, and for more promising ways of influencing your partner's behavior. And as your vision starts to clear—because you gain clarity when you step off these merry-go-rounds—you will see how sharply frustrating and draining the effort has been for you.

Begging, Pleading, Cajoling

As you challenge your partner to look at the harm he is doing, reach for a tone that is calmly powerful. The balance between force and kindness can be a difficult one to hit, but you will get better at it with practice. We regret to say that he will not change through hearing you whine, or plead, or cry (unless you are crying while also speaking with great force and self-assurance, which happens for some people). Showing weakness will work against you.

Now you might respond, "But it should be okay to show weakness to your partner. That's part of being in a loving, trusting relationship." And we wholeheartedly agree. The problem is that you aren't in that kind of relationship. In fact, one of the ways of discovering that you are in an unhealthy relationship is to notice that is has become unsafe for you to show your less solid, more vulnerable aspects. A destructive partner takes advantage of your vulnerabilities to get away with more selfish and immature behavior, or even to deliberately hurt you. And though he may at times show some compassion or caring about the areas where you feel weak or victimized, he will also see those as gaps in your defenses—and he knows he can use them for his own benefit.

Pestering him, treating him like a young child (though he may deserve it), or trying to handle his change work for him will all bear equally little fruit. Although you have every right to bring up the same points over and over again in the hope that he will eventually take action, it's a dead end. He may eventually give in and deal with the specific issue that you are complaining about, but then he'll just stall on the next one, and you'll be haranguing him again. The same principle applies if you make his therapy appointments for him (because he keeps not calling to set them up), or you buy the book he needs to read because he won't get it, or you write the check each week because that's the only way he will go to his abuser group. If you have to take responsibility for his change, the change isn't happening and won't.

The principle to keep in mind is this one:

> **For a man with destructive issues to make deep and lasting changes, a tremendous amount of hard, uncomfortable work is needed over a long period of time. If he can't even get himself to the starting block, he's never going to stick with it through the long haul ahead.**
>
> **He will have to do his own work.**

It's true that above, in Level One, we talked about ways to make efforts to get him to see what he's doing. But these efforts have to have the tone of a kind but unbending *demand,* not a request. Reach for words along the lines of "I love you, but you absolutely have to get what is happening to me (and to our kids) from your actions. And you have to make changes, because this is not an acceptable way for us to live." He needs to hear in your voice that you are taking back your strength.

Here is a list of various other tempting strategies that we recommend you *not* put any of your energy into:

- hiding his alcohol, weed, or paraphernalia
- asking him to "just go once, to try it" to a program or therapist that you know he would need to be with long term
- convincing him that making the changes would be best for *him,* since he's not willing to do it for you
- killing yourself trying to make yourself a better person
- doing favors for him in hopes that he will feel indebted to you, and then asking him to make up the debt by working on himself

- reassuring him that you aren't going to leave him (when he senses you getting stronger)
- reassuring him that you aren't going to stop needing him (when he senses you growing as a person)

The reason the "just go once to try it" is a sinkhole for your energy is that no therapist or program can give a man the motivation to work on himself. They can give the tools, but the desire has to come from him. You may say to yourself, "But if he goes once, he'll see that it's not so bad." But it *will* be bad through his eyes, if not right away then soon. He can't make changes unless the therapist or program pushes him to walk through some dark internal places, and if he's not motivated, he'll just quit when the hard part comes.

Finally, the reason why it generally won't work to convince him that changing is for his own good is that this approach feeds his selfishness, and you can't feed and solve a problem at the same time. Further down the road, if he does serious work, he will realize that making changes is benefiting him. But the initial impetus has to be that he wants to stop hurting you, or that he's afraid of losing you; if he's just in it for his own growth, his energy for doing the work is likely to fizzle soon. So we don't recommend this approach unless you feel that selfishness is not at all a significant part of his problem. (We find that selfishness is almost always an important dynamic in the behavior of men who are abusive, addicted, immature, or personality disordered. It is less consistently present for men whose unhealthy relationship behavior is driven primarily by traumatic experiences or by depression.)

Two Closing Thoughts

First, it isn't your responsibility to persuade your partner to change and grow. Any effort you make in this direction is a gift from you to him—though he won't usually see it that way, unfortunately—and you get to decide how much time and energy to invest. When it is no longer good for you to keep trying, you don't owe it to anyone to carry on. (You don't even owe it to your children—a partner who is harming you is harming your children, too, even if he doesn't mean to, and even if he's mostly very nice to them. Your unwillingness to accept being devalued or mistreated, and your insistence that he has to behave like a good role model for the children, will benefit them in the long run.)

Second, although your anger and frustration may be huge some days, there can also be a lot of hurt and sadness mixed in there as well. *Grief* is a natural reaction to having a partner who makes you feel not valuable or who runs you down. As you work to digest the ideas from this chapter, you may feel grief from realizing that you might not be able to stay with your partner. In the chapters ahead, we will be helping with the process of healing from these losses; but for now, just make room for the full range of different feelings that go through you as the days go by.

EXERCISE 7–6:

Let's work some on creating an image of calm but unstoppable determination. Close your eyes for a minute, or gaze out a window, and see what person (including fictional or movie characters), or animal, or aspect of nature comes to mind that represents this kind of forceful, self-assured energy. Then take that image inside of you, letting it become part of you and seeing how that feels.

After a few minutes, write down some thoughts or feelings you had, or draw a picture that captures the feeling for you.

Finally, choose an object that could represent for you that feeling of calm ferocity, and put it on your desk or dresser, or some other spot where you will see it every day. It could be the drawing you just made, a photograph, a craft, a natural object you bring in from outdoors, or anything else that can help you remember that force inside of you.

EIGHT

Getting Yourself Back to Center

"When I hear people talk about 'me time,' I always think, 'What a joke. What are you talking about? Me who?'"

"I had some dreams, sure. I don't even like to think about that now. It hurts too much."

"I just want some peace. That's all I really want anymore. I can't even think straight."

"I don't have any friends. I used to. I used to go out a lot. I played softball. Now I don't really even want to be around people."

AN UNHEALTHY RELATIONSHIP is like a giant vacuum, sucking your energy, attention, and generosity. Even if you have resisted giving too much attention or too many chances to your partner, your tense stance against that vacuum pull *also* takes energy. You are resilient; likely you have grown so accustomed to the constant pulling on you that without it, you would be shocked at the contrast. Think of how you appreciate the simple nourishing qualities of quiet when a screeching noise is suddenly silenced. You deserve to enjoy that sense of peace daily. In this chapter, we will lead you through a series of exercises designed to help you:

- rediscover what brings you joy
- reinvest in a daily routine that will support you
- rediscover some of the values you hold
- create a Self-Nurturing Plan, including skills for regulating yourself when you feel out of sorts
- create a Parenting-from-Your-Center Plan

If you want to hold on to the clarity you find about your relationship, you will need to shift back to the center and joy of your own life.

WHY YOU MIGHT BE TIRED

Unhealthy relationships can absorb a tremendous amount of focus, and they create a need for recovery time. It takes time to recover from the exhausting arguments in which you spend hours in struggle.

During these arguments, a destructive partner will often treat you as though you are impossible and have lost touch with all semblance of sanity. He might speak as though he has no clue as to what you are talking about while also justifying his actions. This twisted logic is exhausting. How can a person claim that he has not said or done hurtful things while also justifying saying or doing them? Yet the unhealthy partner often does so without hesitation and with a deeply ingrained force of habit protecting himself from facing his impact on you.

"What are you talking about? I never said that to you. But you know it's true, anyway—what am I supposed to do—be perfect? It's always about me, isn't it? I'm always wrong. What do you expect me to do when you come at me like that?"

Responses like these compound your sense of frustration. It usually gets worse from there; he may regard your now even more agitated emotional state with disdain: "Look at you. You're a wreck. You need help. Everyone knows you are crazy."

Being subjected to this is exasperating and exhausting work. Even if you temporarily give up on reaching him in the middle of one particular argument, afterward you'll still need to figure out for yourself what just happened. It takes work to sort through the events and feelings. You find yourself thinking like a scientist or detective, struggling to recall exact words and details because he denies that they even occurred. If you have strong feelings about what took place, trying to remember clearly in the face of his distortions can be very challenging and tiring. You start doubting yourself because his denial is so strong. Also, you may have to spend time reassuring yourself of basic premises; for example, that it is natural that you got so frustrated and angry when he:

- denied saying hurtful things
- then told you they were true anyway
- then said that you were crazy for being mad

And even if you do get clear inside yourself about what happened, it isn't really satisfying, because he doesn't share that clarity with you and you never got your original hurt addressed by him anyway.

Once you manage to talk yourself through what happened in one of these exhausting arguments, and maybe even calm yourself down, you eventually need to reenter the worlds of work, family, and community. Acquaintances treat you as though things are normal. A casual "Hi, did you have a good weekend?" demands that you answer simply, "Yes." Friends generally assume you are in a healthy relationship, so that if you decide to answer more honestly—"We went at it all weekend"—they are likely to reply with comments and thoughts that aren't helpful to you because they refer to the Conflict Stage of a Healthy Relationship Cycle (see Chapter 1), which isn't what you are dealing with. They might say, for example, "Oh, I get too critical, too," making you doubt yourself again and wonder if it really is happening the way you think it is happening.

All of this second-guessing and sorting out is draining.

Also, most women make a kind of bargain with themselves and their social circles. They think to themselves, "Until I am sure that my partner is destructive and until I know what I want to do about it, I'm going to act, to everybody else, as though everything is fine." To do otherwise would be too confusing. But acting takes a lot of work. You have to redirect all your spontaneous thoughts and feelings into a pretend world and act in the ways you think you're supposed to act if you were in a healthy relationship. If your partner is dangerous, you may have to act that way in order to protect yourself from him. Violent partners will use your sadness as evidence that you are accusing them of something, which to them then justifies further abuse. "What's that look on your face for?" becomes a very clear instruction to act as if everything is okay.

There can be further damaging draws on your energy:

- It takes concentrated energy to figure out how much danger you are in after surviving physical assaults or threats of assault.
- If you have children, you may have to confront echoes of your partner's destructive thinking in your child.
- If you have children, you will need to attend to the ongoing emotional aftermath of your partner's destructiveness.
- If you have experienced sexual coercion or assault, you can be left with feelings of numbness, shame, isolation, anxiety, confusion, and anger.
- If your partner has cheated on you, which is, unfortunately, commonplace in destructive relationships, it draws down on your well of emotional energy to deal with the ongoing humiliation, pain, and lack of trust.

These concerns are probably preoccupying your mind; their weight can leave you uninspired, unmotivated, and hopeless. Take heart, there is a way forward. We know how devastating it is to live through these kinds of things. The work you are doing now with this book is an invaluable step toward your freedom from this turmoil. We encourage you to reach out to the helping resources we have listed at the end of the book when you are ready. We have described in some detail the kinds of dynamics that drag on your energies and attention so that we can reassure you that we know what you are up against as you try to preserve your sense of reality and safety in your relationship. The next step for your healing is one that does not come naturally or easily given all the work you have been doing focusing on the relationship. We want you to turn your attention back to yourself. Not the part of yourself that is interacting with your partner. Just you.

You Are Still in There

You have many gifts that you are giving in your relationship. As you have tried to return your relationship to a good place, you have been using these gifts with your partner. You use your humor, your insight, your spontaneity and instincts. We want you to give those gifts back to yourself, to benefit your own life.

EXERCISE 8–1:

Imagine times in your life that you have felt happy. Choose memories that are not about being with your partner. (We know you have good memories of your partner, but for the purposes of this exercise, we want you to choose memories that are about other times in life, or other aspects of life.) You can choose a momentous occasion, a happy turning point you won't ever forget. You can choose a period in time filled with things you like. Think about things that never fail to improve your mood. Maybe you remember swinging on a vine over a lake on a hot day, about to take an easy plunge into cool and fresh waters. Perhaps you remember being stretched on warm sand under a soothing sun. You can choose a moment that fills you with a strong feeling of love, as when your child touches your cheek softly. Or perhaps you can imagine you and your friends gathering at a favorite restaurant. The background noise, the clanking of silverware, their familiar laughter may be the things that carry you to a sense of well-being. Try to imagine being there right now.

Now choose one memory. Imagine it in some detail. Call forth the sounds, the smells, the whole of the happy instant. Once you have it in some detail, continue with the questions below.

What is that sensation like in your body?

How does that happy time register? Perhaps your shoulders feel loose and hang easily. Maybe your midsection feels open as the wide sky. Is there a thread of strength flowing through the legs, or a settled feeling at your seat?

What does this goodness feel like? Does it buzz? Is it smooth?

Take a moment and write some words that describe the way that happy place registers for you in your body.

You deserve more of being in the kind of serene place that you just worked on picturing, and in the state of contentment that goes with it. With your partner, you deserve more of it. When you aren't with your partner—or times when you don't have a partner—you deserve more of it. Your life needs more of this happy freedom. We will support you in coming into a life where these moments don't feel so few and far between. We want you to expand your ability to experience love from many sources. If you have a life filled with support and love, your relationship will not have to carry all the hope you have for a warm, loving life. It will be easier for you to look at your relationship with clarity if you are not thinking, "This relationship is my only possible source of love and happiness."

Do What *You* Would Do

"I was in a relationship. I can see now that it was abusive. I didn't really get how it was affecting me, though my family and friends (the ones I had left, anyhow) sure did. I remember the minute I realized that I'd really lost part of myself. I was at the gas station by myself. I wasn't sure if I should go in to pay for the gas ahead of time or pay at the pump. I realized that I was hesitating because I was so used to hanging back and trying to figure out which move would be the thing that would not piss off my partner. I told a friend about it afterward. She said to me, 'Heidi! Do what Heidi would do.' It was so right on that I wrote it on my hand. I mean, I wrote my own name on the back of my fingers, under my knuckles, H-E-I-D-I. What I had to remember was to get back to me to do what I would do, rather than doing what would make my partner's reactions easier for me."

We're going to take stock now of the things that have brought you joy over the course of your life. It can be hard to remember what means the most to you, and what makes you happy, when you have been so consumed with a relationship that demands so much energy. You might find yourself thinking, "I'm so different now; I don't know what I need anymore." But in order to heal you need to get back to you. You are in there, still. Throughout this chapter we'll be providing exercises to help you figure out exactly "what you would do" and then give you encouragement to just do it!

As we take you through figuring out what you like and need, notice if there are ways in which your partner interferes with your happiness.

What Do You Need Now?

Sometimes, after being in a difficult relationship for so long, you not only don't remember who you used to be, but you're not in a position to do the things you used to do. You may be so drained that you don't have the physical, mental, or emotional energy to ever do what you once enjoyed. For instance:

- Physical Exercise

After a long period in a fearful or consuming relationship, your body might give you different signals. Where before you might have enjoyed going out for a run to blow off steam, now your accelerated heart rate might make you feel panicky. Your racing heart might be followed by feelings that you need to run for cover, fight off a danger, or freeze for safety.

"I started to run, really a slow jog," describes Ginger. *"And then, I just had to lay down. Flat. Right there on the field. There I was, trying to do something good for myself, and I was completely paralyzed with fear. I could not move. I just curled up until I was ready to get up and walk, really slowly, back to my place."*

- Socializing

If your need for emotional intimacy has been unmet for a long time, you might want the time you spend with a friend to be reserved for those who can navigate the deepest depths with you. Casual friendships might be unsatisfying to you now. Being part of large groups might feel overstimulating. Or, alternatively, you might find that you need to take a *break* from intensity. You just want to go out and laugh. If you feel isolated, the warmth of a group could be just your medicine.

No matter where you are starting, you can ease your way into activities in a way that goes at your pace and makes you feel proud and happy.

EXERCISE 8–2: SELF-CARE

In this exercise you have the opportunity to write a practical plan for caring for yourself to follow whether you decide to stay in your relationship or not.

Let's imagine that your dearest friend ever from childhood has found you after a long time of being out of touch. (Facebook finds everyone!) Even though you may feel deeply distracted and do not feel like answering her posts and her calls today, she is coming to your home. It doesn't feel like a good time in your life, but you do want to welcome her. So, it is time to make some space for her and do some planning about what it means to have her in your home.

She, of course, is you.

Your schedule is tight and your partner may not welcome new people, but we are going to find a way to make this happen. Remember, she is you. We want you to think of her as a special, honored person you are thrilled to have around. It can be hard to remember to feel that way about ourselves.

Can you commit to changing the old routine so that you can welcome her back into your life? For now, we will focus on getting her daily needs met. In Chapter 10, we will find out about her goals. We'll find out what has happened to the dream that she had been nurturing for her life.

■ What time does "she" rise? Is there a way to plan soft music for her, or a morning ritual of tea, coffee, water, stretching? Is there some way to greet her for a few moments at the beginning of the day? If spiritual beliefs are important to her, is there a way to set a place where she can spend five minutes connecting to those truths before she faces her day?

■ Though your day may be filled with commitments until evening, are there ways to plan reminders for you to welcome her? The sound of your cell phone ringing, for example, could become your reminder to stop, listen, and be present for your returning dearest friend.

■ What is she eating nowadays? And in what atmosphere?

■ How about reading? What kind of entertainment? What kinds of new things are there that you want to make sure she experiences while with you?

■ How does she relax? Is she a hot-tubber (if there is one around)? Does she swim? Lie in hammocks? Get massages, or give self-massages? Stretch or do yoga? Walk in the morning or evening? Find fresh air?

- What of her creativity? Does she draw or paint or make things out of whatever you have?

- Is color her friend? Does she like to get dressed—the whole act of it, the adornment, the colors, fabric, draping?

- What does her body need to feel good? Does she drink water regularly, keeping herself hydrated?

- How about sleep? Think of the last time you loved your sheets and pillow, cool or warm, or the last time you curled like a cat in the sun. Think of the last time you felt good-tired, the happy tired that makes sleeping a welcome peace. What was it about that day and that time that made the sleep so right?

Please review your answers. Your answers contain elements of a daily routine that will help you feel good. We want you to move toward a life that uses all your skills and respects your loving self.

DON'T WAIT TO GET HELP

Are you reacting to the stress that you are in by doing things that aren't really good for you? Are there things that you do that may get in the way of the Self-Care Plan you have just been making? Returning back to your center can be an especially challenging journey if you are drinking too much, using drugs, or harming yourself in other ways in an effort to make yourself feel better. As you continue working on forming this Self-Care Plan and putting it into practice, we encourage you to make a commitment to getting help for yourself above all other things. Don't wait until your relationship is sorted out to get the support and assistance you need and deserve in sorting out other aspects of your life that aren't working well.

EXERCISE 8–3: THE 5-4-3-2-1

If you react to upsetting situations by getting deeply upset or anxious, by feeling numb, or by retreating deep within yourself, there are things you can do that will help settle you down. You can do this exercise with a friend (by phone or in person) or by yourself. It is important to actually say the answers out loud. If you are in public and don't want to feel embarrassed by talking to yourself, just pick up your cell phone if you have one, and do the exercise while you pretend you are talking with someone on the phone. If you don't have a phone with you, try walking away a little distance and turning your back to get a little privacy from anyone nearby.

Use this exercise when:

- you feel your heart rate accelerate related to something emotionally upsetting and you want to settle down

- you are about to face someone who has hurt you and you feel very anxious and you want to feel more calm and at ease

- you need to focus your thoughts, but you are very upset

Let's try it right now.

1. <u>Look around</u> you where you are right now.

    Name 5 things that you see.
    Now name 4 things that you see. (You don't have to be creative. You can
        repeat.)
    Name 3 things that you see.
    Name 2 things that you see.
    Name 1 thing that you see.

2. <u>Listen</u> right now.

    Name 5 things that you hear.
    Name 4 things that you hear.
    Name 3 things that you hear.
    Name 2 things that you hear.
    Name 1 thing that you hear.

3. <u>Sense or feel</u> something with your body right now. (This refers to what you actually feel with your body, the things with which your body is in contact. This does not refer to emotional states of feeling. A fitting answer would be, for example, "I feel the floor under my foot.")

Name 5 things that you feel.
Name 4 things that you feel.
Name 3 things that you feel.
Name 2 things that you feel.
Name 1 thing that you feel.

This is the end of the exercise. How do you feel in your body? If this technique worked well for you, you will be feeling a sense of steadiness or calm, or at least quite a bit more so than you did when you began.

This technique is an approach you can tell a friend about ahead of time so that he or she can be there to listen to you when a situation arises where you need to use it.

EXERCISE 8–4: JUST BETWEEN YOU AND ME

This exercise is designed to help you feel centered while thinking about someone that upsets you deeply or who has mistreated you.

1. Sit comfortably. Imagine that the person who upsets you is seated across from you.

2. Answer the questions: What is the worst part about it? What is the worst part of why you are upset with this person?

3. Now imagine the thing that gives you the greatest feeling of love or strength.

It could be:

- a spiritual being or teacher

- an animal spirit or animal

- a principle or belief that you cherish or like to live by

- a sacred symbol of love, courage, or strength

We'll call the thing you chose your Protector.

4. Come back to your thought of the person who upsets you seated across from you.

5. Now bring the image of love and strength that you chose directly between you and that person so that you can't see the person anymore. The image of your Protecting Force is completely blocking that person from you.

6. Imagine that your Protector has something very important to tell you about yourself, something that you need to know.

7. What does your Protector say to you?

8. Choose a symbol that will remind you of this Protector.

Perhaps the symbol is a small object that you can carry with you in case you are planning on seeing the person who upsets you. We know a woman who had a few objects that represented her Protector. She had them strategically arranged on a coffee table in her home when she knew the person who has been toxic to her was coming over to talk and they helped her feel grounded and centered during the visit.

How Safe Is It to Be True to Yourself Right Now?

The process of strengthening your ability to return to center can sharpen your awareness—perhaps uncomfortably—of whether or not your relationship is a safe and secure place for you. Use your imagination for a moment now to contemplate how your partner would react if you were to change the compass of your relationship so that it points to true north *half* of the time—true north is *you*. This would mean that your preferences and needs would lead the way about half the time, rather than being repeatedly pushed into the background.

- When you imagine insisting on your own needs and preferences half the time, do you notice any anxiety or fear?
- How does your partner respond when other people give you positive attention?
- What does your partner do when you have opportunities to do things that you like and enjoy?

Answering these questions for yourself may bring up some powerful feelings and realizations. You may well be finding that your needs chronically come second, or that you have a partner with whom you can't be yourself, or both. If so, you now have a good idea of some of the first changes you need to make in your relationship, and you have a right to insist upon these. In the chapters ahead, we will be guiding you on ways to put your foot down—if you can do so safely—to right the balance between you and your partner.

However, if your intuition is that your partner may respond extremely or violently if you refuse to let the relationship stay lopsided, that is a signal that it may be time to use your energies toward making a plan for how to extricate yourself safely from a relationship that has become too dangerous. In Chapter 18, we help you plan to leave when you know your relationship is not going to work for you.

The Financial Cost of Your Relationship

Often in unhealthy relationships, your relationship to money becomes strained. Your financial health and resources can be strained or even devastated when:

- your partner uses your money or credit to feed his addiction.
- your partner's emotional disturbance or chronic immaturity make his thinking and choices around money illogical and impulsive. His choices are driven by anxiety and wishful thinking.
- your partner's abusive values put his needs above yours. This might mean that your partner spends on things that are his priorities without putting resources toward your priorities. It could also mean that your schooling and career have been on hold because his needs came first, or because you need to give your attention to the children. Then you realize that your turn is never coming.

- Your partner uses manipulation, cruelty, intimidation, violence, or threats of violence to coerce you into taking on bad debt or forging bad checks.

You can also lose time, creativity, and energy that you could have been investing in your own work goals if you are constantly attending to the stresses of your relationship. You might, for example, be constrained in a job that does not suit you because you are having to support both of you. Many women are housing, feeding, and maintaining support for destructive men in their lives. It is common for the destructive partner to refuse to acknowledge this, or to do so only with derision. His economic dependence on you can complicate your decisions about whether to leave him, since you feel burdened with the concern of how he will manage with reduced resources.

In a destructive relationship, it is hard to remember your financial values. Prior to this relationship, were you someone who

- followed her credit score?
- used credit cards wisely?
- sought and paid back loans in a way that was planned?
- used a monthly cash-flow plan that determined ahead of time where your money went?
- had an emergency fund, however small, that was growing, to ward off the cost of the unexpected?
- knew her personal priorities for the resources at hand?

We want you to figure out what your financial values and goals are now so that

1. while you are still in with your current partner you can begin to make changes that reflect your financial wishes, and
2. you can use plans that you make now for building your own future if you decide to move on from this relationship

Crisis is a regular feature of the destructive relationship. When dealing with crisis so often, you have to focus on the immediate time at hand. You can lose a sense of the longer-term plan for yourself and for your finances. In fact, you might not get chances to think of the future at all. We recognize that in a destructive relationship you may not have been able to live according to the financial values that you had before. We see that you might not be in a position to live by healthy financial values now. (And perhaps you hadn't really figured out your relationship to money before you entered into this relationship.) You can still figure out your own relationship to money, separate from your partner's.

EXERCISE 8–5: COMMITMENT TO FINANCIAL HEALTH

Please take time to write your responses to the following questions.

- How has this relationship impacted your financial health?

- Do you need help finding, interpreting, and knowing how to improve or keep a healthy credit score? Has your relationship had an impact in this area?

- If your income allows, do you have an emergency savings to which you have access? If so, how is this goal supported in this relationship?

- Do you understand your options for planning for your older years? How does your partner contribute to this plan?

- Do you feel confident in your ability to manage cash flow and budget? In what ways does your partner influence your ability to manage this plan?

- Do you feel confident in handling your tax responsibilities?

- Do you feel confident in planning for and managing any benefits you might be eligible for or receive?

If in answering these questions you are discovering areas where you could use assistance, flip to the "Resources" section in the back of this book and look under "Financial Planning." You don't need to wade into this challenging area alone.

For Women with Children

Parenting a child within a destructive relationship tends to mean making compromises that go beyond what you are comfortable with, and that may not fit what you truly believe is best for your children. Your choices often may become about navigating a path to safety because of your concern about your partner's behavior. For example, you might give your child a consequence for a behavior that you actually find acceptable, in order to save him or her from the haranguing, unpredictability, or even violence that comes from your partner when he is upset at one of the children.

When you feel so compromised, it can be difficult to remember how crucial you are to your child. Your parenting can create an alternative way of being for your child. Your child is learning your reactions, your thoughts, and your moods as an alternative model of how to handle herself so that she doesn't feel she has to become like the unhealthy aspects of your partner. These are alternatives that your child can draw upon for the rest of her life. We recognize that you may not receive thanks or positive feedback—children don't tend to grasp the significance of efforts that a healthy parent is making on their behalf—and you might not see evidence of the benefits of your extra efforts right away. Still, if you protect and respect your children, and treat them with honesty, you can provide a nonviolent, healthy model that will contrast with the destructive one.

EXERCISE 8–6: PARENTING FROM YOUR CENTER

Write your thoughts to the following in order to help you clarify what your parenting looks like when you are not managing the stresses of being with your partner:

1. What is your main goal as a parent?

2. Imagine your child or children. What is it that you adore about them? What are their unique gifts and qualities?

3. Imagine yourself as the most effective, loving parent, parenting them from your highest possible self. Picture your parenting coming from your

deepest values, without interference from a destructive relationship. Take a moment and stand up, if possible, where you are reading. Stand the way you imagine you would stand if you were able to be the parent you want to be. Notice how you stand. Notice the way you hold your face. Your shoulders. How is your voice?

4. In what ways do you believe it is important to support your child? What do those ways look like?

5. What are your child's greatest challenges?

6. What are the ways you need to walk with your child through those challenges?

7. How do you believe in holding your child accountable for negative choices?

8. How do you believe in celebrating your child's many positive choices?

9. What are the ways in which you believe it is important to share time with your child?

10. How far from the way you want to parent are you parenting now? (Answering this question may be upsetting, so take your time and be kind to yourself about what comes up.)

11. Are there ways that your partner's parenting or behaviors interfere with the parenting values you have stated above? If so, what are they?

12. What first steps can you take to move closer to your parenting values? Is there a value that you consider a deal breaker—a value that, if your partner can't agree to it, you know you cannot stay together?

EXERCISE 8–7: THE ELEMENTS OF MY SELF-CARE PLAN INCLUDE:

Please review your thoughts in each of the following areas, adding any ideas that you haven't already written down for your plan for lovingly looking after yourself.

SAFETY
In making commitments to myself, are there any precautions I need to keep in mind to keep me safe from undermining, sabotage, or assault from my partner? (For assistance answering this question, look in the "Resources" section under "Safety Planning.")

CARE OF MY BODY
What reasonable, daily commitments can I make for the regular care of my body?

CARE OF MY SPIRIT
What daily commitments can I make that feed my spirit?

FINANCIAL WELL-BEING
What small goal can I begin to work toward?

MY SUPPORTIVE ROUTINE
What rituals can I include in my day that remind me of the "real me"?

CONNECTION TO OTHERS
What networks, friendships, or groups can I reach out to in my desire to create more opportunity for connection outside my relationship?

WHAT BRINGS ME JOY
What is it that makes me happy at this time in my life? What things—big dreams or small moments—fill me with happiness?

MOVING TOWARD MY DREAMS
In what direction would I like my life to go that will let me know I am doing what my heart desires? (We will be working on this question in depth in Chapter 10, but just put down some initial thoughts now, the things that come immediately to mind.)

MY VALUES AS A PARENT
What are the things I can commit to that reflect my own parenting values?

EXERCISE 8–8:

Complete the blank space in this personal ad with a description of what it is that you really like. Make sure your description suits who you are now in your life. You aren't seeking a partner through this ad; you are seeking yourself, who you are at the very core of you.

Woman Seeking Self:
Courageous woman in relationship who likes _____
seeks to live from her center once again.

NINE

His First Steps

A version of this chapter that is designed for the man to read is available at ShouldIStayOrShouldIGo.net. That version includes spaces for him to write his responses to the exercises and includes other differences. The version you will read below is written for you, not for him; we have included the exercises so that you can know what his assignments are.

B ECOMING A RESPONSIBLE, kind relationship partner has some similarities to learning to play a musical instrument, or learning to speak a new language. Your partner thinks at first, "I couldn't possibly do that—you're asking me to become a completely different person. You're expecting way too much from me." In fact, to his mind it will be like being *required* to learn Persian, or learn the violin; he'll feel not only that it's too much, but that he is being put upon unfairly, that he's being assigned a task that he shouldn't be stuck with.

However, he needs to begin at the beginning and learn what he needs to learn, one piece at a time, just as the aspiring musician has to do. If he focuses on the full size of the project, he'll keep coming up with excuses to bail out. Today, let's say, he's learning to play a simple scale that starts on C, and he needs to stop whining and just do that much.

All of this is work that he has to do himself. You can't take him through

---

The First Steps Toward Change

1. Changing his attitude toward his partner's complaints
2. Understanding his denial, and coming out of it
3. Stopping his retaliations against his partner for raising grievances
4. Making a plan
5. Connecting himself to positive influences for growth and change

---

his steps; we're not teaching a fourteen-month-old to walk. (Though some days you perhaps feel as though you are.)

His first task, the equivalent of that simple C scale, is to start examining the attitude that he takes toward your complaints. From there we will move on to overcoming denial, stopping his retaliatory behaviors, making a plan, and connecting himself to positive influences. Although these may seem like quite a bit, they are in fact just the baby steps, the bare beginning of the change process.

CHANGING WHAT HE TELLS HIMSELF ABOUT THE ISSUES YOU RAISE

We're going to begin with the assumption that you have been complaining about certain aspects of your partner's behavior off and on for a long time. Your grievances may include that he spends more time with his drinking buddies than he does with you, that he's too rough during sex or pressures you to do things sexually that you don't find appealing, that he sticks you with all the housework and child care, that he insults you and acts like he thinks he's better than you are. Whatever you are raising with him, the bottom line is that he isn't hearing it and isn't doing anything to take care of the problems he has created.

He doesn't want to have to look at himself, but you are raising a lot of good points. So how does he escape? The answer is that he has developed an elaborate set of internal messages that *discredit* your perspective, through which he explains to himself why he has no need to take your complaints seriously. He repeats these beliefs to himself over and over, almost like a chant, in order to keep himself convinced. Change and responsibility are like demons that he is trying to keep at bay.

Here are examples of the kinds of things that may go on in his "self-talk," his inner world of recurring messages:

> *"She's just trying to control me like a mother, that's why she won't stop bugging me."*
>
> *"She doesn't know how to have a good time, so she doesn't want me to have a good time."*
>
> *"She's just determined to find something wrong with every little thing I do."*
>
> *"She just doesn't understand men. She wants me to be like a woman."*
>
> *"She ignores all the good things I do, and just notices the bad things."*
>
> *"She's stupid, she doesn't know anything."*
>
> *"She's fucking crazy, there's no reason to listen to her."*
>
> *"She just likes to get on my case because she's a bitch."*

And the list could go on with similar attitudes. Discrediting you is his ticket to running away from himself.

If he is called on these attitudes, he will tend to do one of two things: (1) deny that he thinks that way, or (2) say that it's okay for him to think that way because his belief is true. He may try to engage you in an argument about *your* attitudes and behaviors, switching the focus away from him. You might find yourself, for example, saying, "It's not true that I only notice the bad things you do, I know a lot of things that you do that are good. Look, here are some examples," and you start to list off his strong points or his moments of kindness or generosity.

What has just happened? He has managed to turn the tables so that you suddenly have become the one needing to defend yourself, not him. And he's manipulated you into praising and appreciating him, which is much nicer for him than having to look at his unhealthy actions.

HIS EXERCISE 9–1:

For the next few weeks, pay close attention to the negative messages you collect about your partner. When she brings up a complaint, a criticism, or a step that she is asking you to take, listen carefully to the grievance or request *and do not discredit it.* When you are alone, write down the points she was making, and spend some time trying to take them in. Notice the messages that go through your head about why her issue does not have to be taken seriously.

In order to break his habit of self-talk that discredits you, he needs to start replacing the negative messages with appropriate ones, chanting (internally) the good ones rather than the bad ones as he tries to think through your perspective. Examples of appropriate self-talk for him would include:

"She has the right to bring grievances."
"She has the right to be angry with me."
"She has built up a lot of bad feeling because of things I've done in the past."
"She is trying to make our relationship work better."
"She needs me to make changes so that I stop hurting her (and the kids)."
"Her complaints are just as valid as mine."
"I can deal with this issue instead of shooting her down."
"She's a good person, and she knows what she's talking about."
"How do I want her to feel about me twenty minutes from now? What do I need to do differently to bring that about?"

He has to start working daily on changing his self-talk habits, replacing his destructive attitudes with constructive, respectful ones.

Now, his next line of defense may be to say sarcastically, "Oh, so in other words, you're always right and I'm always wrong, and I just have to accept whatever you say." This stance really amounts to saying, "If I have to take you seriously, I'm helpless to defend myself against you, poor me." Another nice turning of the tables, isn't it?

We don't owe him an explanation when he's manipulating in this fashion, but we will give him one anyhow, so that when he's ready to stop playing games, he knows exactly what the work is that we are expecting from him. When his partner is saying something to him that he doesn't like, he needs to:

- Make a serious, careful effort to understand what she is saying, *even if he thinks he already knows.* He has a history in this relationship of listening poorly and assuming the worst, which he can only correct by shutting his mouth and opening his mind.
- Respond in a thoughtful, fair way that does not include any insults or put-downs, does not accuse her of bad motives, and does not exaggerate or twist what she has just said. His response, even if he disagrees with her, has to demonstrate that he is actually engaging seriously with the points she is making. Sentences that begin with *"Oh, so what you're really saying is . . ."* are off-limits. So are:

  "You're just bringing this up because . . ."
  "You're just mad because . . ."
  "What this is really about is . . ."

- Do more good thinking on his own about what she has said, after the argument or discussion is over. The digestion process should continue for hours or even days. He should be coming back to her later saying things like:

  "I've been thinking over what you were saying and I realize you were really making sense."
  "I'm sorry I was so defensive, and I'm ready now to take in what you were trying to tell me."
  "I've thought about it and I can see why my actions weren't fair, and I'm sorry. I'll make a concerted effort not to do that again." (in reference to whatever her grievance was)

- Not bring up his complaints about her when she is in the midst of trying to raise issues about him. If he wants to talk about his grievances, he needs to bring them up on his own time. Another way of stating this point is that he needs to stop deflecting the discussion away from her concerns onto his, which is an evasive tactic and often becomes an excuse to be nasty.

- Not require her to bring up her grievances in a perfect way. If he doesn't like the way she is talking to him, he can bring that up with her later, but he can't use it in the middle of an argument as an excuse to shut her off and not deal with what she is raising.

Look back up this list and ask yourself, "Is this an unreasonable set of demands? Is this a huge, unfair burden to put on a person? Do these requirements tie a person's hands so that he can't stand up for himself?" Our answer is, *Not at all.*

HIS EXERCISE 9–2:

Write down a few examples of ways in which you have retaliated against your partner or put up roadblocks when she is trying to raise concerns or express her anger to you. Then write down alternate ways you could have responded, drawing from the list above.

Next, write some examples of disrespectful messages you have been running inside your head to excuse blowing her off when she's mad at you. Then write down a couple of positive attitudes toward her, and toward conflict, that you will work to keep in your mind instead. (Draw from the list, on page 179.)

Finally, there may be certain subjects that make him go ballistic if you bring them up, to the point where you have to summon a major amount of courage to dare touch them. From this experience, you may even have stopped raising certain issues altogether, because you can't safely do it, or because the hell he raises just isn't worth it.

Now, however, he's saying he's willing at least to consider doing some serious work. (We're assuming that's the case, or he wouldn't be reading this chapter.) So he has to understand that:

1. He can't make any subjects out-of-bounds for you anymore. You are permitted to raise *any* subject you want to, and he can't scream, tell you to shut up, or get you back for it later. It's time to deal.
2. The very fact that certain subjects are that volatile for him is a strong warning sign that he is running away from himself.

His response to the first item might be to say that there are areas where he feels too raw and sensitive, that the pain is simply too great to be discussing them. (We all have some topics that feel that way.) But he is going to have to give you a chance to explain why this area is relevant *to you,* and what the impact is on his life. He can't shut that discussion off, even if it gets really hard for him.

Let's say, for example, that his mother was an alcoholic, the kind that drank until she passed out on the floor of the hallway. When you try to bring up how upset you are by how much he drinks, he comes unglued and starts to yell things like, "You don't know anything about alcohol abuse! I handle my alcohol just fine! I'm not passing out, I'm not driving drunk, I'm holding down a job! You should have been there when my mom was throwing up drunk and calling me a stinking little shit! I can't believe you are telling me I drink too much, you know how that makes me feel! Leave me the hell alone!!"

What he is refusing to look at (among other things) is that his drinking is having a bad impact on *you,* and on your children. He is acting as though this issue is just about him, but it isn't. (He's also ignoring the reality that drinking problems take different forms, and that the fact that he doesn't drink the way his mother did proves nothing.) It is undoubtedly true that his memories of his mother's alcoholism are a great source of pain for him. It is also quite likely, though, that another part of why the subject sets him off so much is that he realizes on some level that he is getting sucked down the same awful road (which is what point number two above is referring to).

But beyond either of these dynamics, the key point is that he has to come out of the self-centered place that he has locked himself into and start considering your feelings.

OWNING UP THAT HE HAS A PROBLEM

It's been said a million times but we're going to say it again: people can't solve problems that they don't believe they have. As long as he keeps insisting that you are exaggerating the problem, or you're too sensitive, or you just like to get on his case, or that you are actually the one "who is messed up," he can't progress.

What comes up for him when he tries to make room for the possibility that he really does need to get help, and does need to change? Perhaps first he feels ashamed to admit that you have been right all along when he has been so hotly (and disparagingly) telling you how wrong you are. He feels that he's a bad person for having this problem. At the same time, he may look around and see many people who behave even worse than he does—they drink even more heavily, or they treat their wives and girlfriends with even more overt disrespect or violence, or they are even more prone to irrational explosions; so he tells himself, "How serious could my problem really be?"

Lastly, he feels that life will be over if he accepts having the issues you say he has; he feels that all of his enjoyment will disappear if he has to give up his destructive behaviors. From here on, life looks like drudgery and darkness. The substance abuser thinks, "How could life ever feel good if I can't drink and drug?" The person with mental health issues thinks, "How could life be exciting or satisfying without this wild roller-coaster ride of highs and lows that I live on?" The abusive man thinks, "How could I be a happy man if I have to allow my wife to stand up to me, and if she can require me to follow the same rules that I expect her to follow (like no cheating, for example)?"

The reality is that he will get to a much more fulfilling life by turning himself around. Ask an alcoholic who has been sober for several years whether they miss their old partying days, and he or she will usually say, "Oh, yeah, I miss the drama and the fun sometimes, but I wouldn't want to go back to that for anything." They have discovered satisfaction on a deeper level. Ask a reformed abuser whether he would like to get his old life back, and he'll say, "Sure, there's times when I wish I could just shut my wife up the way I used to, but I wouldn't want to go back to seeing her so hurt, and to having my kids not trust me, and to feeling like such a jerk." Ask someone who has overcome manic depression, or a personality disorder, and he or she will tell you, "I can find plenty of excitement in life without those wild swings I used to go through, and now I don't have to be living with a problem I'm trying to hide from everyone." Ask the man who finally grew up whether he wants to go back to being a thirty-three-year-old adolescent, and he'll say, "Actually, it turns out the adult world isn't so bad."

So the rewards will come, but they won't come quickly. First he will have to do a lot of hard work, work that won't seem to pay off much at all; that's why so many men start making changes but then fail to carry them through. Your partner will have to stop demanding instant gratification and stop insisting that the world owes him gratitude and rewards for doing what he should have been doing all along.

On the way—soon, in fact—he's going to have to get some new friends. If he keeps hanging out with his party pals, he's going to keep using, and he's going to keep convincing himself that his behavior is normal since they all do the same things. If he keeps spending his free time with men who speak contemptuously about women, he isn't going to break his own habits of looking down at females as second class. He's not going to get away from the land of denial if he's still surrounded by people who live there.

HIS EXERCISE 9–3:

Write a couple of paragraphs about what is scary or upsetting to you about admitting that you have a problem that has to be overcome. Then put down some of the reasons for believing that your partner is right (even if you aren't really ready to agree with her overall yet—just put the points that you do see down on paper). Third, put down a couple of thoughts about how you would enjoy your life more if you accepted the problem and changed the behavior. Last, go out for about a ten-minute walk by yourself, and let these thoughts and feelings roll around inside you.

SAYING GOOD-BYE TO PAYBACK

Is revenge really as sweet as they say it is? Or is it actually a highly dysfunctional drive, one that keeps spreading more misery around the world and encourages people to find scapegoats for their own unhappiness?

In the context of intimate relationships, the answer is clear: the payback habit is a cancerous one, guaranteed to spread a deeper and deeper level of mistrust, resentment, and ultimately hatred into the connection between two people. It has to go.

If a man deliberately creates a bad experience for his partner, that will not "make her see what it's like," or "teach her a lesson." She will learn only one thing: that she has to obey him and keep him happy, or he will hurt her. Their relationship then stops being one between intimate partners, and becomes one between master and servant, between dominator and dominated. Is this the impact he wants to have on the world, to turn women into servants?

Even if he has only the narrowest, most self-serving goal of trying to make himself feel better when he's upset, revenge still won't get him what he wants. It brings only the most fleeting and superficial pleasure and, like an addiction, leaves the person craving more rather than feeling satisfied. As you may notice, payback-oriented people tend to be miserable anytime they aren't actively gloating.

Here are some typical examples of retaliatory behavior:

- The couple is at a party and she complains that he is drinking too much, so he responds angrily by deliberately getting himself completely (and embarrassingly) hammered.
- The man is sick of his partner pressing him to carry his weight around the house, so he agrees to do the dishes and then "accidentally" breaks two glasses, plus leaves water spilled all over the kitchen floor, to make sure she won't ask him again.
- He is angry that she is confronting him about the demeaning way in which he speaks to her, so he takes off in the car and doesn't come back until after midnight, thereby causing her to worry about him and sticking her with all the work of getting the children ready for bed and tidying the house.

The alternative to payback is that he has to actually live with the uncomfortable feelings that are coming up for him in his conflicts with his partner. He also has to accept her right to disagree with him, to have her own thoughts and perceptions.

There are positive steps he can take to help him resist the temptation to punish her, beginning with *deep, slow breaths,* working on calming his heart rate and coming out of agitation. He should self-impose a *twenty-four-hour waiting period* between the time that his partner does something that makes him angry and the time when he responds in words or actions; this will give him time to cool down and make sure that he makes choices that are not retaliatory. During this time, in fact as soon as possible, he needs to *talk with someone who is a good influence on him;* this person has to be someone who will settle him down rather than further fire him up against his partner, who will press him to think, and who will help him see the conflict through his partner's eyes. If he remains agitated, he should *sit and write* about what happened to help process his feelings. This writing should include some points that are positive about his partner's perspective, even if he doesn't agree with her. He could write, for example, "I believe I'm doing my share with the kids, but I can see why it wouldn't seem that way to her."

This process we are recommending leads us to the following central point in his work:

> He will need, throughout the coming months and years, to be working all the time on improving his ability to take in, understand, and respect her perspective on conflicts, including her ways of viewing *him*.

HIS EXERCISE 9–4:

> Write descriptions of at least two incidents in which you were mad because you were sure that your partner was wrong about something, and it turned out that she was right. Next, write what is hard for you about giving up the payback habit. Last, write at least two examples of times you have gotten her back for things, and put some thoughts down about why your actions were harmful.

The Crucial Distinction Between Aggression and Self-Defense

For your partner to make serious progress on his behavior, he will have to learn to make the absolutely critical separation between *aggression* (actions designed to harm the other person) and *self-defense* (actions designed to pro-

STANDING UP FOR YOURSELF

- naming what you do not like
- speaking angrily (but respectfully)
- explaining how her actions are making you feel
- taking time to yourself, pulling away (but still meeting your responsibilities)
- asking for what you want her to do differently
- withdrawing favors (not responsibilities)

RETALIATION

- saying things that you know will hurt her feelings
- withdrawing in a way that sticks her with work to do, or that ruins plans
- not letting her talk
- giving her the silent treatment
- getting intimidating or scary
- saying bad things about her to other people
- withdrawing your contribution to responsibilities
- trying to "make her feel" what you are feeling, trying to "do the same thing to her that she did to me"

tect yourself). Destructive people get these two all wrapped up together, and tremendous harm follows. Specifically, he needs to sort out clearly the difference between *standing up for yourself* and *getting revenge*. (See box.) It is simply unacceptable to use behaviors from the "Retaliation" list and then say, "I was just standing up for myself." He has to own the choices he has made in the past to use payback, and from here on out he has to make different choices.

Trying to hurt the other person is not self-defense, *even if you think you are just repeating the same thing that you feel she did to you*. Remember "two wrongs don't make a right"? Those ethics apply just as much to adults as to children.

Here's one way to summarize this section:

From now on he has to choose something constructive that he can do with himself when he is mad at you, instead of opting to do harm.

MAKING A PLAN FOR DEALING WITH HIS ISSUES

Deeply ingrained habits—meaning habits that a person has been acting out for years—carry a tremendous force that keeps them going. This force can seem as powerful and tenacious as a human being's will to live. Unless he makes a clear plan for long-term change, he will never break his habits for very long; he will be stuck—which will keep you stuck, too—in a repeating pattern of:

- apologies and promises to change
- then a stage when his treatment of you gets a little better and he meets some of his responsibilities
- then a stage where it all slides backward into his ruts of destructive living

He has no doubt assured you before that he would turn over a new leaf. So what has to be different now is that he is not just going to commit to *what* he is going to change, but also to *how* he is going to change it, and he is going to put his plan in writing for you.

His plan will need to include the specific elements listed in the box below (which we will explain in detail):

The Elements of His Plan for Change

1. The specific behavioral changes he is going to make
2. The specific destructive attitudes that he is going to let go of, and the constructive ones that are going to take their place
3. The types of outside assistance he is going to get, including the specifics of how often he will go for help, how much of his past behavior he will truthfully reveal, how he will pay for services, and how much right you will have to know the details of what goes on in his work
4. The types of day-to-day work he is going to do on his issues
5. What he is agreeing to do if he breaks any element of his plan (this one is tricky, but it will make sense to you when we go over it)
6. How he will keep you informed about his work, which depends on how much you want to hear about it
7. How he will get continued feedback from you about his actions and his progress

---

Let's look at a sample plan, and then we'll discuss each element and how it works:

Kelly's Plan

1. I will stop drinking and smoking weed. I will stop all secret communications with women I meet, and anything that implies to a woman that I'm interested in her or attracted to her. I will treat Renee like she's a valuable person and a high priority in my life all the time. I will commit myself fully to this relationship, and stop acting annoyed when Renee says we need to spend more time together and be more sexual.

2. I'm going to stop my self-talk about Renee being too needy and demanding, because what she is asking for is totally normal and not that much. I'm going to focus on how the rewards of being in a close relationship outweigh the sacrifices. I'm going to remind myself that I'm responsible for my own actions.

3. (a) I will attend an AA meeting every day for the next three months. After that I will go to at least four meetings per week for a year, and then we'll discuss it again. I will get a sponsor by three weeks from now, which is February 15. (b) I will reveal my problem with alcohol and weed to my parents and my siblings, and keep in touch with them about what I'm doing about it. (c) I will talk to a counselor at my EAP program at work about the way I've used flirtations and affairs to get back at Renee for complaining about my drinking, and to avoid committing to my relationship. I will make a plan with that counselor for staying away from those behaviors.

4. I will write in my journal every day about my temptations and about any self-talk that is negative about Renee or blames her for what a hard time I'm having. I will write for at least twenty minutes. I will not use my AA meetings and journal writing as an excuse to not help with the cooking and cleaning or for not being sexually intimate with Renee (e.g., "I'm too busy, I'm too tired from my meeting, etc."). I will e-mail my sister at least twice a week about what is going on with me.

5. If I drink or drug again, I agree that I will go to an inpatient detox. If I have any flirtations or intimate contacts with women, I will move out of the house until (and unless) Renee says I can come back, and not try to take

any of the furniture or other stuff that belongs to both of us. If I skip any meetings or counseling appointments, I agree to move out for at least a month.

6. My journal is private, but Renee can read the e-mails between me and my sister if she wants to. (My sister agreed to this.) At least once a week I will tell Renee about what I'm learning in my meetings, and read her some sections aloud from my journal that I'm okay with sharing.

7. Renee does not want to have a regularly scheduled "feedback time" for now, but I agree to listen without interrupting whenever she has comments about my attitudes, my behavior, or how well I'm sticking to my plan. When this happens, I agree to give her a thoughtful, nondefensive response that day, or by the next morning at the latest.

This sample plan may give you enough of an idea about how to construct a plan, but here are some guidelines.

First, your partner makes the plan; you don't make it for him. If he comes to you with a half-baked plan, don't fix it or rewrite it for him; tell him it isn't a serious effort and give it back to him. If he can't do this much, he'll never do the harder work to come. Minor feedback and additions from you are fine, once he's made a decent start on it.

Detailed, specific descriptions of behavioral and attitudinal changes are crucial. If he writes vague goals such as "I'll be nicer to you," the plan won't help, because he'll just tie you up in arguments about how nice is nice enough. Similarly unsuccessful will be such agreements as "I'll help around the house more" or "I'll keep a better attitude" or "I'll cut down on my drinking." These need to be replaced with such statements as, "I will change at least four diapers a day and vacuum twice a week," "I won't snarl when you ask me to take care of something," and "I won't have more than two beers a week, and no other alcohol or weed." The part where he agrees to additional steps he will take if he falls off his program is indispensable. It may seem odd to have him agree ahead of time to his own consequences; you might ask, "Well, if he can keep an agreement to follow through with certain consequences if he breaks his plan, why can't he just keep his agreement to stick to his plan in the first place?" This is a fair question, and it has two answers. First, if he has agreed ahead of time to accept consequences, he loses some of the temptation to break the plan and then say, "Sorry, I couldn't help it," because he knows the apology is going to have to be followed up with action. Second, if there is a battle going on between two sides of his character, setting up consequences ahead of time can help the Good Side win. And, lastly, if he breaks his plan and then also breaks the agreement about consequences, he has made it unmistakably clear that he is not going to change, which will be sad but clarifying for you.

You do not have to be his monitor if you don't want to be. Sometimes a woman gets sick of having to tell her partner how he's doing, scolding him if he has done badly and praising his improvements like he was a dog at obedience school. *Decide what is best for you regarding giving him feedback.* If you still have energy for helping him through, go for it. But if you can tell that it's not good for you anymore to be putting energy into working on him, then tell him that he is going to have to monitor his own behavior and find other people to help hold him accountable. It's not your job, so don't take it on if you don't want to.

Outside help is indispensable. It does not necessarily have to be professional help if he can't afford that or it isn't available to you. He might agree, for example, to speak three times a week with a friend or relative who you believe will not get sucked into his excuses and will hold him accountable—and you need to check in with that person once in a while and make sure they are not getting bamboozled. He might also use self-help groups such as twelve-step programs (including Alcoholics Anonymous) or Rational Recovery.

At the same time, professional help can indeed be very helpful, and if he is making excuses to avoid it, look carefully at them. For example, if he "doesn't have the money" to pay for counseling, but he does have it for beer and cigarettes, ball-game tickets, spiffier parts for his car, or new golf clubs, he's playing games to avoid getting real.

What Is the Right Kind of Professional Help for Him?

It has become popular in our society to tell one another, "You should go to therapy," as the solution to all personal problems. However, the research on the effectiveness of counseling indicates that a successful outcome tends to come about only when the following conditions are met: (1) there is a particularly good fit between counselor and client; (2) there are clear goals set for the counseling process and a plan for how those goals will be achieved; (3) the type of counseling being used—and there are many, many different kinds—is appropriate for the client's personal style and the specific problems that he or she is having.

Choosing a counselor or group, therefore, depends on what you believe your partner's primary problem is, using the following guidelines:

- **If he is abusive**: The appropriate service for a man who abuses his partner is called an "abuser intervention program" or a "batterer intervention program," where most of the work is done in groups. (In a few states, it is referred to as "batterer treatment," but that term has mostly gone out of use.) This is the right program for him *even if he has never physically assaulted, sexually assaulted, or threatened you*; in other words, even if his abuse does not include violence. If he says, "I'm not going to go sit in a room with a bunch of *batterers*"—a common excuse used by abusers (including violent ones) not to go to a program—then he isn't ready yet to deal seriously with his behavior.

- **If he is abusing substances**: If your partner is abusing alcohol or drugs, he will need to participate in a specialized substance abuse program. The options include: (1) self-help groups such as Alcoholics Anonymous or Rational Recovery; (2) outpatient substance abuse treatment, where he continues to stay at his home at night but gets intensive group and/or individual counseling by day through a hospital, substance abuse clinic, or outpatient counseling service; (3) programs where he stays at the facility for a period of time, known as "detoxes" or "inpatient substance abuse treatment." These options can be thought of as *levels of intervention*, so that a person who does not manage to stop drinking through AA might need to try formal substance abuse treatment, and a person who fails in an outpatient program may need to go inpatient.

- **If he has mental health problems, including effects from trauma**: Most mental health counseling is known as "therapy" and is carried out by professionals known as "licensed clinicians." The most common forms are variations on "talk therapy," where the client sits in the therapist's office and discusses issues. Less common, but growing in popularity, are the "body-centered therapies," which still include some time spent talking but also involve elements of movement, massage, reexperiencing of deep emotions from the past, and other visceral experiences. Some body-centered approaches, such as Sensorimotor Psychotherapy (which has been found to be especially effective for trauma survivors), do not involve any actual touching of the client by the therapist. For people whose mental health problems appear to be rooted in traumatic experiences, such as child abuse, war, sexual assault, imprisonment, and countless other examples, there are the "trauma therapies"; these are new but promising approaches that are not widely available but worth looking for. Finally, there are intensive programs that involve more than one meeting per week and a long-term commitment of as much as two years, the best-known (and most promising) one being "Dialectical Behavioral Therapy." Medical interventions are also present as an option, including psychiatric care and medication. Hospitalization in a psychiatric facility is available for severe mental health crises.

- *If he is severely immature and/or selfish*: Specific services have not yet been designed for men who don't want to grow up, and who don't want to have to think about anyone other than themselves. (If such a program did exist, millions of women would be trying to get their partners into it.) So even though immaturity is not exactly a mental health problem, he will probably need to pursue therapy, for want of another option.

"He Says He'll Only Go to Counseling If I Go with Him"

Our response to the man who says he needs you to hold his hand into the counselor's office, we're sorry to say, is a little blunt: He needs to be a big boy and go in by himself. Couples counseling is not designed to address one person's chronically destructive behavior; its purpose is to help a couple improve their relationship dynamics, communicate more effectively, clarify their desires, and achieve greater closeness *in a context in which both partners are behaving more or less acceptably.*

In a couples counseling context, your partner will be able to spend a lot of time talking about what he feels *you* are doing wrong, blaming his bad behavior on you, and continuing his pattern of escaping responsibility for his own actions. If he is charming and/or manipulative, he may succeed in enlisting the therapist as an ally, and the whole focus of the counseling may shift toward discussing what *you* need to change. We have spoken to many dozens of women who were involved with abusive or personality-disordered partners who have had exactly this experience in conjoint therapy.

Your partner is probably insisting on couples counseling precisely to avoid owning his behavior and the choices he is making. He wants to hold on to his belief that his behavior is your fault, and couples counseling will not convince him otherwise. (It may, though, help to convince *you* that he is too stubborn to look at himself, the one helpful outcome we see from couples counseling where one partner is chronically destructive.)

In a small percentage of cases, the man's reason for insisting on couples counseling is just that he finds therapy a mysterious and frightening process and he wants to be mothered through it. If this seems to be the issue in your case, offer to accompany him to the waiting room, but not in the door of the therapist's office. If he can't take that one small step, he'll never take the far more difficult leaps necessary for him to enter the adult world.

CONNECTING HIMSELF TO POSITIVE INFLUENCES

What we think of as individual behavior is not really as "individual" as it seems. People look to one another for guidance on how to behave, and they tune in to approval or disapproval that they receive from their society and social network. Judgment is passed on our behavior at high levels—laws and police and courts—and at low levels, such as a friend frowning while we tell him or her about something we did. Individuals who behave destructively sometimes appear not to care what society thinks of them, but if you look more closely, you find that they have at least a few people around them whose approval they are winning. This need for social acceptance is part of why drunks tend to hang out with other drunks and why men who abuse women tend to pick friends who are mistreating their own wives and girlfriends (as research has shown). Similarly, men who are chronic cheaters hang out with men who won't call them on their infidelity and will collude with them in keeping the secret from their partners.

So your partner is going to need to change the influences he is surrounding himself with. First, he needs to stop hanging out with, and talking on the phone with, friends and relatives of his who do any of the following:

- avoid responsibility for their own actions, make lots of excuses themselves
- laugh at his stories about his bad behavior, are amused by his self-caused dramas
- join with him in blaming you or in dismissing your concerns
- have the same behavioral problems that he has

He also has to look at what kinds of messages he is getting from Web sites he hangs out on, books he reads, and videos he watches. If he is into pornography, for example, he is absorbing a constant set of messages that support his disrespectful and immature attitudes. He can get the same negative effect from Web sites—there are many of them—that encourage men to believe that women are the cause of men's problems.

So where can he look for people, and for values, that will push him toward growth instead of toward harm? He can:

- make a point of spending more time talking to, or hanging out with, men who have good relationships with their partners and don't speak badly about them
- connect with female relatives of his who are living lives that command respect
- get more involved with his church, temple, or other faith community—if it is a community that promotes respect and equality for women, and if it's a place where people see his issues rather than being charmed by him
- find a mature, responsible sponsor in a twelve-step program
- open himself to more guidance and influence from you
- open himself to more suggestions from you about people or groups he could be spending time around—and about which people to stay away from

In short, your partner has to be willing to unplug his brain from the values, attitudes, and excuses that he has been absorbing on a daily basis and choose an entirely new mental diet to nourish himself with.

We have covered a great deal of territory in this chapter, so let's recap the key beginning steps again: (1) changing his attitude toward his partner's complaints; (2) understanding his denial, and coming out of it; (3) stopping his retaliations against his partner for raising grievances; (4) making a plan; and (5) connecting himself to positive influences for growth and change.

These are all manageable steps, and there is no excuse for him not to take them. They are just the beginning, but an important one. If he isn't willing to make these simple efforts, he can't get to the level where growth occurs. On the other hand, if he buckles down, stops whining, and gets these five points in place, he has at least laid the right groundwork. Whether he will follow through with the more challenging pieces ahead we will see in the months to come.

TEN

Setting "No-Matter-What-Happens" Goals for Yourself

"I appreciate all the help people try to give me to get back to school. But the truth is I want to be with him, and he'll just find someone else if I even talk about studying again."

"Steve told me if I want to take the new job in the new town that he's not moving there with me. He knows how hard I worked to find a really good-paying job, and he hasn't worked in two years. He said he'd move if I got the job, but now that it comes down to it, he says he won't go with me. I don't want to be without him. I think of going, but Steve has really bad depression . . . He's not going to be okay if I leave him."

"What I really want is just to be happy with him. I don't have any other goals."

"I got myself through college. I set my mind to it and made that happen. I remember the woman I used to be. I can keep moving forward."

I N ORDER FOR real change to occur, boxes must be packed," Sherry counsels her troubled women friends. "You have to be able to imagine it and do it."

Sherry is referring to women who live with partners who need to change. Before a partner will undergo the painful work of change, he must know that he risks losing you. He must know that you will not live with him as things stand now. Packing up those bags (perhaps even literally) helps **you** as well as your partner.

- If you set goals for your life that are about your interests and passions, you will have an easier time imagining a life without your partner, in case that becomes necessary.
- If you can imagine a life without him, you can more effectively demand the growth and change that's needed now.
- If you set goals for your life, it will help you build momentum toward a life of more fulfillment, which will benefit you whether you stay with your current partner or not. And if you do stay, it will help you know what kind of support you need from him to help you fulfill your own happiness.

In this chapter, we will explore the many barriers to setting "No-Matter-What" goals for yourself. These include:

1. fear of pushing your partner away
2. the traumatic bond
3. traumatic attachment to the self-destructive partner

We will help you face your fears about considering leaving the relationship. And we will support you in identifying your hopes and dreams.

"I Don't Even Want to *Think* About Leaving"

It can be painful to imagine goals you want for your life *no matter what happens*. It's the last part that stops women in their tracks: no matter what happens. That means imagining not being together. The fear of imagining this comes in many forms:

What If I'm Done with the Relationship?

Sometimes women don't want to look at what they want in their lives because of the fear of what the process will uncover.

"I don't want to talk about my goals," admitted Tammy. "I feel like if I talk about them, then I will have to leave Richard, and I don't want to think about leaving Richard."

Actually, Tammy didn't leave Richard. She made her No-Matter-What Goals and is actively fulfilling them. Richard committed to and is following through with his plan of changing. The jury is out as to whether Tammy will stay over the long haul. What is important to note is that Tammy gets to decide the pace at which she makes choices about her relationship. You get to decide this, too.

What if you overcome the practical barriers to leaving? What if you break your isolation, and plan for safety? What if you feel your grief about all your hopes and losses? If you then stand at that place and look at your relationship, will you still want it then? Many women fear that if they do all of this work, it will destroy whatever love they have for their partner; however, our experience shows us something different.

———————

This work may loosen some of the traumatic attachment you have for your partner, but it will not damage love. It will make way for it. (We'll be explaining what "traumatic attachment" is all about next.)

> You need not fear that this work will destroy the love you have for your partner. It will strengthen your love of yourself and will make a more loving relationship possible.

What If He Leaves Me?

You might fear thinking about your goals because you feel sure that if you make changes or demands, your partner will leave you. And he might. You may have a solid intuition that even subtle changes on your part will result in your partner's abject rejection of you.

And it seems that he can walk away so easily, without feeling any pain. When a chronically immature partner wants to, he can push you away without hesitation. Likewise, an addicted partner, a personality-disordered partner, a partner with trauma can turn off caring for you like a light switch. Because he cannot hold your perspective while experiencing his own emotions or while on a substance, he is insulated from the true emotional impact of his actions. An abusive partner does not want to take your perspective into account. He doesn't think he should have to. He may even be happy to see that you are in pain when he removes himself, because it consolidates his control.

And contrary to what many people believe, it is natural to feel more unbearably afraid of rejection in a destructive relationship than you would in a healthy one. To the outsider, this is counterintuitive. They wonder, "Why do you want to be with someone who doesn't want you to get your needs met? Don't you want someone who is destructive to leave you? Doesn't that make it easy?"

THE TRAUMATIC BOND

For the most part, when the destructive partner leaves you, it does *not* make it easy.

> **Love mixed together with periods of scary behavior or of severe rejection, devaluing, or selfishness can produce a bond that controls you more powerfully than love that is given to you unaccompanied by these kinds of pain.**

Take a moment to digest this idea—that it is natural for you to feel *especially* attached to someone who treats you badly, or who creates a roller-coaster ride of highs and lows in a relationship. We're not saying that you are attached to the bad times; of course you aren't. The reason you come out feeling so attached is that the bad times are bad enough to really *shake you up*; and if someone is kind or loving to you while you are feeling so badly shaken, you will come to feel quite attached. We call this the traumatic bond.

And here's the key point: *this bonding process will go on even if the person who is being kind to you is the same one who shook you up in the first place!* So a man who cycles through periods when he is attentive and affectionate, making you feel deeply cared about, and periods when he is cold and selfish or outright mean to you can leave you feeling like you don't have the strength to leave him.

Some destructive and manipulative people are actually aware of this. "All people, when they are well treated by someone they expected would treat them badly, are more bound to their benefactor," wrote Machiavelli in 1513. His insight into how a ruler might gain and maintain control over his subjects describes the traumatic bond very well. And notice that he was not saying that this works just on women, but on everyone. It applies to children as well, and even to animals. This traumatic bond can be powerful. It can come between you and your children, the family you came from, and your friends. In some cases a bond can form that feels stronger than your commitment to your livelihood and financial well-being. Some women trapped in this kind of attachment see their health and their dreams slipping away, or feel themselves losing their sense of who they are as distinct, fully functioning people.

Women tend to feel the need to work hard to keep up appearances when they are experiencing a traumatic bond to a destructive partner, to put on a good face for the outside world, especially when it seems like other people just don't understand what it's like. If you are struggling with a traumatic bond to your partner, your stress can just be multiplied further if they say things to you like:

- "Don't give up on him; he's trying hard to change!"
- "The children deserve the chance at having a father fully in their lives!"
- "Your expectations are too high. He's a good guy."

How Helpers Treat Us When We Are Traumatically Bonded

For those of us who are attached to destructive people, we feel confusion, pain, and even shame about the strength of this bond. It is often what separates us from feeling understood, and from seeking help and support from others. We may know from experience, for example, how people react to us when they find out that when our destructive partner threatened to leave, *we* were the ones running after *him;* we were the ones who called him, followed him, and begged him to come back. We were the ones who made promises to improve ourselves and be more supportive. We pleaded that we would make him happier; we would do whatever it would take to make him stay.

When friends, family, social-service workers, or criminal justice personnel learn that we have sometimes acted in these ways (as a result of the traumatic bonding we'd been through), their reaction can be to cut off their support.

Some women even get subjected to open (or barely concealed) disgust from people who should be helping us; from their point of view, we are crazy and at fault—which is, of course, part of what the man has been saying all along to justify his behavior.

It's challenging not to get swept up in this tide, and start to blame yourself the way other people are blaming you. "The thing I just can't forgive myself for," confides Yolanda, "is that when he called me when he was out on parole, even after everything, even after the trial—I was already accepted to my graduate program, already completely moved on, I thought—I found myself saying 'yes' to him!" Yolanda holds her hanging head in her hands as she continues. "Now when people look at me *that way* when they find out I was in an abusive relationship, I just think of what I did that day, letting him back in, and how bad it got later. I know they are right about me, even if I have this PhD."

But they aren't right about her! Yolanda's decision was actually entirely natural for someone who had been through her experience. If you have met with criticism from people for having a hard time letting go of your partner, the concept of traumatic attachment can help you to stop blaming yourself.

What you need is someone who understands that this compelling attachment, which feels vital to survival, is the common, predictable sign of the struggles with:

- isolation
- loneliness
- manipulation
- pain
- fear

You need people who can grasp the emotional sense of your experience without recoiling from it.

Reasonable, smart, fully functioning individuals can experience desperate longing for the person who has become their new center by virtue of mixing caring attention and the promise of more, with fear, loss, and, most critically, isolation from other points of view.

EXERCISE 10–1: TRAUMATICALLY BONDED

This exercise is simple. Find something to write with and a piece of paper. We are going to ask you to write your name, something that you have probably been doing since you were about three or four years old. Before you write your name on the paper, grasp your hands tightly together, with palms touching and fingers interlaced. From this new hand position, grab your pen or pencil and now try to write your name.

If your two free hands represented two independent souls partnered in relationship, your bound hands represent them traumatically bonded. Bound in this way, you have temporarily lost your effectiveness. What was it like to struggle to write your name?

The Stakes Seem So High

When you are traumatically bonded, it may be especially difficult to think about the relationship ending. The destructive partner plays upon the illusion that together you have both shared a long, perhaps torrid and emotionally intense history. You seem to have overcome so much together that it would be a waste to throw it away if you left. This idea of a shared history implies that together you have overcome obstacles that stood in your way. It implies that together you have grown. And it creates the sense in you that giving up your relationship with him would be a vast loss.

But in reality, *you* have shared *his* history. He has not met you in your experience, or in your experience of these events. Together you have not faced off obstacles. If he is abusive or personality disordered, he *was* the obstacle. If he was addicted or traumatized, then his struggles became an obstacle to your fulfilling your goals. If your partner has suffered legal or social consequences for his behavior, you may have been the one having to support him through dealing with those effects—but you would not be likely to get any of that same support back when it was your turn to need it. You can't count on him to be there for you about how his hurtful choices and behavior have affected your life. (And anyhow, he probably hasn't done the work of developing insight into what you have been through and its meaning to you.)

What is really at stake is different from what it may seem to be. The real issue is whether you can live a life in which you can identify and strive for your goals. And if your partner is violent or scary, the "real stakes" also means your safety, and the danger you may face when you take the step to leave him and reclaim ownership of your life. (We will address safety issues in Chapter 18.)

If your partner is self-destructive, that, too, can cause traumatic attachment. You fear that if you move toward envisioning a life without him, he will become even more self-destructive. We understand that your motivation in these circumstances is a caring one. You do not wish your partner harm. But please understand that even if you begin to turn some of your focus back to yourself, and stop taking care of your partner as much as you used to, it doesn't mean you care about him any less.

Since you are still deeply connected, it can feel almost unbearable to witness your partner's self-destruction. And you may find yourself deciding reluctantly to give yourself more fully back to the relationship that you were hoping to take distance from, rather than go through seeing the person you love destroy himself. (And a destructive partner can sometimes play upon this compassion by threatening that he'll destroy himself without you.)

But, **you are not responsible for his self-destruction.**

It is another assault upon *you* for him to threaten you with his own self-destruction, and for him to hold you responsible is cruel and utterly mistaken. What he is asking you for, in effect, is to join him on his destructive path.

If your partner is using threats—or implied threats—that he will hurt himself as a way to keep you from leaving, he is behaving abusively. This behavior may not look like abuse, however, because it seems so sad. But underlying this supposedly helpless stance are his abusive attitudes that hold that your well-being is not his primary concern; your role is in service to him, even if it means keeping him company while he actively destroys you both. Abusive and violent values are especially dangerous when combined with severe emotional disturbances that lead to suicidal planning and suicidal threats. These hateful values are the ones that occasionally lead men to kill themselves in front of loving women who are leaving the destructive relationship. They are hoping to horrify and blame the woman for choosing a path of love and freedom.

We need to say this very plainly: **it is not your responsibility, nor is it your fault, if he harms himself.** We don't mean to sound uncaring about his suffering; what we are saying is that his "fix" for his unhappiness would not have worked either. *It is important to know this.* His solution was that you stay with him in the tight, restricted world that he himself could not bear. He has no right to martyr you to his difficulties; your life is precious, too.

You Can Heal

With wise supports for yourself, you can heal from the potent grief that can follow if you have to see him harm himself in response to your decision to move toward greater separateness. Here are some of the steps on the healing path:

- You can honor the feelings of attachment.
- You can sort them out from the feelings of love that you have for him.
- You can grieve his pain.
- You can grieve his tragic act of self-harm.
- You can honor your own loss.
- You can feel pain at the wounds he inflicted upon you.
- You can feel outraged at the cruelty of his blame and rejection.

It may not be his fault that he suffers from depression, but he is responsible for the belief that he has the right to punish you for his suffering.

What Healing Looks Like for Sarah

After years of receiving support from friends, Sarah had formulated her No-Matter-What Goals. When she noticed that her partner was doing some things that were getting in the way of her achieving her goals, she decided to tell him that she needed him to stop what he was doing. Importantly, her partner had changed enough that Sarah felt that she could safely tell him exactly what she saw and how she felt about it. Through her connections to her supportive friends and to her colleagues in her job, Sarah was able to dissolve the traumatic bonds that had previously kept her feeling so stuck in her relationship. She approached her partner free of the panicky feeling that she had to do or say *anything* to make the relationship work out. As she spoke to him, her main interest was in how he was going to listen to her, acknowledge her feelings and point of view, and make choices that would satisfy *her* reasonable needs. Sarah stunned her partner by saying the following:

"I just want you to know something. Just now I pointed out the five times you tried to distract me from the complaint I am making against you. The first time, you tried to distract me by responding to my upset by getting more angry than I was. I didn't let you distract me with that. The next three times, you tried to distract me by bringing up unrelated complaints of your own based on events that didn't actually happen. Maybe you thought I'd get stuck in an argument of whether your accounting of those things really happened. The last distraction was your getting upset for my not listening to your three made-up complaints until you had addressed the thing I brought up.

"I refused to talk about your made-up complaints until you admitted what you were doing. You had good insights, based on my observations of you, into why you do it, your shame, your feelings of inadequacy, etc. And now you feel pretty good.

"This whole thing *did not make me feel closer.* We don't have some kind of warm feeling flowing between us now. You look all soft and warm now. I think you even want to have sex. You feel relieved because you threw up your anger all over the place, and had some good insights, led by me. You had a good cry about your issues, and now maybe you feel loving and vulnerable.

"I, on the other hand, feel even more angry. We never got to talk about the complaint I had to begin with. I also feel tired and bored to death. We are not having a bonding experience here."

Your journey back to center is a journey back to truth. It is a journey toward the truth that you are not the cause of his acts of violence and desperation. It is a journey toward the truth that you deserve a life lovingly supportive of No-Matter-What Goals.

Eyes on the Prize: Setting Your No-Matter-What Goals

We understand that setting goals can be daunting. We've already talked about the concerns you may have about ways that your partner may retaliate against you, or even try to harm your children, if you orient your life toward yourself. We also recognize that it can feel pointless to set goals when you are in deep discouragement or exhaustion—if, for example, you have very small children and are trying to function with barely enough sleep to remember your own name, or if you are recovering from illness or severe injury. *But it is worth it!*

We will be realistic, taking into account the grief, fear, or danger that may arise. And we won't forget the challenging limitations of time and energy that you may have.

EXERCISE 10–2: NO-MATTER-WHAT GOALS

Please write your responses to the following questions. Some women have difficulty answering these questions because they realize that the only hope they have ever had for themselves is to be part of a happy, stable relationship. If this is the case, answer the questions with that in mind, and also play with whatever other ideas come to you.

1. If you do feel your main goal has been to have a happy, stable relationship, what else do you hope for yourself?

2. How would you know you had "enough" of what you need and want in your life? What would it look like?

3. What would you be doing with your time if you could do anything?

4. What ways would you spend your time for fun? Which things would you consider to be your contribution to the world?

5. What ways would you spend your time that would be joyful and new for you—what would you like to learn how to do? What would you like to learn about?

6. What would your ideal partner in a romantic relationship say about these dreams?

7. What would your ideal partner in a romantic relationship do in support of these dreams?

8. Was there ever a time in your life when you were close to living your dreams? If so,

> What were you doing that was bringing you close to living your dreams?
> Do you remember what those sensations were like in your body?
> What was going on in your life that was different than it is now?
> Did you notice things change away from living your dream? When did this occur? What's your sense of why this happened?
> What kinds of things did you tell yourself about leaving the situation that brought you closer to your dream?
> What do you think of those things that you told yourself? Were they accurate?

Share Your Dream with a Friend

Is it possible to find a friend to confide in about this dream of yours? Choose someone who believes in you. If no friend comes to mind, a support group, even a hotline worker under the numbers listed under "Resources" can help you find people who can really be there for you.

You are reacquainting yourself with your dreams. It may feel silly, or embarrassing, to uncover what has lain dormant or unattended to. Perhaps this dream is the very thing for which a destructive partner has mocked you. If so, then it is most important to find it again. It is waiting for you.

You need to share these dreams with someone who is not your partner. There will be important work ahead that will involve your partner, and there will be a time, soon, when you might insist that he show you that he's going to be an active support for your dreams and goals. But for the work we're doing right now, find another friend, one who can focus solely on your dreams. We want this person to ask you not in order to make you feel bad, but instead to help bring these dreams out of the half-light and into the day of your lived life.

Ask your friend to picture you successfully achieving these things. Ask him or her to treat you as though you are fully capable of moving toward what you desire. Ask for emotional and practical support toward these efforts. Your friend can ask you questions such as:

- *What steps are you taking toward these hopes and goals?*
- *What needs to happen to make this dream come true?*
- *What resources do you need in your life to make this happen?*
- *How much of each day can you commit to making this dream come true, to doing things associated with this dream?*
- *How did you do this (week, month, etc.) in setting aside your time? If it didn't go well, what could you do differently over the next period of time that would work better?*
- *What do you need your partner to do in order to make this dream come true?*

Making the Time

Can you set your alarm fifteen minutes earlier? In that time, will you commit to writing in your journal about your progress toward your goal?

You may feel that it is entirely too late, but it's not. Consider that the next five years will happen regardless of whether you begin now. In five years' time, your daily efforts will have moved you closer to your goals. We are asking you to put what inspires you at your core above your other priorities for a few minutes, every day. We ask you to breathe life back into what you feel you are here to do.

If you choose to take this on, consider also giving up some small chore or habit that takes up time in your life. Perhaps there is an online site you visit or a television show that you watch that isn't that rewarding an experience. Maybe there is an acquaintance you spend time with whose connection you do not truly value. There might be places where you can pull out some small time and energy to give back to yourself. It is easier to take on something new, like tending to your own goals, if you simultaneously give something up that is not very enriching to you.

Do you have safety considerations in committing the fifteen minutes to yourself?

What are they?

Are there ways to proceed that would not compromise your safety?

Do you have a secure e-mail account?

Can you find ten minutes a week to write that friend about your progress toward your goal if you can't speak on a weekly basis?

Can you send your friend a private file where you keep your written thoughts, just for safekeeping?

If you have not fifteen minutes anywhere at all in your life that is safely yours, but you are able to read this book, then begin by writing your thoughts in the margins of this book. When you take this time, please guard it with all your growing strength. As you give to it, it will give back to you. You will be clearer. You will see things differently. You will be moving the compass back toward you in your life. It will be so tempting to exchange this time for a thousand other attentions, large or small. It can be the hardest habit to create—*but it is one that feeds your center and your future.*

Your Resources

After writing answers to the following questions, be sure to include these insights in your discussions with your supportive friend.

1. What resources do you have already in your life to move you toward your goals?
2. What things have you done already that are related to the goal?
3. What people have you known or do you know that are connected to this goal?
4. Are there old friends or family members who might have information, connections, materials, or time that could contribute to your goals?

There is a community of like-minded people for you to share your particular vision with. There are always people who do something similar to what you want to do. They have experience, thoughts, successes, and failures to learn from. You can find them on the Web or in the newspapers or through word of mouth.

1. What can you do to take steps toward connecting you with others whose lives resonate with your dreams for yourself?

2. Is there a forum, a meet-up, a discussion group you can join? Are there authors whose work moves you? Retreats or classes to attend?

Grief in the Face of Your New Goals

As you identify your goals, you might feel sad from not having been connected to yourself for so long. When you turn loving attention to yourself, it can highlight the general lack of this loving attention in your life. As these feelings come up, you may feel tempted to turn away from your goals, and chase those feelings away with something unhealthy. But you can stick through it.

We think of this as a grieving period. You are grieving the neglect of the person you had hoped to become. You are grieving the loss of all the love and support you deserved. This pain will pass if you give your grief its time and continue the loving attention and dedication toward your goals. At first, your fifteen minutes of writing about your progress toward your goals could be spent coming to understand what you feel you have lost or lost track of.

Welcoming the Grief

Anticipating a sense of grief can give you time to prepare for the sadness and even welcome it. This kind of grieving can be very healing, signaling room for a relationship with yourself that is more responsive to your needs. Crying, for example, can sometimes be very relieving and bring clarity.

If you saw that kind of deep, hard cry as actually being part of healing, how would that change your view of crying, and of other aspects of healing?

Do you notice any feelings of sadness or grief when you write about your dreams?

If you remain committed to your time to yourself and your steady efforts toward your dreams, you might find that you have less of a desire to distract yourself with unhealthy habits, and feel overall a greater sense of joy, even amid great trials.

EXERCISE 10-3: YOU ARE VALUABLE, NO MATTER WHAT HAPPENS

Now that you have identified your goals for yourself, let's take it one step further. Let's imagine what it would be like to achieve these goals even if you were not in the relationship. In order to do this, let's first remember you.

With or without a partner to engage you, you exist fully.

- What qualities do you possess?

- What skills do you have?

- What is it in your life that makes you most proud?

- What do you find most attractive about yourself?

- When are you most funny?

- If you are a parent, what do you do well as a parent?

EXERCISE 10-4: EMBODYING YOUR NO-MATTER-WHAT GOALS

Imagine a woman you admire. Pick someone that you think is amazing. Choose someone whom you can imagine still being amazing even without a partner. Imagine her in some detail. What are the qualities that you admire? Imagine her talking, sitting down near you, relaxed, doing whatever it is she does, dressed in the way that makes you feel inspired. Imagine for a moment that you got to visit her body, got to sit inside her core, and feel what it is like to be her. Make a note below on what those sensations are like.

- What does it feel like in your legs, your back, your feet, to be her for a moment?

- What are the sensations in your neck and your face, your chest, to be her for a moment?

Now let's imagine you without your current partner. Let's do the same scan of your body.

- When you consider that, what do you notice in your legs, your back, your feet?

- What sensations do you discover at the idea of you without your partner?

Let's switch back to the woman you admired in her independence.

- Note again, below, what you notice.

Switch back to yourself.

- Do you notice anything as you switch your attention back and forth?

- What would it be like to achieve the dreams you have for yourself, but without your partner?

- What would it be like to achieve the dreams you have for yourself, with your partner?

- What commitment can you make for yourself to move forward on your dreams, regardless of what is happening in your relationship?

- What do you need to remind yourself as you do this?

Back in the center of you, in the core of who you are, is a person worth knowing.

Tell us, tell yourself, who you are at your core. Dream her, imagine her back into being.

PART III

ENTERING THE NEW PHASE

ELEVEN

Men's Work: What It's Really All About

A version of this chapter that is designed for the man to read is available at ShouldIStayOrShouldIGo.net. That version includes spaces for him to write his responses to the exercises and other differences. The version you will read below is written for you, not for him; we have included the exercises so that you can know what his assignments are.

I N SITCOMS AND hit movies, selfish and mean jerks turn into angels in the last five minutes. They realize how hurtful they've been acting, they apologize, and their entire outlook softens. And we are left to believe that these magical changes are going to last.

These minidramas that we consume daily seem to be shaping our expectations for real-life relationships. An opinion poll in the United States found not only that a majority of viewers find the solutions to conflicts on sitcoms to be realistic, but also that they believe they should try to use the same techniques that the characters use to solve their own difficulties with people.

Spreading this mythology is like tossing buckets of marbles under the feet of women who are in unhealthy relationships. The reality is that addicted, abusive, or unstable relationship partners change only through deep self-reflection, hard internal work, and thorough reshaping of their daily habits.

This transformation, far from taking five to ten minutes, takes a period of *years* to carry out—if the man works at it hard and steadily. If he doesn't, the change doesn't come about at all.

We want to encourage you to move forward in two ways that may seem like opposites in some ways, but that actually go together well: (1) to understand quite a bit about your partner's process of growth and change so that you can tell whether significant work is happening on his end or not; and (2) to put the majority of your energy into *your own* growth and development, *not* into helping him deal with his issues. Don't let him get away with making your life revolve around him and his ups and downs. The best way to avoid this trap is to work carefully through each of the chapters in this book that is about your work (meaning all of them except Chapters 9 and 11) so that you make yourself your own focus and priority.

We turn now to examining what the nuts and bolts of your partner's work will look like if he gets brave enough to dive down to the depths where things start to count. We're assuming that the man has already laid the preparatory groundwork covered in Chapter 9; he can't skip any of those steps and expect his work at this next level to go anywhere. If he's complaining already about how hard this process is for him, he's going to need to pull himself together, because the more difficult pieces are now coming.

RECOGNIZING THAT HIS BEHAVIOR IS A CHOICE

Men who harm their partners, whether emotionally, physically, or sexually, claim to be helpless. Consider whether any of the following excuses sound familiar to you:

> *"I was so drunk I didn't know what I was doing."*
> *"I was in a rage, and I just lashed out."*
> *"There's only so much a man can take."*
> *"What you were doing reminded me of what my mom used to do to me, and I went berserk."*
> *"You can't expect me to be perfect when I'm that upset."*
> *"The stress of losing my job made me go on a binge."*

"I didn't realize what I was doing. I was out of my mind."

"I was in a blackout."

"You know how to totally push my buttons, then you blame me when I go off."

"I would never have slept with that girl if you weren't being so cold to me."

These excuses are all ways of covering up his problem. The reality is that the behavior of human beings is rarely "on automatic," despite the claims of destructive partners. People *make choices,* and they do so even when they are deeply hurt, enraged, triggered, or drunk. Even in the highest-pressure situations, people's behavior is shaped by:

- their attitudes and values about what is acceptable behavior
- their spiritual and religious beliefs
- their desire to avoid harming *themselves*
- their desire to protect belongings that they care about
- their wish to protect their reputation (how they are viewed by friends, relatives, and the wider public) and to avoid criticism
- their awareness of possible legal consequences for certain acts
- their *goals*—what they are trying to accomplish with their behavior

Here are some real-life examples from cases we've been involved with:

Kyle, who said that the pain of his terrible relationship with his wife drove him into cheating on her, and that it was the waves of intense emotion he was having about her that caused him to use such terrible judgment. Yet he also admitted that getting together secretly with his mistress required lots of advance planning, careful lying, faking sickness, and other stratagems that showed he was anything but "out of control."

Brian, who said, "I don't know what I'm doing after six or eight drinks," yet always managed to continue selling weed no matter how drunk he was, without losing any of his skill as a businessperson, without losing his money or his merchandise, and without getting himself arrested.

Marshall, who came home extremely drunk and beat his wife up badly, leaving her covered with welts and bruises all over her legs and torso. He said that between the alcohol and the rage he was feeling, he went "berserk."

However, when his counselors asked him why his wife didn't have injuries to her face or arms, he answered, "Oh, I wasn't going to do anything that would show."

We have seen relationship after relationship where a rageful man: "goes crazy" smashing things around the house yet manages to avoid breaking anything that is important to him (while he breaks lots of things of hers); behaves in ways that are "out of control" but then quickly covers his tracks when police come around so that they won't find out about the drugs or the violence or the drunk driving; or is in the middle of being verbally and emotionally vicious to her when other people show up, and he switches so quickly to being kind and smiley that those people have no idea what she is so upset about, and she actually comes out looking like the nasty one.

When a man gets serious about changing he has to be willing to look at the choices he is making every day, from the most trivial to the most significant. He has to accept that no one and nothing other than him is determining what he does. If he backslides into drinking, if he returns to abusive behavior, if he cheats on his partner, it's because that's what he decided to do. In short:

> His change depends on his willingness to accept *complete responsibility* for his own actions. He has to stop blaming them on you, on his addiction, on his childhood, or on anything else.

What If He Has Mental Health Problems? Does He Still Make Choices?

Only the most severe mental illnesses cause people to become truly unable to make choices or govern their own actions. If your partner can hold down a job, or can get along with his friends or relatives, or can look more or less normal in most situations, he is in adequate shape psychologically to be fully responsible for his actions. The kind of mental health conditions that leave a man genuinely out of control are on the level of hearing voices and having visual hallucinations that he believes are real, remembering events that never happened, believing harmless people are trying to kill him, and confusing his worst nightmares with reality. Very few women are dealing with a man whose psychological problems are this severe. The more common mental health problems, such as depression, manic depression, and personality disorder, as serious as they can be, do not make it impossible for a person to make better choices if they become seriously motivated to do so.

And that is a big "if." As we saw in Chapter 4, it is very difficult to convince a person with, say, a personality disorder, that he needs to change his behavior because he is hurting other people. He will insist that you are being very unfair to him, and that it's the other people who need to change. And as for convincing him that he is actually harming himself through his actions, he is likely to carry into his old age the idea that everyone else caused his suffering. So although the individual with this level of mental health problem could do better, in practice he won't unless he enters into a process of deep and extended work on himself. And in order to do that, he will have to acknowledge that yes, he is making choices.

Brett, who has gone through two years of Dialectical Behavioral Therapy to deal with his borderline personality disorder, puts it this way: "I realize that I have never acted in any way that would seriously hurt my reputation at work. If I acted on all of the thoughts that went through my head, I would not only have lost my relationship, but also my job and everything I have. I would be homeless. I have a 'switch'—it's my ability to choose. I throw on that switch before I go to work and I can function really well. I finally realized that if I want to keep this relationship, I have to throw on that switch *at home.* "

HIS EXERCISE 11-1:

Write down the story of a time when you told yourself that you "lost control of yourself" and did something destructive. Looking back at that event, how can you tell now that you were actually making choices at the time? Why did you make the choices that you did?

TAKING IN THE HARM THAT HE HAS DONE

"You're trying to make me feel guilty."

This italicized sentence is a line often used by a destructive partner. Here's what he's really saying: "My feelings come ahead of everything. It makes me feel bad when you point out how I've hurt you, so you're bad for mentioning it. Don't pressure me to look at, or deal with, the effects of what I've done."

Meaningful behavioral change doesn't occur in people who lack the strength or the integrity to look squarely at the damage their actions have wrought. The pop philosophy that says, "Forget the past, just focus on doing better in the future" may work well for the baseball player who just missed a catch, but it fails disastrously in the hands of a destructive man. Why?

Because his failure to consider, value, and understand his partner's feelings is a central reason for why he behaved in such hurtful ways in the first place. He can't possibly move beyond selfishness and insensitivity unless he is willing to spend years—literally—developing his understanding of the unjust pain his actions have brought to her life.

This understanding leads us to another mistake in pop philosophy: the saying "Guilt is a pointless emotion, and nothing is accomplished by feeling guilty about something you've done." In reality, guilt is a critical aspect of healthy human functioning. Our guilt feelings exist to alert us to times when we have wronged other people and to motivate us not to repeat those unethical or uncaring acts. The definition of a psychopath or sociopath (known clinically as "antisocial personality disorder"—see Chapter 4) is a person who lacks a conscience; in other words, a person who feels no guilt about having harmed another. *The absence of guilt is pathological.* While it may be true that our guilt feelings about eating too many doughnuts or skipping our exercise programs—in other words, feeling guilty toward *ourselves*—don't usually lead to any positive outcome, the nagging conscience we feel toward others is there for a good reason.

Do we want a man to feel guilty about embarrassing his wife because he got so drunk in front of her relatives? About how humiliated she felt when he called her a "fat bitch"? About the years when he was stealing her money to buy cocaine? About bringing home a sexually transmitted disease because he was cheating on her?

The answer is "yes, we do." Guilt is not an end in itself, but the only way for a man *not* to feel guilty about these kinds of behaviors is to not really look at them. He has to force them out of his mind, minimize them, blame them on his partner, or blame them on women in general. And if he is going to change, we need him to look.

Part of why the alcoholic drinks is, ironically, to escape the pain of the damage that his drinking has already done. Part of why the abuser keeps abusing is to punish his partner for daring to point out how his abuse has hurt her. Part of why the man with narcissistic personality disorder behaves so selfishly is to try to fill a huge internal void he feels, which in turn is caused by the fact that he has driven so many people away over the years. All that effort he pours into not seeing himself is cement being poured into the foundation of his problem.

You don't have to take our word for it. Twelve-step programs for recovery from addiction place emphasis on the importance of "taking a fearless moral inventory" of one's own acts, and doing the extended work of "making amends." Programs for men who abuse women focus on requiring the men to grasp the effects of their violence and to learn to *feel bad* about treating a woman that way. Dialectical Behavioral Therapy, the state-of-the-art approach to overcoming personality disorders, demands that participants immediately

---

The Elements of Facing What He Has Done

- Be able to describe, in detail, the wrongs he has done
- Be able to say a lot about how his behavior has affected his partner, without making her sound hypersensitive, fragile, or overreactive
- Put these thoughts in writing, and allow his partner to keep copies of what he has written
- Give her as much space as she wants, for as long as she wants, to express her hurt, anger, frustration, and other feelings about his conduct, and to let him know what the other specific effects have been on her life (such as financial harm he has brought her, opportunities he has caused her to miss, ways he has harmed the children, physical injuries he has caused, lasting damage he has brought to her trust in him or to her sense of safety in the world)
- Do everything in his power to take care of the harm he has done (such as paying her medical or therapy bills, going back now to anyone he has lied to about her in the past and tell the truth, fixing harm he's done to the home, helping the children cope with emotional difficulties his behavior has sown in them, paying her back money he owes her or that he stole from her, getting a job and holding it down)
- Accept that there will be aspects of the harm he did that he *can't* fix, and that his partner has a right to express anger and bitterness for a long time about those effects

stop behaving in ways that make things worse; then they work on the skills of preserving relationships by learning to consider the implications of their choices. As Brett says, "When she's mad at me, I have to stop and think about my skills. I take a moment and ask myself, 'How do I want her to feel about me in twenty minutes? How do *I* want to feel later about this interaction? She's got every right to be pissed off at me. I have to remember everything I put her through.' Thinking in that way goes against all the negative voices in my head—but those voices are going to get me divorced. And I want to be with her. I want her to trust me."

The list in the box is useful in trying to find out how serious your partner is about changing. He may begin by claiming helplessness: "I know I've done things I shouldn't have, but there's nothing I can do about them now—she just has to forgive me and move on." But there are things he can do about it; the list above shows him many things he can do, and needs to do.

HIS EXERCISE 11–2:

Do some extended writing (filling a few pages) about how your partner has been affected by your unhealthy behavior in the past. Make it honest, and face your actions bravely. Let her read it when you are finished *if she wishes to*. If she does read it, be prepared to listen nondefensively to any reactions and additions she may have, or new pieces she wants you to write about.

GIVING UP THE BARGAINING HABIT

No one gives up unhealthy behavior patterns without a fight. Your partner had reasons for developing his issues, and those will not vanish; as a result, a big part of him is going to be keeping an eye open for opportunities to go back to his familiar ways. One way he may do this is by trying to *cut deals* regarding his change, which might look like any of the following:

- telling you that he has made big changes, and that it's unreasonable for you to expect him to change even more

- saying that you don't appreciate how hard he has been working on himself
- acting as if a period of behaving appropriately gives him license to behave badly now (for example, he gets drunk and then says to you, "But I've been on the wagon for a long time, you shouldn't be so mad, you don't appreciate how well I've been doing")
- using his change as a bargaining chip to force you to do more to please him, such as "I quit smoking weed like you wanted me to, so now you should quit hanging around with your sister so much, like I've wanted," or "Okay, I'll stop yelling and calling you names about how messy the house is, but then you've got to keep it cleaner"
- managing his alcohol or drug problem by *bingeing,* where he doesn't use for weeks at a time but then gets himself hammered enough in a weekend to make up for all the time of not partying

Each of these bargains deserves a response. First of all, there is nothing unreasonable about your expecting your partner to completely stop his destructive behavior. In fact, he is the one being unreasonable by suggesting that you should be willing to endure any of it. What he's really saying is: "Because I treated you so badly in the past, you should accept some mistreatment now, as long as it's less than it used to be." Or, to put it even more starkly: "You can't complain if I steal a little of your money today, because I used to steal *a lot* of it." Logical? Not terribly.

We would, in fact, argue the opposite; we believe that the fact that your partner has behaved badly in the past gives him even *less* license to do so in the present, because you are already injured by him and he has no right to poke you in the wounded places.

Similarly, you don't owe him gratitude for treating you the way he should have treated you all along. If he wants to congratulate himself for how much he has changed, or if his friends want to give him a prize, that's great, but he shouldn't come around looking for credit from the person he has hurt. If someone is holding you on the ground with a foot on your neck—speaking metaphorically—you aren't going to thank them when they step off and let you get up. The immature guy thinks he should be admired for finally working a steady job, the partier thinks we should be so impressed that he finally stopped snorting coke and smoking weed, the abuser wants us to shake his hand for not threatening his wife and calling her disgusting names.

Good behavior, even if it continues for weeks or months, does not earn a man a gift certificate that he can then redeem for a day of acting like a selfish or scary jerk. And this is exactly what we recommend that you say to him if he starts trying the "but I've been good for so long" routine.

Nor does it earn him the right to control or change something he doesn't like about you, or to demand that you cater to him more, King of the Castle style. This style of bargaining is called "quid pro quo," which means if you want him to do something for you, then you have to do something for him. If he tries to run this bargain, the best response goes roughly like this: "When I insist that you be a good relationship partner, I'm not asking you for a *favor*; I'm asking you for my *due*. You don't get to demand anything back from me in return for you being a decent and responsible human being."

Untangling this bargain leads us to a critical point to highlight:

He has to make his changes *unconditionally* or they absolutely will not last. He is changing *because it is the right thing to do*, and therefore it cannot be done with the expectation that you will do anything in return.

These bargains are warning signs of change that isn't happening. The guy who stops drinking because he thinks then you'll go on a diet, or who stops calling you a slut but expects that in return you will stop having conversations with male friends, or stops stealing your money but feels that in return you should give him some, is going to be back to his old ways eventually, probably pretty soon.

Making Meaningful Apologies

"Why do I still have to be hearing about this? I already told you I was sorry. What more do you want from me, a pound of flesh?"

Does this person sound like he's sorry? Not very. In fact, he is creating the impression that he used his original apology as a way to placate his partner and get her to leave him alone, and never really understood what was wrong with his behavior.

Let's consider an example. Maryellen is having a difficult pregnancy and

THE CHARACTERISTICS OF A MEANINGFUL APOLOGY

- He sounds like he really means it when he says it.
- He makes a serious commitment not to repeat the behavior.
- Even after he apologies, he gives you the time you need to explain to him what was wrong with what he did and how his actions affected you.
- He shows signs over time of making a serious effort to grasp why you didn't like what he did.
- He respects your right to have additional bad feelings about the event that come up later, especially when something triggers the experience for you.
- He respects your right to demand that he *do something* about what he did.

THE CHARACTERISTICS OF A USELESS APOLOGY

- He insists that his apology should be all you need from him.
- He blames you for not feeling finished with the event, insisting that it's your job to put it all behind you.
- He doesn't back up the apology with much (or any) action.
- He keeps doing the same things over and over again and then apologizing again.
- He switches into the victim role if you remain angry or mistrustful about something he did, and makes it sound like you're being mean or unfair to him about it.
- He acts annoyed if you point out that his apology didn't sound heartfelt.
- His apology sounds hurried or unfeeling, or he retracts it later.

the doctor tells her that it's essential that she get some exercise. She and her husband, Luke, agree that three days a week he is going to hurry home from work to look after their two children while she goes to the gym. But only the second day into this agreement, Luke gets offered some high-paying overtime and accepts it (without asking Maryellen), so she remains trapped in the house all evening. Maryellen expresses her fury to Luke when he finally gets home, and he ends up apologizing before they go to bed. Two weeks later Maryellen says something to Luke about feeling under stress about their financial situation, and he snarls, "Well, we wouldn't be in this position if you wouldn't have a fit about me getting in some overtime."

Luke's comment is a *retraction* of his earlier apology; he's now saying she shouldn't have been upset by what he did. He has just demonstrated, also, that he never did bother to think carefully about her needs and feelings (or the needs of their growing baby), and instead stayed mentally locked onto himself. Luke has switched the issue from being about Maryellen's need to exercise, and his need to honor his agreements, to being about her "having a fit." He has revealed that his original apology had nothing behind it.

Accepting Her Anger

A succinct way to summarize Luke's thinking is: "Maryellen has no right to be angry at me. Her anger is ridiculous. I'm going to put her down about it." One of the most consistent characteristics of men with destructive issues is the frequency with which they dismiss and discredit the anger that their actions have caused. This discrediting tendency is often worsened by a man's negative attitude toward women's anger in general; he may be contemptuous of women when they are angry, perhaps doing demeaning imitations of them or making them sound irrational and hysterical.

Therefore, one of the central pieces of work he has to do is to learn to respect, reflect upon, and respond appropriately to women's anger, and to his partner's anger in particular.

HIS EXERCISE 11–3:

Write your partner a thoughtful, detailed letter of apology about one of the hurts you have done to her that she has complained about the most. Follow the elements above of what makes a meaningful apology, including writing out your commitments to what you will do differently in the future. Then, follow through on this commitment in the months and years to come. Give her the letter *if she is interested in having it.* Accept any reactions she has to the letter, including accepting her right not to react at all.

What Is a *Real* Man Like?

Sooner or later, a man who is interested in becoming a responsible, kind, sober partner is going to find himself struggling with insecurities about his manhood. As part of that process, he is going to have to come to terms with the mixed messages he has absorbed about masculinity over the course of his life, beginning when he was very young. We find that men's unhealthy behavior patterns are highly connected to their gender identity, whether that plays out in obvious ways—as with men who batter their partners because they don't believe women have any rights—or plays out in much subtler ways, as with the man who won't stop drinking because he feels that without his party buddies he would lose his status as "one of the guys."

Our society's messages about manhood include some powerful binds that leave almost every man feeling that he isn't man enough:

- He is taught that he should be a good provider and a responsible family man BUT he also learns that he should value his male friends more than women and children, and spend his free time with them.
- He knows that he is supposed to be the strongest and the bravest BUT in reality only one man can be the strongest and the bravest, so that leaves all other men not quite up to snuff.
- He hears that he should be able to "handle his liquor" (which means he should be able to drink a lot) BUT he also gets the message that he shouldn't drink too much and especially that he should avoid the shame of being an alcoholic.
- He learns that he should not open up about his feelings or "show weakness" emotionally BUT his pain sometimes (or frequently) becomes more than he can endure.
- He learns that a man should never back down from a fight BUT he also learns that he's supposed to keep his family safe, and his aggressive behavior can endanger his whole family.
- He learns that a real man has to have lots of money, power, and women BUT his efforts in that direction are leading him to hypertension, drug or alcohol addiction, illegal behavior (such as drug dealing, embezzlement, or taking bribes), and cheating on his partner.

- He learns that men are intellectually superior to women and shouldn't take women seriously BUT without accepting substantial leadership and guidance from women—including his partner—he's never going to turn his life around.

Many positive, constructive messages about what it means to be a man are also part of a male's socialization, but they get interwoven with pro-violence and antifemale training (see the box below). Your partner needs to take on the project of untangling this knot inside of himself.

MESSAGES ABOUT MASCULINITY

HEALTHY	UNHEALTHY
Men should be courageous. They should fight for what they believe in, and fight to protect those whom they love.	Men should never be afraid. They should never back down from a threat or challenge.
Men should be tough, and be prepared to endure hardship for the good of their loved ones and communities.	Men should be unfeeling and unemotional, and especially should not cry.
Men should be protective of those they love.	Men should view women as weak and incapable of protecting themselves.
Men should be good providers for their families.	Men should have the privileged position, so the best things (best food, best leisure, best "toys") should be reserved for them.
Men should treat women with respect.	Men should control women, look upon them as lesser, and use them for sex.
Men should be good, loving fathers.	Men should be the disciplinarians and should toughen up their children.
Men should be proud.	Men should ruin their own pride with shameful or dictatorial behavior (e.g. drunkenness, violence toward women and children), undermining their own dignity.
Men should be prepared to make sacrifices so that their families and communities can be well.	Men should be focused on what they can get for themselves.

Looking at the surface, you might think, "What does a man's internal conflicts about his masculinity have to do with smoking weed, or calling names in an argument, or having a narcissistic personality disorder?" But closer examination almost always reveals that the contradictions above are playing a role, and he will need to work through these societal pressures and build a new definition of what it means to be a "real man" in order to come through as a loving and responsible partner.

HIS EXERCISE 11–4:

Spend some time writing about what you think a "real man" is like, and how such a man should live. Which messages have you been taught about manhood that you believe are good ones to follow? What unhealthy messages have you been taught? Which men in your life should you spend less time with because they promote an unhealthy version of masculinity? What women in your life should you open yourself up to to accept more influence from?

Next, look back through the box on the previous page. You will find that you were taught each of these beliefs, even though the ones on the right contradict the ones on the left. Consider where each of these messages, both the good ones and the bad ones, came into your life from. Your father or stepfather? Male relatives? Your friends? Your faith community? Television shows? Popular songs? Sayings?

LEARNING TO REGULATE
HIS OWN EMOTIONAL STATES

As we discussed in Chapter 4, people with mental health difficulties or a history of trauma commonly have a poor ability to manage the emotional stresses of daily life. Small frustrations or setbacks can send them into paroxysms. They may cycle, within a period of just a few hours, between elation, depression, rage, withdrawal, and hysterical laughter. A person who lives in the center of an emotional tempest is exhausting to live with, and can't achieve enough internal calm to do the hard work involved in transforming behavioral patterns. We also explained in Chapter 4 about the internal splits that certain mental health problems can cause, so that the different parts of the person are not integrated; learning better emotional self-regulation is one important part of how a man can overcome these splits and form a consistent center to his self.

We do not often see people make much progress in this arena except with high-quality professional help, such as your partner might find from a Cognitive Behavioral therapist or a therapist who is trained in "emotional regulation" or "distress tolerance." However, if he has no way to pay for this kind of assistance, or it is not available close enough to where you live, he might also work with the book *Don't Let Your Emotions Run Your Life* by Scott Spradlin.

The skills that he needs to work on developing include:

- mindfulness (the ability to stay conscious of what is going on around him even when he is upset)
- ways to calm himself (for example, to go off alone for a few minutes and settle himself back down, rather than using that time to get himself even more worked up)
- how to better focus on the other person's perspective in an argument (rather than just "freaking out" and trying to rip their perspective to shreds)
- meditation
- body awareness techniques (such as yoga, watching his own breathing, and many others) to help him tune into his physiological processes and reactions

His complaints about you can't be excuses for him to fly off the handle. Even if he has a justifiable grievance, he still must take the proper steps of: (1) bringing himself back to center emotionally, and then, (2) raising his complaint with you in a reasonable way that doesn't involve screaming and doesn't communicate hatred or contempt.

You may need to establish an agreement with him regarding how you two are going to proceed when he "loses it" emotionally. For example, you might have an agreement that anytime you can see that he is turning disregulated and irrational, he has to walk off and be alone for ten minutes, and can come back when he has pulled himself together. (Remember, as we discussed in Chapter 9, that an agreement of this kind should also include an agreement about what he will do if he breaks the agreement, such as refuses to leave the room when you tell him he has gone off the deep end.)

Replacing Destructive Attitudes with Positive Ones

Since emotional difficulty does not automatically lead to bad behavior—many people with mental health problems or trauma histories nonetheless treat other people with kindness, avoid abusing substances, and maintain an ethical system—it also follows that emotional healing does not lead directly to good behavior. In the early chapters of this book we described in detail the role played by attitudes in causing men's problems with abusiveness, and in contributing to their problems with alcohol, immaturity, and personality disorder.

When you put your partner under pressure to deal with his issues, his first fallback position may be, "Okay, I'll give in and open up about my emotions and inner struggles." This can be a positive step, but it can also be a way to avoid looking at, and reforming, his ways of *thinking*. You will need to keep redirecting your partner's attention back toward his need to change his values and beliefs, including his way of viewing you. **Attitudinal change is indispensable; without it, no other improvements will last.**

You, and he, can refer to the following list of changes he needs to make to his internal messages:

INTERNAL MESSAGE	NEEDS TO BECOME
"I lose control of myself, I'm helpless."	"My behavior is a choice that I make."
"My partner is a bitch."	"My partner is a human being worthy of respect 24/7."
"She expects too much from me."	"I need to meet my responsibilities."
"I can't stand this."	"These are the kinds of challenges everybody has to deal with."
"Looking after the kids is a burden."	"I'm so lucky to have this time with our children."

"Look at all my partner's faults."	"I'm going to focus on what I appreciate about her."
"She owes it to me to have sex with me."	"Intimacy is never her obligation"; or "My history of behavior hasn't exactly been a turn-on for her."
"She shouldn't be so upset with me"	"I'm lucky she's still willing to give this relationship a chance, given how I've been."

If you feel motivated to write a list for your partner of what you feel his most chronically unhealthy attitudes have been, by all means do so. Then he can, as part of his work, write down what the corresponding proper outlook would be for each of the items you gave him, following the model we've given above.

HIS EXERCISE 11–5:

First, begin by making a list of destructive attitudes you have had in the following categories:

1. Reasons you tell yourself why you are helpless about your own behavior

2. Reasons why you have to drink or drug, or why no one should ask you not to

3. Negative views of your partner, including unfair demands and expectations you have had about her

4. Reasons why the world is responsible for your difficulties

Next to each item you write down, put a new, positive attitude to take instead.

Second, monitor your own thinking over the weeks ahead, and when you notice a destructive attitude, write it down, and put the corresponding healthy attitude next to it.

Note well that this exercise will rapidly become counterproductive if you use it as an excuse to catalog your partner's faults, feel sorry for yourself, or be sarcastic. Do this exercise as a sincere effort to look at yourself or don't do it at all.

FOLLOWING THROUGH ON HIS PLAN FOR OUTSIDE HELP

Did your partner seem willing to go to therapy at first, but over time he has started to make more and more excuses for skipping, such as complaining about the money or saying the therapist isn't that good? Did he say he would get a sponsor in AA but he doesn't take initiative on speaking regularly with the person? Did he agree initially to sign up for an abuser intervention program, but now he's starting to say that he doesn't really have time for that, or that he thinks he can manage his behavior without the program? Was he seeking trauma services, but now he's saying he can heal on his own?

Our message here is simple: he has to follow through on getting proper help for himself, and without you dragging him kicking and screaming each step of the way. If he could grow on his own, he would have done so years ago. In fact, *no one* changes from chronic unhealthy behaviors, or heals from serious trauma, alone. Promises that aren't backed up by concrete action go nowhere.

If he needs to switch therapists, or change sponsors, or make some other adjustment to the plan he made (back in Chapter 9), he has to follow these steps:

1. He has to work out a new plan that you are comfortable with, and to which you agree, and
2. *He has to follow his old plan until the new one is in place.* In other words, he can't quit therapy while he finds a new therapist, and he can't skip talking to his sponsor while he chooses another sponsor.

We have watched many times how the man backs off from his plan for outside help, then starts to not keep certain other aspects of his agreements, and then goes back whole hog to his old ways. This is the most slippery of slopes.

DEVELOPING, AND KEEPING TO, A DAILY PRACTICE

Because your partner's unhealthy habits have become ingrained, his change process is akin to the work involved in turning someone who never exercises into a fit athlete; he will have to have pieces of work that he does *every day of the week* or he will not progress. This program should be written up and posted on the wall in a place where he can see it easily, and should specify which actions he will take on which day of the week. Depending on his behavioral history, it might include such elements as:

- making the decision each morning that he will not drink that day
- reading a set number of pages from a book he is working through, and writing some thoughts about what he read
- calling his sponsor or attending a meeting
- giving you at least three thoughtful appreciations during the day
- meeting specific household and child-care responsibilities
- thinking each morning about how he will, for that day, replace abusive attitudes he has had toward you with respectful ones
- attending an individual or group therapy session
- meditating
- attending his abuser program

There are other daily commitments that his plan might include, based on what his core issues and chronic behaviors have been. Some items might appear on his schedule every day of the week, while others (such as attending therapy or a support group) might be one or more times per week on specified days.

Brett describes his practice in this way: "Every day before I get out of bed I say to myself, 'I have a borderline personality disorder.' I'm not putting myself down; I'm just getting it straight. Otherwise, I get back into really distorted thinking. I know it isn't my fault that I got this way, but it's my responsibility to keep my head clear and not keep being selfish or mean."

We wish we could say that your partner will definitely succeed if he works seriously through all the elements of this chapter, and of course we can't. But we can say that if he isn't refusing to work on any of the pieces, and if he is willing to be answerable to you about how he is addressing each of the areas we've covered, he is at least putting himself in a position where change is possible.

Any process of transformation includes a long series of ups and downs. You will undoubtedly have days of wondering whether your partner is making lasting progress, and whether it's all worth it for you. In the chapters ahead, we will help you answer these thorny questions. We would love to see your partner turn himself around, but what matters most to us is *you*.

TWELVE

Why Your Growth May Bring More Answers Than His

"If he could just own up to what he's done, I'd be satisfied with that."

"I finally figured out he'll never see my point of view."

"When I look at it all, I can honestly say, I don't deserve this. Not one bit. I deserve better."

I

T'S NOT SO simple to shift your focus away from your partner's progress— or lack thereof—and onto your own. The lion's share of your thinking time, and of the time you have free to talk with friends, is probably taken up with figuring out what's going on with him, venting your frustrations about his actions, and trying to calculate what improvement he might be capable of. This book itself has been at least half devoted to analyzing your partner's issues and laying out a plan for him to overcome them— and about what this all means for you.

What makes it so hard to make yourself the center of your thoughts? First, depending on how destructive your partner is, you might not be finding it safe to take your eye off the wrecking ball. Second, you might not feel like you have much energy left. Another compelling reason is that it is hard for some women to step away from the nurturing role. When women are giving nurturers, good things can and do happen. However, nurturing and attending *to yourself* must make it back onto the top of the priority list—or get there for the first time.

Giving yourself over to something greater than your individual needs, giving yourself to the well-being of others, is an act of love. It is the cornerstone of many spiritual and healing paths. However, women do not typically end up at this essential concern for others after decades of intense focus on themselves; rather, that is usually where they begin. We encourage you to step back from giving yourself to the well-being of your partner. Step into your own growth.

MAKING YOURSELF YOUR OWN PRIORITY

Why is it that so many women spend so much time working on their relationships? Perhaps it is because women readily make meaning in their worlds through connection with others, through relating to others in a way that is different from how most men typically relate. Perhaps this valuable and praiseworthy tendency comes from how women are socialized. Whatever its cause, this shift toward making yourself your own priority can be challenging, especially if it seems that to begin this shift at all means you must be willing to give up your relationship.

We know that you want him to grow. In this chapter, we will explore ways in which your own growth can bring you more answers than his. We will look at:

- how your changing expectations will open you up to buried feelings and new possibilities
- how your changing focus will reward you and propel you forward
- how your own acknowledgment and clarity will help heal you

YOU CAN SET YOUR STANDARDS

Sarah was making plane reservations for a conference at which she was a speaker. Her partner, who happened to be well-off and did not need to work, was listening to her phone call. He sneered defensively when she hung up the phone: "I hope you don't think that *I* am going to pick you up at the airport."

Some months later, when she told him she was leaving him, he asked her what it was she thought she was looking for. She replied, "Someone who would actually look forward to getting me at the airport after having been away."

"Do you *really* think you will find that?" he scoffed.

"Then I won't be in a relationship until I do."

Sarah did find a new partner. She was pleased when he eagerly asked her what time she was returning from her business trip, and asked if he could pick her up. She said yes. When she disembarked, he was holding aloft one of those signs, like those with passenger names held up by taxi drivers; only this one read MOST BEAUTIFUL WOMAN ON THE PLANE.

Clarifying your needs opens up possibilities for you to seek what you deserve. As you begin to move the focus of your life toward your own goals and ambitions, your perspective on your partner and on your relationship will shift in important ways. You are likely, for example, to find yourself more willing than you would have been before to risk letting go of a relationship that you are sensing is based on the hope of change rather than on actual change. In return, you can have the clarity and certainty of your own worth. Feeling your value and owning the wisdom of the lessons learned from a relationship that was not good for you will help move you forward. Either these new insights will lead you to insist on new agreements for the relationship you are in, or they will lead you out of that relationship, and then will form the standards you will have for the next one.

CHANGING THE RULES

Your growth can sometimes disrupt relationship agreements that you share with those around you (agreements that are usually unspoken, but still important). A destructive partner may push back against the areas of growth of which you are most proud. He might interpret your new standards as a direct attack against him and everything he considers right. The new rules that arise out of your loving attention to yourself are likely to undermine the selfish, disrespectful, or even violent rules he is used to.

"I'm sick of this bullshit!" complained Brian to his old friend. "I've stopped going to the strip clubs three times a week; I'm coming home to be with her and the [three small] kids. I've been sober for years. I'm going back to the gym. I quit all my bad habits. I'm busting my ass for her for *three whole months* and still—no sex! This is bullshit!"

Brian's abusive and narcissistic behaviors are deeply ingrained in his relationship to his wife, Hailey. To Brian, it is preposterous to consider that his going to the gym and being present in the evenings to care for his own children *does not even begin* to constitute supporting and meeting his wife's needs. He can't even imagine that these current improvements aren't nearly enough to somehow magically erase the decade and a half that he spent on a self-centered cloud, abandoning (and demeaning) his partner. He fully expects that his recent progress—not toward doing anything amazing, just what he should have been doing all along— should produce the intimacy that would lead to the goal he craves: sex.

As a few more months passed while Hailey sought out time to reconnect herself with long-lost friends and her growing new identity, Brian grew impatient. When he pressed her to find out if her feelings of detachment from him and their old life had changed, she said no. He asked to proceed with a divorce. He complains to all who will listen, "Can you believe what she did to me after all of these years?"

Over all those years, Hailey had been growing—without even realizing it. She was forced to draw on deep wells of her own strength in order to take primary responsibility for three small children. She created her own network of friends and supports that held a vision of her and her dreams, propelled by Brian's absence. After a long time, she finally shifted her view about Brian. She began to see that she didn't want to spend the rest of her life with this person. Even though they had committed themselves to arduous periods of couples' work and individual growth, Brian had really only moved a small distance from the abusive attitudes that had driven his addictive and intimidating behaviors; so even though he appeared to be changing how he acted, his underlying thinking still seemed largely the same as it had been. The new insights that Hailey found and shared with Brian didn't shift his perspective much over the years, as she had hoped. But those insights did give her back to herself.

Sometimes you do not need to make a decision, because you become the answer.

The longer you are able to face honestly

- the truth of what you feel
- the facts and emotional realities of what you experience
- the things you have given up
- the desires and dreams you have in life
- your own strengths and capabilities

the less you will have confusion about which way to go and what to do. This clarity happens because it is your feelings, your perspective, your way of seeing—you—that changes. In this way, *you* become the answer you seek.

GIVING UP TRYING TO CHANGE HOW HE VIEWS YOU

Staying in the struggle to change your partner's perspective about you, your issues, and your responses to him may be one of the things that binds you to him. What if you were no longer struggling to establish the truth of your own goodness?

A destructive person has terrible difficulty taking responsibility for what he is doing that is so harmful; he finds solace in exaggerating or inventing problems of yours, rather than dealing with his own. Oddly, he feels that if he can make it look like what has happened is equally your fault, then none of it is his fault at all! In this way, he tries to magically mitigate the impact of his own self-centered or addicted choices.

When you attempt to address his destructive behavior, you probably have encountered a reflexive response from him along the lines of "Well, what about the way you . . ." or "At least I never . . ." (Sometimes he may point to things you did that were indeed mistakes, but that is entirely beside the point—he's just throwing whatever he can at you to deflect accountability.)

Lara describes how when she confronts her husband about repeatedly cheating on her, Joseph attacks back with the non sequitur "At least I'm not a murderer!"—because Lara had confided in him about the terribly painful choice she'd made years earlier to have an abortion. This is an example of how destructive people can keep your secrets on hand to attack your spirit whenever they find it necessary to avoid dealing with their own selfishness or cruelty. Whatever it is they point to need not be related to the argument. It does not need to have a basis in fact. When there is a basis in some fact, it is often combined with fabulous lies and distortions, so that the accusations become so skewed as to no longer resemble fact.

These kinds of attacks naturally stimulate the desire in you to dismantle his outright fabrications, his contortions of sequence and context, and his taking of shreds of truth and then totally distorting them. You want so badly to establish your truth, as anyone does in that situation.

But what you can lose sight of is that you will unfortunately never win the argument, because the destructive person is not interested in establishing your experience or your truth, especially if it reveals his own deficiencies.

The destructive person is committed to arguing with you and muddying your clarity about what actually occurred and what he has done to you. Above all, he does not want to meet with you on a plane of reference that includes your innocence or your well-being; he feels that he absolutely must make you guilty of things just as bad as what he has done—or guilty of having caused him to do what he did. His responsibility is too painful for him to bear and cannot be tolerated. You must be equally unwell and at fault, or he must at least be significantly better than you in the assessment.

As with the example of Lara and Joseph, sometimes a destructive partner can reach for the most deeply private or sensitive issues to use against you, especially if he senses that you are making advances in your healing and growing stronger. *But even there, at your most painful places, your growing clarity about yourself can make you less vulnerable to these assaults, or even get you to a place where they don't confuse you or slow you down at all.* His nasty tactics will have less and less emotional impact on you over time, especially if you make your healing a high priority.

"He called me stupid and uncoordinated. And you know what? This time it was *great*," said Denise. "It was great because I didn't even flinch. I knew. I just *knew* it: I'm not stupid and I am not uncoordinated. Never have been either, and never have worried about being those things. I wasn't even insulted.

I thought it kind of foolish of him. He'd miscalculated. It was the first time he didn't hit the mark." Denise has gotten to the place where she is no longer interested in convincing her partner that he is wrong about her. She is now committed to learning about herself for her own growth.

If there are things you have done in the past that you genuinely feel bad about, you can take steps to attend to those issues, but we recommend strongly that you not involve your partner in that process at all. Opening up about your mistakes leaves you exposed, and until he has made huge changes, your partner can't be trusted with that kind of vulnerability in you. So work out your feelings about these past events inside of yourself, and with other people. Put your efforts into:

- digesting and learning about your vulnerabilities and mistakes (by your *own* definition, not by his)
- knowing your context—by which we mean, remembering to really take into account the emotional conditions you were living in at the time, and the daily situations you were having to face, understanding and accepting fully the beliefs you held and the choices you made at the time
- being willing to address with other people the things you may have done to harm them—which may mean having to deal with certain events repeatedly over time in ways that are meaningful to them and for the time that it takes them (not you) to recover from your errors

This last point you could think of as similar, in a way, to steps we ask your partner to take in dealing with the harm he has done to you; these are actually basic principles in how anyone needs to right wrongs they have done. (You can also follow these principles in apologizing to yourself about self-harming things you did, and healing your loving connection with yourself.)

If you proceed in this way, you will establish your own well-being—because the amends you make to others will be healing to them *and to you*—and you'll reduce your vulnerability to destructive attacks because you will have removed from your conscience some of the weapons a destructive person can use to make you feel bad about yourself.

FOCUSING ON YOURSELF PAYS OFF

As we explored in Chapter 4, you may have discovered that you have your own issues that you need to attend to. You may have opened the door to healing past issues. Perhaps you are looking at harmful habits you have developed as a means of soothing yourself, or are making a commitment to deal with addictions you've developed. If so, you have probably noticed that it's hard to attend to these things adequately if you are constantly being thrown into upheaval by the twists and turns of your current relationship.

When you look at what it takes to press and support your partner through his changes (while he fights you all the way), and then contrast that with what it takes to work on your own changes, you can see that working on yourself will reap benefits you can rely on and build upon. You can be confident that the growth you bring about in yourself will last—so you know it's worth the effort.

MOVING AWAY FROM "WHY?" AND INTO WHAT YOU DESERVE

Knowing what you actually need—and have needed all along—can be more important to strengthening yourself than knowing *why* your partner has not given you what you deserve. You might have thought that what you really needed from your partner was to know the reasons why he acted the way he did, what drove him to attack you, to turn on you. Maybe you hold hope that his own work will reveal these things to him, and that he will bring these answers to you as the fruits of his labor and the thanks for your loyalty. Even if he does grow to the point where he can do that, knowing more about what you truly deserve and reclaiming the path to your own joy will still give you more relief than the acknowledgment you long for from him.

Over time, life with a destructive partner shapes our expectations. It becomes unrealistic, perhaps even ruefully laughable, to expect the kinds of respect, focus, and attention that we might have taken for granted before being in this relationship. When we break our isolation and spend time with friends, coworkers, family members, and supportive allies who treat us with respect and kindness, it can refresh our whole outlook on who we are. And this kind of treatment is nothing more than the minimum we all deserve.

EXERCISE 12–1: WHAT YOU DESERVE

In this exercise you will write a letter to yourself. The letter is not to actually send or to show to your partner; it will be a letter that you write to yourself, as though it were from him. Through this letter, you can give yourself the acknowledgments you have craved.

Before you write, let's look at an example from a woman named Suzanne. In this case, Suzanne decided after writing the letter that she did want to show it to her husband, who was doing some serious work on himself. He then used her letter as a starting place for writing his own letter to her. The letter you are going to read is the one that Suzanne received from her husband.

Here is a point that might surprise you, however: Suzanne reflects, "You know, it isn't what you might think to get a letter like this. When you are going through all the bullshit, what you think you need more than anything is for him to just see it and say it, but it isn't all you need. For me, the deeper part, the real deep crying, came from when I wrote it myself. That was for my own healing. That's when I understood what I'd been given, and what I really deserved. The big shift in me happened before I got this letter from him. It came when I got it from myself."

Before writing this letter, Suzanne's husband had stopped his destructive behaviors for more than a year, and had been actively participating in group and individual healing and accountability activities. He had multiple issues to overcome, including post-traumatic stress disorder, a borderline personality disorder, and a collection of abusive attitudes and beliefs.

As you read, notice what follows the sections that begin:

- "You needed me to . . ."

- "I should have . . ."

- "It was my job to . . ."

Dearest Suzanne,

These are things I need to say, want to say, and am now able to say. If I don't succeed in wording it all exactly right, please know that my intentions are good, and above all, I don't want to hurt you any more than I already have.

It's been difficult and painful for me to face all the ways I have failed you as a friend, lover, fiancé, and husband. However, my program has helped me to take an objective look at my behavior and give me clarity on how I behaved through the course of our relationship. I have a sense of hope for what our relationship could be in the future, a real sense of the possibilities.

I have taken a very long and hard look at the past and I am trying to see myself in as uncompromising a way as I can. For all the ways I have harmed you, in thoughts, words, actions and inactions, knowingly and unknowingly, I apologize most earnestly.

I am so, so sorry:

For punishing you and judging you about your previous relationships. For eliciting trust and then using information obtained through trust against you. You needed me to hear about your life with interest and respect. You needed me to get to know you through the experiences in your life, and to honor you and those experiences. I was supposed to recognize that I was lucky to have the woman who had the wisdom and learning of all those experiences in my life. I was supposed to support you as you healed whatever needed healing.

I am sorry for becoming coercive, belligerent, and narcissistic when you found out you were pregnant. I met this unmeasured spiritual, biological, and emotional experience with complete contempt for you and our future together. You needed me to be a supportive, consoling, present partner who made you feel safe and loved. You needed me to make it clear that we together would sustain any of the turmoil of the situation and we together would celebrate its gifts. You shouldn't have had to go through that experience alone and abandoned.

I am sorry for pinning you to the ground and hurting your wrist. You were trying, again, to reach through to me and get me to speak to you, talk to you and accept your love and closeness to me. I violently rejected you. You needed me to envelop you in my arms and console your wounded heart from the damage I had caused over and over.

I am sorry for taking for granted your time, love, affection, letters, surprises, cards, dinners, and gifts. There were many times over and over when I rejected what you were giving me through the mail or through the touch of your hand or your heart. You needed me to recognize and acknowledge your gifts, your love, your hand in a way that reassured you of our love and the devotion you selflessly gave to me over and over. In turn, you needed to be filled up in the way you were persistently attempting to fill me up.

I am sorry for locking you out of the home and looking at you through the door's window while I did it. It was disrespectful and full of contempt. You needed me to console you, to be present and work out what was wrong and be responsible for what I had done wrong to create such an abusive episode.

I am sorry for the times I humiliated you, rejected you, and abandoned you in front of your family, or my family or friends or strangers. Being drunk and abusive the night of that concert and my rage about your conversation with another man in the art gallery. You needed me to let people know that I stood firmly and centered in our love and that you are a person that I respect, cherish, and adore. You needed me to get over myself and into us, into your interests and your right to explore them.

I am sorry for not giving love that would sustain us both through hard times. That is the failure to fill your heart with the certainty of my reliability, which would have become the unassailable foundation for your joy in our relationship. This was my job. Otherwise, I was just taking from your love and your reliability. You needed it all to come right back to you.

I am sorry for putting my needs first at the expense of yours, over and over. I am sorry for rejecting and humiliating you when it was my responsibility to ensure you were the center of the plan, of the moment, of the day. My refusal to move where you wanted to go, to rent that house; my fiddling with my car instead of making love, insisting we go home on our honeymoon, canceling our trip to the West. It was my job to make these plans together and not dismiss your ideas, your desires, or your wants in ways that would have celebrated us and helped us become more whole, intimately.

I am sorry for blaming others for my shortcomings and faults. I went through years of therapy, with little movement to show for it, blaming my parents and others for the way I behaved or you for the way I had behaved. I should have owned my behavior and apologized over and over for it but, more so, I should have changed by showing you the love you so deserved all through the years.

I am sorry for not being romantic and spontaneous and for ruining trips while traveling. I am sorry for not showing you that no matter where we were, I was demonstrating my love for you and enjoying our life together as one, as an intimate partner. You needed me to reach out and show you love, hug you, kiss you, look into your eyes. You needed me to enjoy the ride or the trip to wherever it was we were going. You needed me to find you, know about you, and fill you up with love.

I am sorry for failing to shove aside all my consuming fears and risking all I knew in my limited world to act on your behalf, in the name of loving you. I am sorry for abandoning you over and over when devotion demands our connection to be sacred and inalienable. I have been immature, self-centered, selfish, and abusive, continuously, and over time. I cannot apologize enough. There is no apology that can salve the wounds I have caused to your being—but I offer it fully.

I am sorry for subjecting you to my family, people who are emotionally and physically abusive, mentally ill, and not in recovery—all of whom were demeaning, humiliating, dismissive, judgmental, and tried repeatedly to make you feel bad. My family should have invited you in, made you feel welcome, honored your contributions, given back what you gave them, and I should have made sure you were safe and loved during that process.

None of these things that I did were your fault. They were my fault.

On a sheet of paper, write your first thoughts at reading the excerpts from the letter to Suzanne.

Now draft elements of the letter that you feel you deserve, following the structure and questions provided below. It is important to write in detail about what it is you needed from him and how that collides with what he actually has given you in the relationship.

One of the questions below will help you consider whether there is anything you can do, whether inside or outside of your relationship, to help you remind yourself of what you need and deserve today. We're not saying that you can change your partner's behavior by knowing exactly what you need from him; rather, the question is meant to help you heal from being treated badly, by finding ways to help refresh your image and memory of what it is to be cherished and treated well.

1. You did not have the right to . . .

    What I needed was for you to . . .
    Today, what I deserve is . . .
    One thing I can do that will remind me of this is . . .

2. You should never have . . .

    What I deserved was for you to . . .
    Today, what I deserve is . . .
    One thing I can do that will remind me of this is . . .

3. I want to forget the time you . . .

    Above all, I needed you . . .
    Today, what I deserve is . . .
    One thing I can do that will remind me of this is . . .

EXERCISE 12–2: THE LIFE YOU WANT

First, write how it is that you want to feel (rather than the ways you may have been made to feel) about the following aspects of yourself:

    my history
    my hopes and dreams
    my talents

my body
my spiritual life
my family of origin
my parenting (if it applies)

Now consider these questions:

1. How much does your current relationship help you feel how you want to feel?

2. How much does the rest of your life—friends, family, spiritual resources, neighbors—support you in feeling how you want to feel?

TURNING YOUR ENERGIES BACK TO YOU

Over recent months and years, you have extended yourself to do some or all of the following:

- understand your partner
- learn about his moods and challenges
- gauge how volatile he is
- cajole him into a lighthearted mood
- see whether extreme efforts on your part can divert him from striking out at you in disastrous emotional or physical ways

This work may have helped to keep you emotionally, or even physically, safe, but it does not strengthen you and meet your needs. You might have learned to cajole a lighthearted mood out of him. You probably have figured out if it is possible to use extreme efforts to divert him from his disastrous striking out at you. When you give your compassion in these ways to someone who often devalues you, you are using your precious creativity, humor, and life's energy to eke out the occasional good times. All of those resources in you, unchained from such arduous work in your relationship, would free you to enrich your own creativity and well-being.

You could be just as caring, attentive, patient, and understanding with your own life and goals.

Your untapped physical abilities and talents need nurturing and expression. All of the skills you've gained in managing his limitations could be used, for example, in a professional or volunteer setting that credits and honors your gifts. You may be able to heal and deepen attachments to other people, relationships that may have fallen into the background or developed tensions over the years, and that now sorely deserve your loving attention.

WITHSTANDING A STORM OF CRITICISM

You may experience that certain relationships with relatives or friends get more difficult as you become increasingly clear about what you need to have happen with your partner. Your choices might not make sense or seem right to them, depending on their own ways of looking at emotional disturbances, abusive attitudes, and addiction. If your partner has had a manipulative style, telling people you care about lies or distortions about you, you may have the additional challenge of having to unravel the messes he has made for you. In Connie's words, "We were separated, and I came over to clean up his dishes and make food for him for the week. I was feeling for him, you know? And while I was there I heard him on the phone telling someone that I was back, trashing his place and eating him out of house and home!

"I got up and left without a word. I walk out, and then my cell phone rings, and it's my twenty-three-year-old son calling me. And all he wants to know is how could I treat the poor guy like that!"

When you shift your attention back to your point of view, you are in a stronger position to weather the storms of unfair criticisms that can sometimes follow growth. If you are clearsighted, you will be in a better position to continue to insist on what you need, in spite of the lack of support.

Women often don't get celebrated and supported the way they should be for putting distance into an unhealthy relationship, or for making steps to end it. The pressure to stay comes through in comments like "She's leaving? Again? Another relationship goes down. What is wrong with her?" or even "How could she abandon him?"

Well-meaning people sometimes insist on taking neutral stands in talking about unhealthy relationships, saying things along the lines of "There are two sides to every story. You never really know what goes on in a relationship." If you have had to listen to similar comments, you have probably found that they sting; "neutrality" is not actually neutral, because it harms the person who has been mistreated (and subtly supports the person who was destructive).

Finally, women who want to hang in there and try to right a destructive relationship don't tend to be admired for their commitment and dedication. You might hear people say, "She's got bad self-esteem and she's in denial," or "What is she doing with him anyhow?" Or they may even take her partner's side as she tries to get him to deal with his issues: "She's got him whipped now—you see how angry she is with him?"

To keep these ignorant responses from getting under your skin, you will need to keep returning to the truth that you know, and to your faith in yourself. We hope you will keep working on building your strength, and there are many more exercises still to come in this book to help you in that direction.

THE LIONESS ROARS

As you grow, expect to feel outrage. Once you see all you have given, and what you have been given in return, you ought to be good and mad. And for a while. You may have other emotions such as loss or grief beneath your anger. But you may also just be good and mad.

Your anger can serve as a cue to when your boundaries are being violated. Lots of violations? Lots of anger.

The depth of rage you may carry about your relationship doesn't mean you are destined to stay angry forever, or to be angry all the time. Give your anger its expression several times a week in ways that are not destructive or unsafe, such as yelling when you are alone (or with a trusted friend), pounding a mattress, or moving vigorously. Writing or drawing about your anger can also be a powerful outlet. Plan for physical activity that feels nonthreatening to help you express some of the physical effects of being angry.

In these ways you can develop a relationship with your anger, learning and welcoming what it is telling you. If you welcome anger as signaling something to you, it can become very instructive. For example, you may find that your outrage about the recent violations you have endured awakens memories of other violations that happened earlier in life. Your rage might uncover earlier anger and pain, beneath and mixed in with it all.

As your healing continues, your relationship to your anger will grow and change. If you haven't been experiencing much of it, we recommend that you prepare yourself for it, teaching yourself to draw from its lessons as your clarity expands.

Joyful Sexuality

As you start to feel better overall, you may feel an awakening of sensual aliveness, including sexual feelings. Don't be surprised if your partner isn't among the images that are included in your fantasies. Unless he has radically changed, why should he be? The feelings that are awakening in you are natural expressions of life's joy. They come from your growing sense of ownership and safe connection to your own self. Only those who support this new relationship will be naturally part of it. You might feel interested in women. You might feel interest in men you never would have considered before.

The awakening of your sensual life is entirely positive, and we hope you will take that view. At the same time, the decision of when to actually act on these feelings is a tricky one, especially when you are in the midst of feeling very stirred up about the relationship you have been in. Consider waiting to engage in new sexual relationships until you feel that you have come to clarity and have made choices about where you are going with your current relationship.

Secret Treasures

"This is an amazing journey!" Darlene announced to her friends. From the outside, her life is in upheaval. Her partnership as she knew it is ending, and her family is not supporting her. Still, she knows what has happened and why she is making the new choices that she is, and she feels excited. She is starting to feel reconnected to her goals and her well-being. She feels like she's found her own treasure.

Like Darlene, you will come to feel the growth of deep connection to your intelligence and your abilities. Once you are putting your energies toward goals that are obtainable and that depend only on you, you will start to feel effective, sane, useful, and connected to the world. In a destructive relationship, so many of our efforts led to nothing but more frustration. This can make us feel ineffective and isolated from the fruits of our labors. As a smart, effective person, you will have a whole new way of setting foot into your world.

We are excited for you. Your own treasure is there for you. In our eyes, the outcome is certain: you will become your answer and you will shine with it.

THIRTEEN

Are We Really Getting Anywhere?

H OW MANY TIMES in your life have you heard a woman (a real one, not a character from movies or television) say any of the following?

"My partner used to be so mean to me, but he's nothing like that anymore. He's been kind and patient for years now. It's like night and day."

"My husband used to drink like a fish, but he stopped and now he never overdoes it. I don't even worry when he goes out."

"My boyfriend struggled for so long with feeling suicidal. But that's all in the past, and he is in good spirits most of the time now. He's a new person."

"My partner wanted to be looked after like a little child, and it was driving me crazy. But he really grew up, and he carries his own weight now. I just don't feel that sense of being burdened by him that I used to have."

We would guess that you could count on one hand the number of times you have encountered a story like one of these. Although it is not uncommon to see people make some improvement to their character, their habits, or their well-being, we are much less likely to find cases of individuals who transform themselves into something dramatically different from who they were before. Certain core aspects of people's character tend to endure over the years.

This principle applies even more to people who are repeatedly destructive to their partners in relationships. Regardless of the underlying cause, patterns at this depth are profoundly difficult to overcome.

As we have discussed, the chances increase when a man is willing to take a serious look at himself, involve other people in his change process, and work on his issues for a long time—for years, realistically speaking. But even if he undertakes the work in earnest, it will still take time before you can feel sure that his reforms are going to stick.

One of the cruxes of this book, then, is the following tension:

On the one hand, people who aren't willing to stick with a relationship through some hard times end up with no lasting relationships, and they miss some chances to be with a person who had potential.

On the other hand, many women end up feeling that they poured precious years of their lives into struggling to get a man to change, only to have to accept eventually that he simply wasn't going to.

We want to see you avoid both of these pitfalls and find a course down the middle of these two risks.

In this chapter, we are going to provide a collection of guideposts to apply in figuring out whether your partner is moving forward, and how far he might be willing to go before he digs in his heels. But we would like to ask you first to consider a couple of important questions; your answers to these will shape the way you use the directions and formulas that will follow.

ONE: HOW MUCH CHANGE IS ENOUGH?

The tactic that the men we work with most employ to keep their partners waiting and hoping is to make minor changes. Ironically, the longer a man resists addressing anything that his partner wants him to deal with, the more mileage he can get out of finally making a little move; the woman comes out feeling like, "Well, at least he's doing *something,* that's better than before. Maybe now things will start to shift."

The longer you have been battling trying to get him to deal with his behavior, the more that minor improvements that he makes will play with your emotions.

One way to avoid this trap is to keep your attention focused on how far he still has left to go. Let's begin exploring the question:

EXERCISE 13–1:

Make a list of *all* the changes your partner would need to make in order to bring your relationship to a point where you could be happy and satisfied staying in it. Some questions to consider while you do this include: What behaviors that hurt you would he need to stop? How thoroughly would you need them to stop? (Go down to once a week? Go down to twice a year? Never happen again? Answer this for each hurtful behavior.) What positive behaviors that are missing would he have to start to exhibit? How often would he need to do these positive things?

Next, write some about whether you feel willing to settle for less. What if he moves forward enough that you get half of what you are asking for? Will that be adequate to convince you to stay with him? Which issues feel negotiable to you, and which ones feel nonnegotiable?

The destructive partner is generally looking to disrupt his life as little as possible; a big part of him would rather stay in his ruts. Your husband or boyfriend will therefore test you to see what level of change he has to make to placate you. *Unless you get clear within yourself regarding what you are willing to live with versus what is a deal breaker for you, your partner may play games for years, making changes that don't go far enough and don't last long enough.*

Here's an example of how one woman decided her limits and standards:

"If he hits me or raises a hand to me ever again, our relationship is over for good. This is true even if it happens five years from now out of a clear blue sky. Ditto if he ever calls me c—, wh—, or sl— again. I'm willing to struggle along with other aspects of his verbal abuse for a couple of years, but I have to be able to see progress, and I'm not sleeping with him for a month each time he does it. And I'm not staying with him unless he gives me appreciative comments and affection almost every single day."

Don't follow this woman's model; you have to live by *your* standards and do what feels right for you. *And we fully support you in putting everything and anything you need to on the "This Can Never Happen Again" list.* You have no obligation to put up with any destructive behavior or mistreatment of you, especially given how much you have already been through.

However, it also won't help you if you put items on the "This Can Never Happen Again" list but then make excuses to yourself for not ending your relationship the next time your partner does something from the list. Try to make realistic decisions about the extent to which you are prepared to put your foot down at this point. Clarifying your standards will only be helpful to you if you go forward with living by them.

Two: How Much Energy Am I Willing to Put into This Struggle?

As your partner goes through the ups and downs of working on himself, you will feel pulled in with a vacuumlike force to devoting huge efforts to helping him, pushing him, and demanding action from him. Becoming his teacher and enforcer can become a full-time job, and in some ways your partner will like that outcome because it means you are staying completely focused on him. You may find that playing that role feeds you for certain periods of time, giving you back some of the power that you lost when he was in denial. Fighting with him can be a way of feeling closer to him, as long as the tensions seem to be leading to more productive outcomes than before. However, we would like to see you ask yourself frequently whether this process is still good for you. As we discussed earlier, *you can decide to quit this process before you feel ready to quit the relationship itself.* This decision leads to a stand that sounds something like: "I'm still hoping that our relationship can work out, but I can't be involved anymore in fighting with you about what you work on or don't work on, and I can't work anymore on trying to explain things to you that shouldn't have to be explained. So you go off and do your work and leave me out of it. I'm not even going to tell you anymore what you need to be working on. If you actually start to make some deep changes, I'll be able to tell."

We are not saying that this is the "right" way to do things. You can be very involved in his change process, or not at all, or somewhere in between, based on what you feel is best for *you*. The chances that he will make lasting changes are about the same regardless. What matters most is to decide what level of involvement is right for you, and *honor your own limits,* whether your partner honors them or not.

How to Recognize "Changes" That Aren't Really Going Anywhere

A man with unhealthy behavioral patterns (including self-destructive ones), does not change from magical awakenings, or promises, or waking up in a better mood, or deciding one day to be a nicer person. Your partner's transformation can only be brought about by hard work over a long period of time, serious self-reflection, development of empathy, and overcoming self-centeredness. Mystery and poetry do not play a big role here; we're talking about hands-in-the-mud, no-nonsense, committed work that is not much fun, but that can carry great rewards over the long haul.

As you struggle to make decisions about how much time and energy to invest in keeping your relationship alive, we want you to know how best to read your partner's progress—or lack thereof.

He's Not Really Changing His Thinking

You will recall that early in this book we examined the kinds of thinking that contribute to, and often outright cause, destructive relationship behavior. A key question to evaluate for yourself, therefore, is whether your partner is really turning his attitudes around, or whether he is just making the behavioral changes you have demanded of him—doing what he's told, in other words. Is he behaving better, but not getting the reasons why these changes are necessary? Is he trying to placate you so that you'll stop complaining about him or threatening to leave, but he's not really willing to look at what's wrong?

He's "Cutting Down" on His Addictive Behavior

An addiction is, by definition, a set of behaviors that the addict cannot manage. Layer upon layer of long-standing habit, desire for immediate gratification, inner emptiness, self-centered attitudes, and deep self-loathing override the addict's judgment. He will engage repeatedly in behaviors that he knows will have terrible consequences; logic has vanished from decision making.

So how is this person going to "use less"? For any of us, the entire concept of cutting down on a behavior means that we are able to recognize what is harmful about the behavior, think clearly about the negative effects that will result if we continue, and develop a clear sense of what the "correct," lower amount would be. If you become aware that you eat too much fried food, for example, you can use your health consciousness to motivate you to decide how many times a week is acceptable, and more or less stick to that. But it is the very nature of addiction that the person cannot see with that kind of clear vision, cannot figure out where appropriate limits are, and cannot follow a healthier plan with any consistency.

So whether your partner's addiction is alcohol, pornography, weed, or compulsive sex, if he "cuts down" on his use that will usually mean that nothing is changing. Once he's gone through a few cycles of trying to cut down, you can conclude that he's going to have to get off the substance completely. The right amount of use for most addicts is no use at all—that's the only amount he can manage in the long run. And if he is a "sex addict," that means he gives up all sex that isn't with you (including all masturbation that involves looking at any images of other women)—completely.

Of course, when people are addicted to food they can't just give up eating, which makes recovery quite a bit trickier. But the underlying principle still applies, which is that people do not overcome an addiction as long as they keep playing games with using "once in a while" (which for a food addict might mean the "occasional" binge, for example).

So if your partner is getting drunk less often, or drinking less overall, or smoking less weed, or spending less time on Internet pornography sites, or losing less money on the lottery and other kinds of gambling, he's probably going fast down a dead-end street—and taking you with him. If he doesn't succeed after one or two tries at cutting down, it's time to cut it out completely, whatever "it" is.

He Minimizes His History of Unhealthy Behavior

Listen carefully when your partner sums up his issues, whether he's talking to you directly or you are overhearing him telling other people. Beware of statements that sound like:

"I drink more than I should sometimes," when the issue is that he has a history of drinking until he passes out, spending important family money on alcohol, driving drunk, and behaving irresponsibly because of his alcoholism.

"She says I'm disrespectful to her," when the issue is that he *is* disrespectful to you (it isn't your imagination, as he is implying), including when he calls you names, makes fun of things you say, demeans you in front of other people, undermines you with your children, and more.

"I have some emotional problems," when he has a history of losing jobs because of his inappropriate behavior at work, can't maintain any successful friendships, invents things you supposedly did that actually never happened so that he can discredit your complaints about his behavior (by saying you're just as bad as he is), and has explosions that look really extreme or nutty sometimes.

"I've had to work on overcoming my bad temper," when the issue is that he has been physically scary, has thrown or punched things around the house, or has even been directly violent to you.

He Is Avoiding You and/or Avoiding Intimacy

One of the central themes in the change process for a destructive partner is his inner process of grappling with his responsibility for his own actions. He will continue, and probably for a long time, to have a great deal of inner dialogue in which he is arguing to himself that you caused him to behave the way he did and that you have exaggerated the problem. One way that you can get an indication that the wrong side is winning this internal debate is if he is keeping emotional distance from you and making excuses not to be physically close and sexual. The message when he pulls away is "I resent having to behave better, so I will make you pay for those changes by shutting you out." He still wants to punish you for calling him on his issues.

He will put his withdrawal in another package, saying things like "I just don't trust myself yet to behave well if I'm close to you," or "I have to be focused on working on myself right now, so I have to take distance from our relationship for a while." With occasional exceptions, we find that these excuses are simply that—excuses. He is remaining in his selfish rut, and making what are only superficial changes. Secretly, he still thinks you are the problem.

If you are comfortable giving him some space for a while, there's no harm in going that route. But do notice that, once again, your needs and desires are being put aside so that his needs can come first. You don't want to let that continue for very long, since you've done a lot more than your share of the giving already. Besides, in some ways you can't really tell if he's working on himself seriously unless you challenge him.

You Are Being Careful Not to Upset Him

We were interviewing a woman named Clara one day about her husband's process of change. Clara was reporting that her husband, Ian, had not been yelling at her or calling her "bitch" and the other degrading kinds of verbal abuse that he typically used, and that the past three or four months had gone well. We asked, "Have there been changes in how he handles it when you get mad at him about something or stand up to him?" Clara reflected for a few moments, and then replied that she didn't know, because she'd been careful "not to rile him up while he's working on himself." In other words, Ian hadn't necessarily changed at all; the one who had changed was Clara, who had become extra cautious and compliant, even more than she was when Ian was abusive.

Unfortunately, there's no way to tell whether your partner is really changing except by seeing how he handles the bad periods: the times when he hasn't slept, when his boss chews him out, when he gets criticized, when you tell him how sick you are of his messes around the house, when you have a medical crisis and he has to look after the children for three days, when he doesn't get his way about something that is very important to him. Consider yourself a schoolteacher; if you aren't testing your student once in a while, you aren't going to know what he's learned.

He Declares That He Is a Changed Man

If your partner announces that his work is done, it has barely begun. Overcoming destructive relationship behavior takes years; many experts on the subject believe it takes a lifetime.

A number of personality aspects, which together we will call "ego," undergird a man's chronically selfish or unkind relationship behavior, whether it is rooted in addiction, abusiveness, immaturity, or mental health problems.

These aspects include some mixture of arrogance, superiority, becoming angry and dismissive when called on faults, being a "know-it-all," and listening poorly to the feelings and opinions of others. For a carrier of these traits, the very fact that he continues to think that *he* is the best judge of how much he has changed shows how little he actually has. When he gives himself an award for having overcome his issues he shows that he has not developed the necessary humility to treat his partner well in a consistent way.

Be aware that some men develop the language of humility without truly getting unstuck from ego; in fact, we have sometimes seen a kind of "I can be more humble than you can" competitiveness, an outstanding irony indeed. So don't just listen for him to say the right words; watch for real changes in his ability to value, and learn from, your perspectives—including your perspective *about him.*

Two behaviors are especially loud warning sirens of a man who isn't changing:

1. He says that you don't recognize how much he's changing, and that the problem is that you are perceiving him incorrectly and not appreciating the work he has done.
2. He says that because he has made such good changes, now it's time for you to make the changes that *he* wants.

He Wants Credit for the Improvements He Has Made

Consider this irony: If a mother makes dinner six nights a week, the family tends to stop remembering to even say "thank you," because the cooking just comes to be viewed as part of her job. Meanwhile, if the father makes dinner one night a week, it's a big deal! Family members thank him so much, and are impressed by his contribution! In other words, the less you do, the more credit you get, because your efforts seem special rather than ordinary.

Your partner may look for this kind of lopsided credit, expecting congratulations for doing a tiny fraction of what you do, and wanting a kiss on both cheeks for being less hurtful and selfish than he used to be (like the proverbial batterer who thinks he should receive a medal because he stopped beating his wife). For him to make real change, he has to accept that he doesn't earn special points for doing what he should have been doing all along.

It's Still All About Him

One of the similarities between immaturity, addiction, abusiveness, and personality disorders is that they all allow a man to live absorbed in himself. When he then enters a process of "self-exploration" and "working on himself" and "taking a hard look at himself" . . . well, it's still all about "self," isn't it? Some of the most important work he needs to do is to stop being so fascinated by himself, and start understanding much better the experiences of others.

"I'm going through a lot of feelings right now" needs to give way much of the time to "I'm thinking a lot about how things must feel to you."

"I'm really working on myself" needs to make space for "I'm changing how I treat other people."

"I'm facing some things about myself" needs, much of the time, to instead take the slightly different form of "I'm facing how I have harmed others."

"I'm spending a lot of time thinking about things" needs to make more room for "I'm taking action to address the wrongs I've done, and to contribute more to the lives of others, especially my partner and children."

In short, he can latch onto "healing" and "recovery" as a way to actually stay pretty much the way he was before, selfish and self-involved. Real change means *taking action* toward being more loving, more caring, more generous, and more empathic—in other words, focusing more on others and less on himself. (And this tends to be particularly true for men, who are socialized in our society to be self-involved and expect things to be done for them.)

Your Gut Instincts Are Telling You He's Not Really There Yet

While all of the above factors are worth applying to your partner's progress, it is also important to listen carefully to your own inner messages. If a voice in your head is saying, "I just don't buy it," or "Something about this new version of him just doesn't feel right to me," or "My intuition tells me this isn't real," *listen to what your instincts are telling you.* Don't ignore them, because they are sending you crucial information.

There are many excuses for dismissing your gut feelings, and other people (including your partner) may press these excuses upon you, along the lines of:

"You are reacting to how hurt you feel about things he's done in the past, so it's hard for you to believe that he's changing."

"You are afraid of things going bad again, and you're responding from that fear."

"You have to learn to trust him again."

"You are stuck in the past."

Our professional experience is that these explanations don't often have much validity. If you don't trust him yet, it's because he has a lot of work left to do to prove himself trustworthy. If you are afraid of what he might do, it's because you can tell he could easily go back to his old self. Don't let people tell you the problem is with you. When it's really safe to be close to him again—assuming that day comes—you'll know.

EXERCISE 13–2:

First, go back through the bold headings in the section you just read, and make a check mark next to the ones that fit where your partner is these days. Then write your feelings about viewing his progress in this light.

Next, write a few thoughts about some area of life in which *you* have made progress in recent months, whether your partner has moved forward or not.

Signs That He May Be Buckling Down to the Real Work

Let's turn now to the other side of the coin. What moves on his part would demonstrate that he is doing some real work?

He Surrounds Himself with New, Better Influences

Is he pulling people around him who will help him move in a new direction? If he's going to stay sober, he's got to start spending his time with people who don't drink or drink very little. If he is going to overcome abusiveness, he has to stop being around friends and relatives of his that look down on women or who treat their own partners disrespectfully. He has to find men to be around who will demand that he treat women well, including you, and who are responsible fathers. If he is going to overcome a personality disorder, he has to give up the habit of charming everybody into thinking he's a great, well-put-together guy. In place of that habit, he has to spend time with people he is honest with, so that they know how much he has been dishonest in the past, and know how distorted his perceptions have been. He has to have friends around him who won't fall for his manipulations, won't let him blame you for his problems, and will help hold him accountable.

He's *Really* Listening to You, and Valuing Your Opinions

We're not looking for little improvements in how he listens to you; what is called for is a sea change, a complete transformation. He needs to:

- completely stop interrupting when you are talking (including not making faces, which is a way of interrupting).
- ask you questions to express his interest in your thoughts and draw you out.
- remember things you tell him (and we ask that you not buy the "I have a bad memory" excuse—if he bothers to make an effort to remember, he can do it).
- demonstrate that he is willing to have your thoughts and opinions *influence* his thoughts and opinions (which means he gives up the habit of swatting down things that you say as if they were flies, and instead takes them in and lets them create growth inside him).
- focus fully on what you are saying, and not rushing you.
- not keep switching the subject back to himself.
- respond *consistently* in ways that indicate that he considers your thinking to be valuable and intelligent (including that if he disagrees with you, he expresses his disagreement in a way that does not send the message that his opinions are superior to yours).
- follow up in future conversations on ideas, ambitions, and dreams that you have expressed earlier, and show that he is supporting you.

One of the outcomes of this deep change in how he listens is that he should *get to know you*. You should be able to feel him coming to really understand who you are. In the past you may have thought, "He really knows me," but he didn't really; he collected knowledge about you, but it was always going through his self-centered filter. Now he has to do the work of making it be about *you*.

He Takes Charge of His Life and His Change Process

While we do want to see him become much more willing to learn from you and take guidance from you than he has been in the past, it won't help if he turns into a little puppy dog. If, for example, he switches from arrogance and aggressiveness to an exaggerated passivity and dependence, asking you all the time, "How am I doing? Am I treating you okay? Do you think I'm on the right track?" you will find quickly that he's driving you as crazy as he was before. He has to stop pretending that he is helpless and lost. (This includes, by the way, that he needs to stop making excuses for not making serious efforts to get a job, if that's been an issue for him.)

If he starts to take proper care of himself without your having to bug him about it, that's another good sign. He should be getting himself to his therapy appointments or his abuser group, getting proper exercise, calling his sponsor and getting to meetings, eating well, getting enough sleep, all without any pestering from you. And he should be meeting his other responsibilities, whether paying bills or taking care of his elderly parents or performing well at work. It isn't real change unless he starts to be a big boy about it.

He Has Given Up the Victim Role

Has he stopped feeling sorry for himself? If so, that is a step in the right direction. He should be thinking much more about how his behavior has affected you and other people, and much less about how hard his life has been for him. He should be validating the steps you have taken to stand up for yourself— including times you may have left him or threatened to leave—instead of whining about it. He needs to get that your decisions to tell other people what he was doing, or to file for divorce, or to call the police, or to do an intervention were all *necessary*, and were the products of his bad behavior. He should even start to recognize how these kinds of actions are actually in his best interests, because they push him to get help.

He Takes Meaningful Actions in Support of Your Goals

Talk, as they say, is cheap. A destructive man who is serious about changing starts to take concrete action to be behind you, *including actions that may work against his own interests.* Is he actually helping to pay for that training or college program you've been wanting to do? Is he coming through with spending more time with the kids (and making that high-quality time, not just putting them in front of a video) so that you can have the time you need to do things for yourself? Is he willing to postpone some of his own dreams in support of yours?

We're looking for actions on his part that move beyond self-interest. If he's offering to help pay for your cooking class, or your weight-loss program, that's self-serving. He needs to be willing to get off the couch and take steps that make a significant difference in the quality of your life, without looking for any reward for himself.

He Demonstrates a Commitment to Long-Term Change

Quick fixes are easy. We want to see signs that he is willing to work for years on becoming a better person. And that includes that he should show a deeper understanding, with each passing month, of what his behavior has put you and your children through, and how it has affected other people.

A FEW OTHER WAYS TO MEASURE HIS CHANGE

Here are some other methods you can use to get a read on how far he has come, and how far he may still have left to go:

- Read what he has written in response to the exercises on the Web site versions of Chapters 9 and 11. See if he has put effort and thought into the work, or has been perfunctory, and see if he is owning his actions or still making excuses. Look for how deep he goes.
- Get reads on him from other people who are aware of the depth of his issues and who won't be enthused about minor improvements. Ask them especially for signs of work he has not yet done, or of backsliding into his old ways of thinking.

- Do things that are important to you that you have given up in the past because he didn't like them. See how he reacts as you reclaim your right to freedom in these ways.
- Stop taking care of things for him, including not cleaning up his messes (both literal and figurative ones), and see what happens.

EXERCISE 13-3:

Write a few thoughts in response to these questions: What does your "gut" tell you about how far your partner has come? Does it feel like he still has a long way to go? Does his work feel genuine so far (even if it isn't enough), or are you concerned that he's faking it? If you were to rate his progress on a scale of one to ten (with ten being a hugely changed, loving partner), what number would you assign him at this point?

If you have children, do they seem to be sensing any change in your partner?

SOME QUICK GLIMPSES INTO HIS INNER WORLD

Women approach us frequently with questions about what is going on inside of their men as they grapple with change. We're hoping this mystery will start to become clear without us, because your partner should be letting you in on his thoughts and feelings more than he used to—or at least more honestly than he used to. But we're happy to share some signposts to help you find your way down these foggy roads.

He's Feeling Loss

Your partner is not losing anything of substantial value by leaving his unhealthy ways behind, but he feels like he's losing his closest friend. He doesn't handle grief well; he's used to chasing those feelings away with partying or abusiveness or disconnecting from reality. Now, because he's under pressure to stop using his maladaptive habits, he's having to sit with grief and let it be there, and this is new for him. He is squirming inside from the newness of it.

A couple of years from now, if he keeps working seriously, he will start to see that his change has not only benefited the people he loves, it has also made his own life a lot better. But in the meantime he will have a hard time seeing it that way.

He's Feeling Powerful Urges to Mess Up His Life Again

He wants to cause a disaster, for a number of reasons that include:

- Disaster is exciting, despite how painful it is, and he is hooked on adrenaline. He feels like he'd rather be miserable than have to deal with calm and stability, which make him very uncomfortable.
- He's convinced that he's going to cause a disaster sooner or later, and he can't stand the suspense of waiting for when that will happen, so he figures he'll relieve the tension by doing it now and getting it over with.
- He feels exposed, as if people can see inside him, now that he's acknowledging the depths of his issues. He wants to run back into hiding, which means back to using and back to acting "out of control," which he feels cover him up.
- He is so accustomed to blaming other people for his problems that accepting responsibility for his own actions is overwhelming him. He really wants to go back to making everything someone else's fault—especially yours.
- He really misses partying, or whatever his addictive behavior was, and all of his longings, unmet needs, and desires to escape emotional distress are still caught up with the addiction. So he is really wishing he could go back to it.

He Feels Like He's Letting You Win

Remember much earlier in the book when we talked about how your partner may tend to confuse a relationship with a football game, especially if he is controlling or abusive? This outlook takes time to overcome. So in the short term he feeds his change process through that same filter; he feels like owning his problem means victory for you, since you were always saying that he was messed up and he was always hotly denying having a problem. It's driving him a little crazy to have to accept that you were so right and he was so wrong.

He Wants to Wake Up and Discover That Actually the Issues Were Yours

Even if he's quite serious about changing, the reality is that he will struggle for years with the question of whether he was truly responsible for his own actions, or whether you were driving him to drink, cheat, threaten, and so forth. He really wants it to come out the second way, not the first. So, as we said before, there's a steady debate going on his head.

He Feels Like He's Not Being a Real Man

We took you into the world of men's insecurities about their masculinity in Chapter 9. As he works to change, these insecurities will sharpen, and he may often have voices in his head telling him that he is abandoning manhood and that you are turning him into a woman. (And unfortunately he may find Internet sites that support that distorted thinking—the Web has many fanatical antifeminist sites full of paranoid ramblings about how women are trying to "emasculate" men by demanding that they stop behaving destructively.) He's having to figure out a new way to think about what a "real man" is like.

He's Trying to Figure Out What Love Is

As he moves gradually out of his destructive rut, he begins to find cravings awakening in him to be in a really loving relationship. But he also feels that he has no clue how to do this, and he finds the idea of being that intimate—emotionally, not just physically—frightening. (This is true, by the way, even if he was already one of those "sensitive" or "New Age" men; many destructive men masquerade as being way into openness and honesty and self-discovery and spirituality. But when it comes to living it in reality with a female partner, not just playing the role, they freak out.) So he has to start, almost back at the beginning, trying to reach an understanding of what love is and how it works between two partners.

We explain these dynamics to help you not feel mystified about him, but we don't want to create the impression that you can relieve him of these struggles. These are inevitable aspects of his change process. For him to succeed, he will have to go through these internal battles over and over again, and the good side will have to win each time or he will backslide. In other words, he will have to make a deep commitment to not giving in to his urges and his unhealthy attitudes, and waiting until he is back to clarity before he acts.

EXERCISE 13–4:

This exercise is about striving to "clean" your own energy from a preoccupation with your partner's change, now that you have taken in all the information in this chapter. Choose an activity that is soothing for you, such as taking a bath, going for a walk, listening to music, or calling a friend. Spend twenty minutes or more on this activity *and each time you find yourself thinking about your partner, gently shift your attention to something else.* You can reflect on your work, your friends, or your children; you can think about a novel you've been reading or a movie you've enjoyed lately; or you can choose to quiet your mind and not think about anything at all. Don't get mad at yourself if you realize you are slipping back into dwelling on your relationship; just shift your attention back onto other subjects, without scolding yourself. Notice how good it feels to be thinking about other things, or about nothing at all.

FOURTEEN

The Pros and Cons of Giving Him Time

"I just want to know for myself that I've done everything I can in this relationship."

"I'm not ready to make a big decision about leaving, but I do want a break from this."

"He's doing really well now. I can't say the same for me."

"This is not the life I imagined I would have."

IF YOU DECIDE to give your partner time to change, it could be just what you both need. Over time, you could get a substantial number of your needs met. You could have him participate actively in the healing you require. He could use the space to do his own changing and healing. Together, you could orient yourselves on the course of a healthy relationship. You might find the way that moves you both forward in your lives and in your love.

However, if this most positive scenario comes to fruition, it will be because you have given your partner not just time but *your* time, time that isn't coming back to you. You won't be in this same season of your life when the time pays off—if it does. Your children and family won't be at the stage they are at now. Your resources, your well of energy and hope for all of that out-of-reach love from your partner, will not be the same. And, you will change during that time.

So we want to see you prepare yourself adequately so that the giving will be a true gift. You will, of course, have goals in mind, namely your partner's healing and his engagement with you as a healthy, loving person. But the tasks required for him to make sustainable change are daunting, and you need to be aware going forward that there is a significant chance that your partner won't be willing to make the level of change that you need from him. It is in this light that we encourage you to be clear that the giving of your time is a true gift; it's fine to give it hoping for a loving return, but we don't want to see you go forward counting on that outcome.

Instead, it's important to move forward from a standpoint where you believe you will be okay either way; then you can witness his progress or lack of it, and determine whether it makes sense for you to continue giving him more of your precious time. Watching awarely and seeing clearly the ways in which he deals with his issues, and the ways in which he avoids that work, will change you. There are many ways in which giving your time to your partner's change process can change you.

Let's begin looking at some of the costs to you of standing by him, hoping that he's going to finally take his issues seriously. As you review the bulleted points below, note which ones you feel are happening for you, and in what ways.

- **Your natural sense of hope and resilience** may be wounded in the ways that we have explored earlier. Giving so much loving attention to your partner without much return is like a slow leak in your energy reserve tank; hope for a life filled with love can fade, to be replaced by a desperate longing for love and connection.
- **You might lose sight of your own set of standards in the relationship,** compromising even your basic emotional needs because you are so busy sorting through and managing your partner's dramatic ups and downs, with only short periods of rest in between. With all that work at hand, you have been pulled away from addressing what you actually want in your relationship. The standard becomes "He's not as bad as he was," or perhaps even "It doesn't devastate me the way it used to."
- **You might lose your sense of joy and creativity,** for all the reasons we have just been describing. Expressing your vision is the core of creativity. You must have an audience that is receptive in some way, even if it

is an inner audience. When you have internalized the destructive audience, you become bound up by a sense of rejection. You feel stopped before you even start.

- **You may miss opportunities for yourself,** and lose out on necessary personal changes because you are no longer attuned to your inner signals regarding your own needs and desires, as you have become so outwardly focused. Living with a destructive person is like living with a constantly loud, blaring horn. How could you hear your own subtle, inner symphony? You are just trying to turn off the damn horn.

- **You might have a confused sense of what the real signals of change are,** since you have been promised changes for such a long period and they never materialize. His promises may be honest and heartfelt, but he lacks any real grasp of what it takes to overcome the profound issues and wounds that he faces. It's easy to misinterpret these honest pledges as being signs of change in themselves. And your confusion can be compounded if he keeps making changes but they rapidly fade away each time, or he makes small changes but they aren't nearly enough.

- **You might have an inaccurate sense of who you are,** because your partner so often responds to you in ways that don't at all fit with what you are actually giving, saying, or doing. Being in a relationship with someone whose perceptions are so distorted can start to throw your own vision out of whack. It's like looking too long into a funhouse mirror. You can't get an accurate reflection of yourself back.

- **You might have a growing fear of being "alone"** from him telling you that you are unlovable, unworthy, and inadequate. The prospect of being without a partner takes on a new meaning when you are in a destructive relationship, because you are already longing for intimacy, and may already be isolated as well. From inside the relationship, it seems that life without him would be even more painful than the situation you are in. (In reality, once the traumatic bond dissolves significantly and your life is filled with other loving connections, including to yourself, being alone can be filled with joy and renewal. You could rediscover who you are as loving, worthy, and invaluable. Your possibilities for partnership could open.)

- **You might not be the friend you want to be to others,** because you have so little time to devote to your friendships.

- **You may have a sense of frustration and impatience** in your dealings with people, because you feel not known and not seen, and feel that your generous sharing of your life and time is not being acknowledged for what it is worth. You might be irritable and short from having been attacked over such a long period of time that you no longer have a place of rest from which you navigate the sometimes frustrating world. You might become intolerant of people disagreeing with your opinions because you've had to live with so much devaluing of your thinking that your value as a person seems like it's at stake.

- **If your partner is self-destructive, giving him your time might increase your sense of obligation to him.** If his style is to be less self-destructive for certain periods by channeling his unhealthy energy toward harming you, you may feel that you have to sacrifice yourself. Sacrificing yourself may seem less painful in the short term when you can ward off, temporarily, the self-destruction of someone you love. The longer you are with the self-destructive partner, the longer you have the sense that you are keeping him going. But the reality is that you are both actually sinking; he may be sinking more slowly than he would without you, but you are both sinking nonetheless.

- **The longer you stay, the harder it may be to find support** from people around you when the time comes that you do feel ready to talk to other people about how this relationship is dragging you down. You may have had many reasons not to reveal what was happening: you were afraid of how he would react if he found out what you said; you wanted to figure it out more yourself first because you don't know what it all means and where it is going; you didn't feel that you could open up about the hours of arguments or the scary threats. It's tempting to just say you are "fine" and move as best you can throughout your day with incredible (and unnoticed) strength.

EXERCISE 14–1: DIGESTING THE COSTS OF WAITING

For many of you, there are more than a couple of these that are true. Before you continue, we want you to know that you can heal. You can recover your sense of joy and creativity. You can have a life filled with friends and support. You can feel your patience and kindness again. You can recover your sense of who you are. You can have wisdom lead your life.

Circle the items on the previous page that you see happening in your life. Then write your thoughts in response to these questions:

Do any of these stand out as being especially true for you? If so, which ones, and why?

What is it that you notice yourself seeing, doing, thinking, or feeling that demonstrates any of the bullets previously described?

How do the things you just described demonstrate a change for you? Are there significant moments that come to mind that signal to you a shift in yourself—a thought about a way you used to be and a way you are now?

Successful but Unbalanced

It can come as a shock to many women who have decided to give their partners time that even the successful outcomes are often still quite unbalanced. A partner who changes significantly arrives at the beginning of a new connection with you. He has benefited from the growth that you, in many ways, have upheld on your shoulders. By staying connected and supplying him with hope and consistency, you helped move him forward. You provided an accurate reflection of the causes and impacts of his problems and choices. He got to be at the center of your attention almost all the time, whether for behaving well or for behaving badly. Your efforts helped him move forward while he was getting at least some of his desires and needs met. At the very least, he has had a great deal of attention, even negative attention, heaped upon him. Entire lives were likely organized around his wants and his emotions. Plans and feelings were arranged around the rise and fall of his changeable demands. Even the sporadic presence of his more winning, funny, charismatic, or simply loving and attentive self were given more than their due. And now, if he's starting to come out somewhat from, say, his mental health problems or his drinking, he may feel like a new world is opening up before him.

You, on the other hand, are not necessarily going to view the beginning of this healing connection with the same sense of accomplished arrival that he does. Unless you have extended Herculean efforts to also build a world that has sustained you deeply emotionally, spiritually, financially, and physically all along—a world of connection and enrichment that feeds your soul and well-being—you will quite likely face this new stage of the relationship as a parched and exhausted survivor staggering out of the desert. You have a deep need for rest and replenishing. You may have great demands—wholly justified and reasonable ones given how much you have been giving and how little you've been receiving in recent years. But when your partner starts to realize what is being asked of him, he may suddenly show signs of not having changed quite as much as it appeared; he may slide back into feeling sorry for himself and making it sound like you want too much from him.

And professionals sometimes buy into this view. "It's just sour grapes," comments one renowned counselor of veterans with addiction and PTSD issues. "The veterans get sober and better, and their wives don't want to celebrate that. It's all about the past for the wives; they need to learn to just move on and see where their husbands are today."

These outrageous comments add a second wound to the already beleaguered partners of the veterans. The veterans' treatment should be preparing them for the repair of the damage they wrought. The repair needs to be done in the way that is meaningful to the partner, and for the length of time it takes her to recover. The healing of the relationship gets under way once she can safely get good and mad at what he's done. The impact of the past should finally be acknowledged and embraced, along with all her well-deserved fury.

Equal Isn't Equal

Because your life has been in so many ways put on hold while your partner started dealing with his issues, you may feel that it isn't fair to you for things now to go "back to fifty-fifty"—when it never was fifty-fifty! Unless the changed partner turns his focus and attention to you for a significant period of time, the costs of the time you gave, even when he's successful, will be detrimental to you. For at least a couple of years, your needs and goals need to come first. When a structured, long-term commitment toward centering the relationship on supporting you is part of the plan, the chances for your own fulfillment and growing happiness are much better.

What Does Good Enough Look Like?

If your partner has a significant amount of healing and change before him, it is important to realistically assess what it is that you are waiting for. What is enough for you? What are the changes, small and large, that fuel your desire to give your time to your partner? What is it that you will see or hear that will tell you the wait has been worth it?

After you read Rosa's thoughts, consider your own responses to the questions that follow.

"I just wasn't ready for it," says Rosa. "I mean, to him, he's come a long way. In the old days, he was, ninety percent of the time, miserable, edgy, angry, and scary, and ten percent of the time, an all-out terrifying lunatic.

"Now he does really well at his job, but he's miserable. He is real hands-on and loving with the kids, but he's also short with them. There's only so far they can go with him before he just cuts them off and they have to come to me. I can't actually turn half the parenting over to him—because he can't really handle it the way a parent needs to take it on.

"And then there's me—you know, he thinks he's doing great, compared to what he used to be like with me. He's all shut down most of the time and then once in a while he comes out of it and smiles and is funny and loving. Nowadays, it's ninety percent of the time he is stressed, unhappy, and kind of robotic, but not doing anything mean toward me. Let's see, to be honest, I get five percent of that loving and funny person I fell in love with. And the last five percent, well, he's either on the edge of being a stubborn, defensive pain in the ass or he's actually being one—but no, not crazy like he was.

"He's been working on this for almost ten years since he got out of the service. I thought he deserved a chance and I saw him moving forward. You know most guys don't even try, and here he was, giving it his all in program and therapy and counseling with me.

"It's hard for him when I bust his bubble and tell him that ninety-five percent stressed, miserable, and the occasional aggressive destructiveness is not good enough. He shakes his head and compares himself to the abusive tough guys, the out-of-work addicts, or the guys who just came back

and turned their families into the combat zone. It's hard for me to tell him that yeah, well, those guys aren't the standard. Not for me. I feel awful. It really comes down to whether this is enough for me . . . I'm glad he's doing better, but, is it what I want? I know I don't want it like this . . ."

EXERCISE 14–2: HOW MUCH CHANGE IS ENOUGH

Write your thoughts in response to these two questions:

1. What are the changes, small and large, that fuel your desire to give your time to your partner?

2. What is it that you will see or hear that will tell you the wait has been worth it?

The Pros of Giving Him Your Time

There can sometimes be advantages to giving your partner your time so that he can change.

- You might use the time to construct a plan of exiting as safely as possible, with as many sound emotional and financial resources as possible—this is especially important if your partner is violent or threatening, or has indicated that he will get financial revenge on you if you leave him.
- With a dangerous partner, you might use the time to hope that he loses interest in you so that he is the one to leave you, which can be safer.
- Giving him your time might give you the space to become very clear about what is happening; going through repeated patterns can give you the opportunity to identify them, prepare yourself emotionally for them, and see the range of his abilities.
- Giving him your time can allow you to manage major life transitions, such as caring for infants or very small children, or dealing with a relative's sickness and death, with fewer disruptions than leaving might entail.

- Giving him your time can allow you to articulate for yourself what exactly your "deal breakers" are so that you are more prepared to insist upon change, and to reinstate for yourself your standards and your clarity.

- Giving him your time, when safety is not an issue, can allow you to detach yourself from the intense care and responsibility for him, and reestablish yourself as a priority, even while in the relationship.

- Giving him your time can assuage the voices in you that say, "What if . . ." or "I have to . . ." These voices can't be heard and these expectations met until you can meet them squarely and feel confident in your conclusions.

- Giving him your time, if things are noticeably improving, can connect you to the love, hope, and expansive feelings you felt when you first met.

- Giving him your time, if things are noticeably improving, can afford you some of the acknowledgment and healing that you desire and deserve.

- Giving him your time can help you feel certain of yourself as a person who has tried everything, who is committed to relationships, who believes in giving people a chance.

- Giving him your time can give your children a chance to be in an intact family. (Of course, the costs can quickly turn too high for you, and for your children also, so be alert to when the costs start to outweigh the benefits.)

- Giving him your time can spare you the pressures of having to go through finding a new partner and building a new life.

EXERCISE 14-3: LOOKING AT THE BENEFITS FOR YOU OF WAITING

Write your thoughts in response to these questions:

1. Do any of the items on the bulleted lists above stand out for you? If so, which ones, and why?

2. What is it that you notice yourself seeing, doing, thinking, or feeling that demonstrates the accuracy of any of these for your situation?

Next, reflect for a moment on Anne's situation. Her testimony below demonstrates the mix of emotions and feelings she has as a result of a destructive relationship to which she gave her time. This is a relationship that she currently feels is a good one.

"I stuck it out. I can say things are better. Mostly, I did it for the kids at first. And then, they got older and I decided I couldn't do it any longer. The time really helped me sort out what was going on, in spite of how he had everyone fooled. I told him what needed to change, but I wasn't really thinking he would change. I was done with it, though. I felt a huge amount of grief.

"He was demeaning, kind of threatening, but I didn't feel unsafe. That doesn't mean it didn't get awful. When it was bad, it was endless, all his defensiveness and arguing all the time about things I'd never said or done. It was so much work. He ended up getting diagnosed with something—I don't really believe much in that stuff, but I do know he had a history of bad things happening to him. And he was such an arrogant jerk. Really selfish, though he always played it like he was being wronged. He had all of these ideas about what he had to do and who had the right to tell him whatever.

"So, I gave him one week to show me something really good. He volunteered to go to this men's group. I never thought he'd stick it out, but he did. And he went to Al-Anon. Then he went to therapy.

"The thing is, he is loving to me now. I can feel he really loves me. I run a program where I work with teenagers, and sometimes they are rude to me. He volunteers there on some of the projects. He tells those young guys that I 'kicked his ass and gave him a life' and that I deserve nothing but respect. It chokes me up when he says it. He's good to me.

"But sometimes, honestly, I still hate that guy that he was. He has heard it all from me, many times, but the truth is, I don't think he really knows what it was like. Will he ever get what it was like to be on the other side of his hatefulness?

"I still don't understand how a person can be like that—how they never really see that they don't have the right to go after you like that, to go after you till it hurts. It's madness. It's crazy and it's a whole other world. I remember it, and I get so pissed off about it still. I can't stand the thought of that part of him. I remember looking at him and he knew that I knew that no one in the world would see how crazy and hateful he was but me. He'd get a glint in his eye—like he was enjoying that. That's looking into the eyes of evil.

" I have changed. Now I always think that there is that part in people, that potential to choose evil, and I'm always on the lookout for it. I also don't think that being kind and understanding helps when you are face-to-face with that kind of evil. Now that I know what it is, I know you have to walk away from it. No, run. If there is anything left of him that's good, he'll come after you with the good. If he's mostly evil, then you be careful to sneak out quiet as you can—and then run."

What part of Anne's testimony stood out for you? Why?

What events, feelings, or thoughts will you look for that will be a sign for you that you are giving too much of your time to your partner?

What are the things that you want to keep or nurture in yourself, whether you give your time to your partner's changing or whether you decide not to?

PAYING FOR YOUR ANGER WITH YOUR TIME

Sometimes, women make the decision to give more of their time because they are not sure if their own anger is at least partly responsible for the difficulties in the relationship. You might wonder if your partner deserves more time because you have not been perfect yourself. Our experience is that the destructive man's issues will not be affected, except perhaps very briefly, by having his partner be less angry or more patient with him. So even if you have sometimes vented your frustrations at him, or had times of responding to him from your own places of emotional disturbance or trauma, your decision to give your time to his change is a gift of great value, and it must be treated as such by the both of you.

SAFETY

If your partner has shown violent behaviors or values, your thoughts about how much time to give him to change are no doubt colored by your efforts to figure out which path is the safest one for you and your children, and you may even be concerned about whether your partner would harm your friends or relatives.

In this case, factors influencing your decision might include your awareness that leaving would:

- open up the possibility of having a life that nurtures you
- increase the probability that you will be safer from assault
- give you the opportunity to heal from any sexual humiliation, coercion, and violation
- increase your chances of being able to raise your children in a nurturing and nonthreatening atmosphere

We recognize that you have to balance all of these weighty advantages against the risk that your partner's response to being left will be to stalk you, or try to go after custody of your children, or try to do you even greater sexual or physical harm than he has done in the past. We urge you strongly, if your partner shows signs of being of this style, to be in touch with a hotline for abused women (see the "Resources" section) and to carefully craft a safety plan before attempting to flee.

If you live with these kinds of circumstances:

- You may be hoping that his violence will ease off if you comply absolutely with his demands.
- You may have found a formula of appeasing him adequately that seems to be working for now to gain respite from his all-out attacks on you.
- You may be trying to use the time to save enough money to plan a realistic escape.
- You may be using the time to find yourself support to break the isolation that makes the takeover of your own state of mind possible.

In addition, you may be hoping that the periods of loving sanity will last just because they are so much better than his madness; you may be struggling to grasp your partner's repeated destructiveness.

We are not criticizing any of these reasons for waiting, or any of these strategies for trying to protect yourself from a violent partner. There are no doubt times when these strategies are necessary. However, we worry about the ability of these approaches to keep you and your children safe in the long term; therefore, it is important to keep reevaluating for yourself the question of whether it is more dangerous to stay or more dangerous to leave.

EXERCISE 14–4: GIVING TIME TO A VIOLENT PARTNER

Write your thoughts in response to the following questions:

1. When you reflect on the considerations of giving a partner who is violently destructive time, which ones stand out as thoughts you have had in the past?

2. What were the circumstances? What are your reflections on those thoughts?

GIVING YOUR PARTNER TIME WHILE STILL MOVING FORWARD

Sometimes women decide to take a break from their relationship by creating an agreement that does not dissolve the whole relationship but gives some room to take a break from the unhealthy dynamics. It is a way of giving less of yourself while still giving your partner a chance to make some changes, as Darlene explains:

"He started to come home drunk again. I couldn't take on the whole idea of leaving my marriage. He had changed over the years, for the better with his attitudes toward me. I knew he'd been through some stuff, but he didn't want to go to therapy or anything like that. When I saw he started drinking again, it all seemed to unravel. He says he doesn't

remember the things he says when he's drunk, but I do. The truth is that
I will never forget them. But I couldn't do it all at once. I couldn't just cut
things off completely. It was too much. So I figured I could take a break.
For a while, I spent more time at my parents' house, just to feel normal,
just to soak that in. I slept over when I could. I knew I couldn't stay with
them forever, so I found an apartment and set it all up. It was important
for me to say to myself that I wasn't leaving my marriage, I was just tak-
ing a break."

Darlene set the terms of the break. The terms included that they were not
seeing other people romantically and they were not filing for divorce. She did
not decide at the outset whether she would file for a separation; their children
were grown, so she didn't have to worry about custody and visitation. The
break gave Darlene time to reconnect with herself. The time alone also presented some challenges. Darlene had to find her own rhythms again. She had
to reinvent her own way of taking care of herself and of loving herself.

There were so many questions that kept coming to her while she sat in her
small apartment. What did she really think and feel about her relationship?
What were the specific changes she required of her relationship in order to
consider moving back?

Darlene needed to create connections to others so that isolation would stop
seeming like the choice that stood in contrast to going back; if she were to go
back, it shouldn't be from sheer isolation.

She needed to find the feeling of competence in living her life that comes
from responding to her own life's demands with undivided energy, rather
than having her attentions consistently divided and turned toward her partner's behaviors and issues. Everything began to seem simpler. It became easier
to remember things at work and to organize her thoughts in general. She
found that she needed more of this.

Darlene's partner had always created tornadoes of drama and high-
running feelings. She needed to even herself out in the quiet and see how
things looked from a backdrop of rest and easy rhythm. In that space, she
found herself filled with grief over her partner's shocking return to substance
abuse. She saw the unhealthy ways in which he was dealing with his own
emotional disturbances, and felt the loss for the loving person he had been.
Darlene did not avoid the pain, but sought out support to allow herself to feel

all of the love, all the loss, and the sense of relief. This mixture of giving her partner time, while giving it to herself, helped her find her clarity.

EXERCISE 14–5: TAKING A BREAK

Write your thoughts about these questions:

1. If you are currently struggling with whether to give your partner more time, does taking a break, or creating some distance while still in the relationship, have any appeal to you?

2. What are your thoughts about this strategy?

3. Of all the considerations in this chapter, which ones stood out for you as most important in your own relationship?

4. Which ones stand out as things you that you consider as relevant or useful now in your relationship?

5. Based on how you are viewing things today (and recognizing that this may change tomorrow), how much time and energy do you feel is right for you to invest in getting your partner to change and in pursuing that process with him? How much longer do you want to give him?

THE TIME TO STOP WAITING FOR HIM IS NOW!

Sasha was bravely participating in a weekend retreat for people struggling to heal from the effects of loss or trauma. About halfway through the Saturday session, she got up the nerve to raise her hand in front of the sixty participants and ask the workshop leader a question. "I feel like I'm outgrowing my boyfriend," she said, "but I don't want to. We've been together for over five years, but I've been thinking seriously about ending our relationship. Then I start to feel so guilty. I love him and I just hate the thought of abandoning him."

The leader invited Sasha to stand up with her in front of the group, and then said to her, "I want you to imagine that your partner is in the room with us today, watching and listening. I want you to talk to him aloud, saying these words:

" 'I want you to come with me, but I can't wait for you any longer."

"And I'd like you to repeat this phrase to him several times over."

Sasha said the phrase aloud five or six times, and let the feelings that arose wash over her (including the tears that sprang from her eyes after the third time she tried it).

The workshop leader wanted Sasha to experience that moving on with your own life does not in any way show lack of love for your partner. If you have told your partner clearly what you need, you are offering him the opportunity to grow with you. The choice is his, as you have so generously offered it to him. If he chooses not to come along, that isn't your fault.

> The decision of when to *stop waiting* for your partner is a different decision from the one about when to *leave* him.

It is possible to leave your partner but remain attached to waiting for him. Have you, for example, ever known someone who ends a relationship but then months or years later still can't commit fully to a new partner, because he or she is still hoping that their ex is going to turn up healed and transformed? They got away from the relationship, but they haven't been able to let go of the desperate hoping for that person's love.

And just as you can leave but keep waiting, you can do the opposite: stay and move forward. What does this mean?

- You let yourself build closer and closer relationships (nonsexually) with women and men in your life whom you care about, and stop holding back from them for fear of making your partner feel jealous or threatened— his insecurity is his problem. (Unless he's dangerous, of course.)
- You start imagining a life of which your partner is not the centerpiece, and you don't choke those thoughts or fantasies off. You perhaps even start imagining what it would be like to be with a different partner.
- You put at least somewhat less energy into your relationship, and rechannel it in other directions such as your work, exercise, or other interests.
- You pursue skills, insights, classes, or any other form of widening of your life that you have been craving.

- You stop fighting the changes that you can feel happening inside of you. When you find yourself having political opinions that are different from your partner's; or you start to think you might want to change your life by living in a different area or by changing the kind of work you do; when you start to consider making some changes in how you are raising your children; or when shifts are happening inside of you that you can't even put words to—you just sense that you are becoming a different person than you used to be—these are all signs of *growth* and *expansion*. People in relationships, especially in destructive ones, often stifle these signs of growth in themselves, because they are afraid of their partner's disapproval and they are afraid of outgrowing him or her. *Stop holding yourself back.*

You might be seriously considering leaving your relationship, or you may feel years away from taking that leap. Either way, the time to unleash your own growth and development is *now*.

EXERCISE 14–6:

Reflect some on the messages you have received over the years, including during your girlhood, about the following issues. Try to write some about what you've been taught, or what friends, relatives, or advertisers have told you, whether you agree with those values or not:

1. Doesn't a woman have to censor or erase certain aspects of who she is in order to be in a relationship with a man? What sort of things does she need to avoid? (Did you ever hear, for example, "You'll never have a man if you do such-and-such"?)

2. What does it mean for a woman to be single? Can she be complete without a man? Can she be happy "on her own"? Shouldn't she avoid any substantial periods without a partner?

3. Do these messages seem to be different for men? Is it more acceptable for men to be single, or to be in relationships that are casual?

After writing for about ten minutes (or more if you want to) about the questions above, write down at least one goal you want to set for yourself for how you want to keep these messages from controlling your life.

EXERCISE 14–7:

Rewrite the following sentences, filling in the blanks. You might have more than one answer.

1. "For a long time I've thought that I was [some description of something about you], but now I'm starting to wonder if actually I'm more like [ ]."

2. "Other people often assume that I'm [some way of viewing you], but actually I'm more like [ ]."

3. "I'd like to let the world see more of [some aspect of yourself that you keep hidden].

Then write at least one goal for yourself of a way that you want to stop holding back on your growth or development.

In the long run, you don't want to be with a partner who prefers that you be stuck. (Do you?) So if he responds critically to your growth, or launches into self-centered whining, he's revealing aspects of himself that have to change. A healthy partner is thrilled by watching your life take off.

Expanding your own horizons also helps you to heal. As we will examine in detail in Chapter 21, recovering from the harm done by a destructive partner involves a combination of internal and external work, an interplay between emotional healing and concrete action. By leaping forward with your development, you feed the "action" side of the equation in a way that can make a large contribution to easing the pain of what you have endured. (And we'll be teaching some techniques for the internal healing side, to help keep the recovery process in balance, which we find brings the fastest path to well-being.)

And even though your partner may resent your growth and perceive it as a threat, the reality is that he stands to benefit, too. By holding you back, he also holds himself back. When you start to fly, he can catch the stream behind you—if he chooses to.

You are going to shine. Full speed ahead.

EXERCISE 14–8:

Write a letter to your partner (just as an exercise, not to actually give to him) in which you describe your decision to move forward with your own progress. Tell him the spheres of life where you most want to grow. (Work? Personal relationships? Health? Learning? All of these?) Tell him how much it would mean to you if he would decide to get unstuck and really move forward also. And then explain why your growth can't wait on his.

It's important that you not show your partner what you write, because you may unconsciously change how you express yourself if you are writing with the thought that he will actually see it, and then the writing wouldn't have the same healing impact on you. *Later,* if you want to, you can write another version of the letter to give to him, assuming that it is safe to do so.

Remember that an abusive man can become dangerous when he realizes that his partner is thinking seriously of leaving him, or even that she is growing beyond his ability to control. Choose carefully how much to let him know about what is going on inside you. For more guidance, see Chapter 18, "Entering Freedom After a Destructive Relationship."

PART IV

MAKING THE BIG DECISIONS

FIFTEEN

Why You May Feel Worse When He Improves

"He's really doing better, but what does he want? A medal for acting like a decent human being?"

"He never really told me what exactly happened with the other woman. He said it's all behind him now, he's sorry, and we should just move forward. But I don't know if I can."

"It's not all in the past. It's like it was yesterday."

"It's finally, finally going good. But I'm not really in love with him anymore."

WHAT DO YOU imagine it would be like for you if some (or all) of the following started to take place:

- Your partner finally recognized how unfair and unhealthy his behavior toward you has been.
- He admitted to you, accurately and in detail, what he has done, without shifting the blame onto you.
- He described the impact of his actions on you in a way that showed that he got what things have been like for you in this process.

- He was able to put into words how strong you have been, how loyal, and how good to him, and acknowledge that he has been attacking and damaging your best qualities.
- He stopped the behaviors, for a period long enough to convince you that something real was shifting.
- His friendships and acquaintances changed to reflect new values that were healthy.
- He was honest and frank about his past behavior toward you to people who matter to you.
- The focus of the relationship shifted to repairing the harm you suffered.
- The joint energies and resources of your partnership were committed toward your dreams and your aspirations.

"Then everything would be all right," asserts Yolanda.

"Oh, no, it wouldn't," warns Yvette in her support group. "He'd just be setting you up, saying what you want to hear, acting that way so he can get you back good and then go right back to it."

What If the Change Is Real?

Yvette's suspicions are reasonable, given how frequently destructive people engage in semblances of change. But what if the improvements are genuine? In this chapter, we will examine the powerful feelings you may have if your partner starts to do some significant work on himself, and his way of being in your relationship starts to shift. Beyond the relief and bliss one might imagine, feelings may come up that can present almost as great a challenge as living with a destructive partner. You may be surprised to find yourself feeling rage, or grief, or even a loss of interest in your relationship. In addition, you may feel guilty that you have these other feelings. Let's look at why you might find it harder than you expected when he starts getting better.

EXERCISE 15-1:

Let's recall the letter of accountability that Suzanne received from her partner that we read in Chapter 10. The letter actually continued on, asking Suzanne's permission to move the relationship forward into a period of repair. As you read the remainder of the letter:

1. Circle things he writes that would make you feel suspicious if they came from your partner.

2. Circle parts that you feel moved by when you imagine your partner writing them to you.

Suzanne,

I know that it's not possible to change the past. I am hoping that with goodwill and good intentions, I can start to repair the harm. If you can believe how much I love you, I hope you accept my apology, even though I don't deserve it and this I truly mean.

I am trying to be very diligent and aware of the harm I have caused and how I caused it. As removed from my wisdom as I have so often lived and as inadequately as I have engaged in loving you, I have always and entirely loved you to my greatest ability—even as that ability was terribly impaired. Please forgive me.

I am prepared to listen now, without judgment, to the truth of what you have lived. I really want to know how you feel, the extent that you want to share that with me. I won't make excuses or try to justify my behavior.

I recognize that in place of the innocence that you deserved, the life you have lived with me provided so much pain that you, through your own endurance, have filled it with strength and insight. You likely have known for years these things about me and no doubt have articulated them for yourself with accuracy and elegance. That represents an additional burden that was put upon you—to have found your way alone through the labyrinth of loss. I owe it to you to name for you what I have done and, with the naming, take the full responsibility.

You have always been a rich, shining spirit, a bright intelligence, a fierce heart, and an adoring lover and partner. It has been a gift to have the chance to be your partner, one that, for many reasons, I could not honor in the ways required of me.

I have the hope that the kind of love I am capable of embracing can reach the woman who fell in love with me. I honor the fact that you found your power and way without the strength of the partner you deserved next to you at every challenge. Rather, every beauty you have, you earned on the merits of your own enduring spirit. I made your life hard, perhaps in ways that seemed unbearable. You bore it—you grew in spite of what I gave you, and what I took away, and you are flowering today.

I do want to try again, to embrace you completely and to stand strong for you and with you. I want to heal our relationship. I want you to be honest with me and I want to be there for you with all my heart. I want to be with you in a way that your forgiveness might grow and in a way that you feel completely and utterly adored, cherished, and seen for all the beauty, strength, and gifts of love you possess.

I have always loved you more than I can say; I will always love you more than anyone. You brought love into my life, you brought beautiful children into my life, you devoted yourself and your energies to my heart and I want now to return that to you, with your permission.

I am aware of the impact I have had on you throughout our relationship and how hard you have tried over and over again to get my attention to understand how much you love me and to understand how much damage I have caused you repeatedly. You have been devoted, unselfish and utterly, unbelievably patient. You have every right to be angry for decades if you want and I would not question that. It's my job to cherish and adore you, and to make up for all the harm, loss, and pain I have caused you. I will hold the space and be present. I am truly aware of the misery I have put upon you and am truly aware of the responsibility ahead to make amends for these years of pain and anguish. I really do love you.

The Words Are Fingers on the Wound

Reading this letter may bring tightness to your throat, or tears that well up from the heart. You might experience a mixture of relief at being seen and grief over the sheer pain of what you've endured. You might feel rage at having been treated this way, rage at being denied the acknowledgment you deserved for so long. You might feel a sense of despair at the thought that you will never receive a letter anything like this from your partner. You might be entirely suspicious at the assertion "You have every right to be angry for decades if you want and I would not question that," as it would be hard to imagine a destructive partner keeping up such a position for five minutes, never mind decades. There may be other sections that alert your suspicion, given your experience.

Acknowledge whatever you feel, and know that if you identify with any or all of the completely different sentiments, that's okay. It's perfectly normal to have a myriad of emotions—even conflicting emotions—when your partner attempts to change and make amends.

MAKING ROOM FOR RAGE

When Suzanne first received the letter from her partner, she enjoyed a brief period of relief. But soon she was overwhelmed with deep and abiding rage. She noticed that there were so few women to talk to who could understand this. When she shared the letter with her trusted friends, she noticed that they were either shocked to read of the things he had put her through and remained angry with him on her behalf, or they were deeply moved by the growth and hope that they saw in the letter, reflecting on how desperately they themselves longed for such growth in their own partners. Both responses felt unsatisfying to Suzanne, because her feelings were so much more complicated and mixed.

Suzanne should not have been treated so badly to begin with; that was definitely the first thing she was pissed off about. But more, Suzanne was outraged at how much work it had taken her to get her partner to this place. Now that she could finally stand atop the mountain and look down, she saw how many obstacles her partner had placed in her path, how she had made her way up a hellish climb with him fighting her the majority of the way.

The whole enterprise looked like a terrible waste of her energy and love. She knew, to a certainty, that he would never have done the same for her. She looked down and back and knew all her heartrending pain was not felt by anyone but herself. Suzanne was not merely angry. She was filled with raw, soul-shaking rage.

So, if what you have long hoped for finally occurs, what can you expect to feel?

Hello, More Anger

You might find yourself reliving all the hurt and pain in your relationship; you're recounting to yourself all the cascade of lies and deceptions, all the hypocrisy, that are now suddenly clear. Likewise, if your partner has a history of cruelty and selfishness toward you, you undoubtedly had a plethora of issues that were impossible to raise with him over the years; and if now he's beginning to own up, you may feel the accumulated effects of all those issues, large and small, that he refused to address at the time.

"It's all in the past," one unversed in such projects of repair might say. But rest assured, if the past in all its patient detail rushes forward as though it were moments ago, don't be surprised, and know that you deserve to be heard and answered in complete.

If, as part of an effort to repair your relationship, your partner reveals an affair, he no longer has the right to claim that those details are his private province. Where he and the other women met, when they met, how far and to what extent their expressions of devotion and commitment unfolded, the rationale behind his choices, and his changing orientation toward you—all of these are your business now *if you want it to be*. Their relationship did not exist as legitimate relationships do, on its own terms; it existed *inside your* relationship, was *made possible* in many ways by your relationship. Every shift occurring during that illicit relationship affected you and your life deeply. And those details may make you even angrier, even more outraged, perhaps to the point that you need some distance from the relationship. Such is part of the work of repair.

We are not, however, advocating that you insist upon sexual details, as you might want to at first. The reason why we advocate caution is that later on, you might regret the specific images and thoughts that his confessions will plant in your mind. They might continue to burn in your imagination long after and simply make you feel bad.

It does help to know what kinds of deceptions your partner engaged in, including how extensive and complicated his lies were; this will help you know the kinds of changes in thinking and feeling that you need to look for in him.

Knowing exactly what he is capable of gives you clearer and specific ideas of exactly what needs to be changed.

In order to feel emotionally safe in the relationship again, if you ever do, you will need to know what specifically has changed. There are many answers you may feel you need to hear from him:

- How does your partner sense when he is distancing himself from you?
- What does your partner know about what triggers these feelings of distance from you?
- What attitudes and beliefs does your partner have now about your role in his life? How are they different from the old ones?
- What does he believe is an appropriate and constructive course to take when he is feeling distant from you?

EXERCISE 15–2:

GOOD AND MAD

This exercise is about discovering a safe and satisfying way to express your anger. How do you usually express your anger? Do your actions harm you, your health, or others in some way? If so, we'd like to encourage you to try on some different ways of releasing your feelings.

Look at the list below. Please choose one or two that you have not tried. As you try them, keep asking yourself what is the worst thing about what you are so angry about. See which thing helps release your pent-up feelings.

1. Take a bat to a dead tree stump.

2. Bury your head in the pillows and yell out everything you ever wanted to say about what is making you angry.

3. Dig your pen into the paper of a notebook, carving the words to what makes you most angry.

4. Find a place where you can safely bellow—deep woods, hilltop, empty beach.

5. Bang drums for a half an hour.

6. Get a dozen eggs and smash them in the woods, one at a time. The animals will appreciate you, and there's something about seeing the delicate shells shatter and the bright yellow lost that sums it all up just right.

7. Growl. Yes, growl. Try it for a while. Change the guttural noises.

8. Kickbox.

9. Take a fast walk in the rain.

10. Take a lipstick and decorate your mirror with everything angry you want to say.

11. Go running and sprint as fast as you can.

12. Write down what makes you angry on a sheet of paper and then rip it to shreds until you tear it into tiny pieces. Then throw it up in the air like confetti.

We know a woman named Jane who had collected every sweet and loving note and every card her partner had ever given her in a special box. "When I found out what he did, I couldn't sleep. When it was time to stoke the fire of the woodstove that I use to heat my house, it occurred to me— the box. I wasn't all worked up. I took that box, and I looked at each thing. They all seemed so innocent. The handwriting, the little notes I'd saved. Keeping this box was like me keeping the relationship going. There I was, protecting, holding on tight to evidence of love. And there he was, destroying it. I put each one of those things in the woodstove. I watched them burn. It felt great."

What Embracing Your Outrage Looks Like

If your partner is honest about the project of repair, then his open arms must embrace your outrage. You deserve to feel loving focus and attention coming your way even when you are not making him happy by being so upset.

When you are in the process of repairing your relationship, you might find that in moments of happy closeness, you are reminded of a similar situation in the past when your partner was destructive. You may recall the contrasting unhappy time in vivid detail. In your current happy moment, you deserve to be held, and to be loved while bringing up the devastation, disappointments, and destruction of all the times in the past that you were mistreated. A truly changed partner will have a new agreement with you. Gone will be the old, perhaps unspoken, agreement that held that in good times you were not allowed to mention previous disappointments at the peril of destroying the moment: "Not now, when we were having such a good time." During the repairing process, you will be able to move from happiness, to sudden misery and grief, back to happiness with the focus remaining gratefully and lovingly on you and your continued presence in the relationship. This journey through the grief is part of your healing from your many losses, and deserves welcome.

EXERCISE 15–3:

> Imagine you are enjoying a happy time with your partner when you suddenly are reminded of the pain of the past. Write down what you need him to do now in regard to his past actions. What do you need to hear at this time? What does he need to do to comfort you now?

OTHER FEELINGS YOU MAY EXPERIENCE

Grief

You may also notice an acute sensation of loss, even when your partner, the same person who wreaked havoc, starts to make real changes.

"Where were you before when I needed you?"

"If you could do this now, why couldn't you then?"

"It was still me, the same person you now adore, and you treated me like garbage. How could you?"

"You never could have done for me what I have done for you. Why should I stay now?"

These gnawing questions may have answers that can be understood intellectually, but those reasoned answers fail to satisfy the grief and the loss you may be experiencing. You may ask them repeatedly because you are actually grieving the cruelty and the loss of your sense of safety and decency in love. Allow yourself time to grieve in response to the rhetorical cry of "Why?"

Loneliness

Even when your changed partner looks back on his own behavior with an appropriate sense of being disturbed by what he's done, you might also feel a sense of isolation. The very same person who denied there was ever anything wrong is now seeing himself through your eyes and casting the same judgment on himself that you fought for. You might feel alone with the memory of the person he was. You may wonder why it took so much for him to see what you saw all along. The sudden quelling of the battle leaves many questions, the foremost among these being: Does he remember who he was? He must not forget who he has been, because you won't. He can't spend a moment congratulating himself in front of you about how far he's come or what a great job he's done. He needs to save that for conversations with his own private support people.

Instead, he must recognize all the pain he caused when he refused to acknowledge his destructiveness. He must stand with you whenever memories of days past cast a shadow on whatever progress he is making. Even as he moves forward toward real and significant positive change, he must be willing to shine a light on his past transgressions so you don't feel so alone in your grief.

Mistrust

When your partner responds lovingly in situations where he had formerly been destructive, you may find yourself reacting with mistrust. To be assured that this is a reliable person, you must be confident in his ability to see himself honestly, and not just for the moment. He has to be able to remember what he did and its impact on you even while he engages with you in a new way. If he can do this, then you may find yourself relaxing into a bond that you can rely upon.

Your partner might soften in a moment when he would have been defensive in the past. He may freely offer embraces that were so infrequent before— after all, this should make you happy, shouldn't it? Isn't this what you wanted all along? Maybe so, but you might just not be feeling it for him right now. He might have to really convince you that he is accepting responsibility for his own acts and issues, and for the suspicion you now feel. And he will need to keep offering himself up repeatedly until you are ready to truly accept him. If he is changing, he will do it.

Lack of Interest

The long period of struggle with your partner may have changed you in important ways. At the juncture of repair, when your changing partner is ready to engage with you, to get to know you, to create a new bond that has your interests and well-being at its core, and even to invest significant energies into building up your diminished inner resources, you might find yourself not interested in him as a partner. All the drama over his destructiveness can make it seem like you have more in common than you do. Once it blows over a little, you may find yourself realizing that you don't really have the basis for a relationship.

While your partner had been actively using his substance, or perpetrating his violent attitudes and beliefs, or living a divided and constricted life, he has not been maturing. Though he may now be at the beginning of this journey, you might be so far along on yours that you no longer find a connection that inspires you to further devotion. You don't feel in love with him anymore.

You might feel guilty about this. After all, if your partner has actually made significant changes, you know how rare that can be and how many times you thought that only if he changed, you would be happy. You may have been thinking that a deal was in place: you would give your time and energy to him and he would work to change, and then you would stay together and live happily ever after. In reality, he needed to do that work on himself whether you were going to stay together or not. And you might not feel spontaneously loving or interested in your changed partner. If he has moved toward greater health, then perhaps you two can have a healthy friendship. And if he insists that you have to either be partners or have no relationship at all, then perhaps he hasn't really changed all that much.

Retired Cheerleader

Certainly your partner's efforts merit support and congratulations, but you might no longer want anything to do with this role. You could have a very limited patience for celebration of his changing, whether it is his sustaining his sobriety, or refraining from assaultive or demeaning acts. It's understandable if you don't feel like celebrating the fact that he's doing what he should have been doing all along.

Further, feeling like you have to congratulate and encourage him forces you to stay in the role of giver, focusing on your partner as you've had to do for so long. Just as he underwent a process to cease his denials in order to improve, you will have your own process. You have the right to decide that your process is enough work without the added job of cheering him on.

BECAUSE YOU SAY SO

No process of change occurs in a straight line, moving forward, with no slipping into old habits. Your partner might show negative shifts in attitudes that are subtle, but significant to you, because they represent a way of thinking that was the underpinning of the maddening carousel you have just left. His backsliding will, of course, make you feel worse, even though overall he is getting better.

Especially if he has an emotional disturbance, it is important to establish with your partner and any supporting professionals that *your* expertise as the keen observer of your partner's subtle shifts will be considered the default accurate assessment. His ability to notice when he has gone off course is not reliable. As we recommended in the previous chapter, we hope that you will establish an agreement that for a significant period, of at least a couple of years of repair and building a relationship anew, *your* assessment of his appropriateness will prevail. Our presumption is that you now have a finely tuned sensibility for where and when your boundaries are being crossed.

When there are periods of regressing to destructive, constricted ways of being or violent values— and you point them out— it is almost a guarantee that your recovering partner will deny it. When you contradict him and remind him of your agreement that your assessment prevails, he may retort:

"I'm not being defensive! I'm not sarcastic! I wasn't being demeaning!"

"Does this mean you are always right?!"

For a significant period, yes, you must be the arbiter of these assessments.

———

After all, if his own judgment and clarity were good enough to rely on, he wouldn't have handled your relationship, and his life, as badly as he did.

EXERCISE 15–4: NOT ANOTHER MINUTE

If, when you read this chapter, you found yourself thinking, "Maybe I've had it with this process. I don't want to see any disrespectful attitudes, any violent beliefs in my relationship." Or maybe you thought, "I'm done with the intense mood swings and the periods when he's so cold and distant, or "I don't want to think about or worry about whether he's drinking anymore," then this exercise is for you.

Draw a clock. At the top of the clock, where the "12" would be, draw a little figure of yourself as a baby. Over at three o'clock, draw a little figure of yourself as a girl. At six P.M., draw a little figure of yourself as a woman. Over at nine, draw yourself as a vibrant old sage of a woman. Back above the baby draw a tiny heart or halo or question mark to symbolize whatever you think comes to you after you die.

Then get a pen or pencil. Try to find a highlighter. If you have young kids, find their markers or crayons. (There's usually one between the couch cushions.) Color in—in gray or black, the amount of time on the clock that you have had to deal with:

- disrespectful attitudes directed toward you

- violence directed toward you

- lack of emotion, withdrawal, or exaggerated reactivity in your loved one that limits your life

- substance abuse in a loved one

In your highlighter or light crayon color, color in the amount of time on the clock that your life has been primarily free of these things and filled instead with respect, safety, expansion, and good natural rhythms.

When you are done coloring, write your thoughts to the following:

1. What time is it for you?

2. What do you want to do with the rest of your time?

HE'S FEELING GOOD—YOU'RE NOT

When your partner starts changing for the better, he'll eventually have some happiness and strength to bring home. He'll have joy to share. And yet, you might not be so happy. Because you gave him so much of your time and energy managing him when he wasn't doing well, you quite likely weren't able to deal with your own wounds, or attend to your own life the way you needed to. Now maybe you aren't satisfied with your career, or you are simply run-down. You might not feel so happy that he's feeling pretty good until he uses his good energy to support you in ways that matter to you.

If your partner is in recovery, he might be welcomed into a whole secret club. AA or other substance abuse recovery crowds will open their arms to him, offering him stories, jokes, camaraderie, and dramas that you are not privy to. He will be meeting and embracing "friends," having supportive social contact that specifically excludes you. You can expect that at least the first six months of addiction recovery will be unbalanced. Your partner will be expending far more energy on maintaining recovery than on your relationship. But following that period, if he is not able to commit as much time to the care, nurturing, and repair of your relationship as he does to these friends, then you may rightly feel that you are not getting your needs met satisfactorily.

EXERCISE 15-5:

What are the absolute limits that you expect in your relationship as your partner changes for the better? What are your deal breakers?

Look back over this chapter. What concepts stood out as new for you? What are the most challenging for you to look at?

SIXTEEN

Rules for Saving the Savable Relationship

A DIFFICULT BUT PLAIN truth is that much of the advice about relationships that you will find on the "Psychology/Self-Help" shelf of your bookstore is just plain wrong in cases where one partner has a history of repeatedly harming the other, whether through addiction, chronic devaluing, cheating, or outright abuse. Here are a few examples of commonly accepted wisdom, treated as virtual fact in the talk-show world, which will actually feed an unhealthy future for the kinds of relationships we are writing about:

- *"Both partners have equal responsibility for making the relationship work."*

Nope—the person who has behaved destructively has a much greater responsibility, and the relationship can't become a healthy one unless he's prepared to take that on.

- *"Each relationship partner has to focus on evaluating his or her own faults, and stay out of judging the other person's."*

Nope again—the person who has lived with the destructive behavior needs a break from stewing about her own faults, which her partner has most likely already harped on for years. Moreover, she will probably have to be calling her partner on his issues, because he has already shown that he won't face them unless he is repeatedly confronted.

- *"Issues from the past need to be left in the past."*

But wait—what happened to the famous (and very wise) saying "Those who forget the past are condemned to repeat its mistakes"? And how exactly can healing happen if we can't address the past?

- *"Don't shame your partner about what he has done—you'll just make him feel bad about himself."*

Do we really want to continue the centuries-long mistake of encouraging women to be silent? Don't we want to see men who are tearing lives apart challenged forcefully about what they are doing?

Once one partner becomes chronically cruel or demeaning to the other, once a power imbalance is established in a relationship, once profound lies start to be told, the regular rules for dealing with predictable, healthy relationship conflict have to be tossed out the window and a whole new plan put in place.

In this chapter, we are zeroing in on one particular phase in an unhealthy relationship: the period when the partner who has been destructive has admitted that he has a serious problem and is agreeing to take steps to turn himself around. If you are here, there is at least some part of you that feels that your relationship may be savable; we hope, for your sake, that it turns out indeed to be. But we only want your relationship to be saved if it's worth saving; that is to say, if it can become a relationship in which you receive what you deserve. In order to create the best chance that your wish will come true, your partner (and to a lesser extent you, too) will need to closely follow ways of thinking and acting that are, as we have seen, in stark contrast to much of the advice from the world of self-help.

At the end of this chapter, you will find—for the first and last time in this book—an exercise that we are proposing that you and your partner do together. *Don't do this with him if your instincts tell you it's a bad idea.* (We'll remind you of this when we get there.)

Let each of these principles soak in for a moment as you go through them.

Some of them may be surprising to you, but you may find at the same time that you feel happy after reading them, a sense of relief that you don't have to follow old dictums that really weren't right for you.

THE PAST MATTERS

We recommend that the following statements be off-limits:

> *"We're putting the past behind us."*
> *"None of what happened matters anymore."*
> *"We're making a fresh start."*

While it's true that you don't want to live in the past, you also want to avoid getting too distant from it. When destructive people, or those whom they have harmed, forget what has come before, it comes around again. We borrow the caution from AA, "Don't forget where you came from."

Therefore, you and your partner will have to do a kind of balancing act. On the one hand, you can't be endlessly rehashing the past and reacting to it as if it were the present. On the other hand, you have to keep the past beside you, give it a kind of presence in the room at all times. Neither you nor your partner should go too long a time without mentioning what his behaviors were like, and what the harmful impact of his actions was on you and on your children. This is sobering and helpful for the truly recovering destructive partner, and may be deeply relieving for you. You will know when you don't need to hear it any longer.

A related principle here is that *the facts matter*. We often hear the opposite being argued—that in a relationship it only matters what each one *feels* about what took place, and that you each have your "own reality." We're not sure how wise this thinking is for *any* relationship, but it is most definitely misguided when it is applied to a relationship where one partner has caused great harm. The blurring of the facts allows the destructive person to escape accountability for his actions, minimize the impact those actions have had, and avoid learning the necessary lessons. And it sets the partner up—you, in this case—to always seem irrationally angry, mistrustful, and overreactive.

The statement that no one has a perfect memory and therefore "the truth lies in the middle" is a misleading one, because when people hear this they picture a point that is halfway between the two people's perspectives. But the place "in the middle" between a destructive man and his partner where the truth lies is usually going to be far closer to her perspective than to his distorted and self-serving one.

> **If you and your partner cannot reach at least reasonably close agreements as to what took place during critical events in the history of your relationship, you cannot safely trust him not to repeat those kinds of behaviors in the future.**

Thus, one of the rules for saving the savable relationship is that if your partner can't get to a clearer memory of his actions, *he needs to at least be prepared to wholeheartedly take your word for it* regarding how he behaved, and stop saying (or implying) that you are making things up or exaggerating them.

HE NEEDS TO COME CLEAN WITH OTHER PEOPLE

Does your partner have a history of manipulating and misleading people around you? Most people who have the kinds of issues that this book is about engage in what we call "splitting" behaviors. Your partner may, for example, have lied to people about his addiction or his emotional instability in order to convince them that you were unfairly criticizing him, and he may have succeeded in getting friends and community members to feel sorry for him about it. You may have experienced having people you cared about suddenly distancing themselves from you, based on what they were hearing about you from him. He may simultaneously have been poisoning your mind against those people, persuading *you* not to trust *them*!

It's his job to clean this mess up now. This step can be, for him, one of the most embarrassing aspects of his change; having not only to admit to people that he really does have the problems that you have been saying he has, but also that he has been lying to people about it, and about you. But he cannot save face in this critical area. Not only does he owe it to you to fix the splits he has caused, he also has to make people aware of his issues so that they won't let him get away with the same behaviors in the future.

You might also want to warn people in your life that he has a history of splitting, and ask them to please let you know right away if he speaks badly of you or tries in subtle ways to get them to believe that something is wrong with you. The idea is for people to warn you as quickly as possible if he is slipping back into habits of harming your relationships or your reputation.

You Can't Make Yourself Trust Him

Your mistrust of him is not "something you have to get past," though he and others may tell you so. He has to earn your trust, and he has to do so over a long period of time. Why does it take so long?

- because he has had other "good periods," so it will take an extended time, probably at least a couple of years, before you can tell if this time is any different from those
- because some of his breaches of trust have been so severe that they shake the foundation of a human connection to the core, so he has to build it up from the bottom (through such betrayals as cheating on you, lying to you, or harming you physically or sexually)
- because he has caused you deep emotional wounds, and those wounds take quite some time to heal—and they take even longer to heal if he triggers your memories of those events, which he is likely to do from time to time

There may come a time—but don't rush it—when you start to feel that your partner has really done everything he can to rebuild trust, and that you have to make certain shifts inside yourself. But the crucial Rule for Saving the Savable Relationship at this point it that *the decision that you need to do that kind of work has to come from you*. He is out of line if he starts saying, "You should be able to trust me by now."

Similarly, you may come to feel over time that you have, indeed, become overly reactive to certain things he says or does. Being mistreated or devalued by a partner can trigger earlier times when you were abused, or awaken memories of having alcoholic parents, or pour salt in various other wounds. It will be helpful for you to expand your awareness of when you are in the grip of feelings from other times in your life. On the other hand, it is impossible to make a complete separation; all of us move through life reacting to our pasts in various ways and there is no way to overcome that altogether. It is easy to become self-blaming and overly vigilant of yourself. Feel your way to a balance; you don't want to make your partner the scapegoat for all of your internal pains and dissatisfactions, but you also don't want to minimize the hurt he has caused. Above all, you don't want to harm your relationship with yourself, which is your most important one.

The Rule for Saving the Savable Relationship that applies here is that *he doesn't get to tell you when you are being overreactive, or analyze you regarding which parts of your feelings are about your history with him and which parts come from other places.* Statements from him along those lines are off-limits; those are determinations that only you can make, and that are your business.

Are you cheering? Underlining? Don't hold back. These are very healing principles, unfamiliar though they may be.

THE RELATIONSHIP NEEDS TO TIP THE OTHER WAY

Suppose that you worked harvesting tomatoes in a two-person team. Your coworker was lazy and rude, so each day you would have to cover nine rows of plants while she took care of only three. You would complain bitterly from time to time, but nothing would change. Finally, after months of working your butt off, staying late many days, and developing problems in your back, you complain to your boss, and your coworker is put on warning that she could be fired. She comes to you and says, "Okay, from now on, we'll each cover six rows. That will make everything fair, right?"

But it won't. You're still left with the aching back, with the sadness of the times you had to miss your kids' soccer games because you had to take care of her work, with the exhaustion. If we're really going to think about fair, your coworker is going to have to cover nine rows for a few months, while you do three. In fact, that's the least she would owe you; she might also have a responsibility to pay your chiropractor bills, and come in to work early sometimes to cover for you so that you can make up some of the time you lost with your children.

This way of viewing fair exchange and accountability is often not popular with psychologists and self-help writers. You may read a book on relationships that advises you to let go of your old resentments and just focus on the present. A therapist may tell you that it's immature to be too concerned with what is fair. Friends may tell you that you're expecting too much from your partner if you demand that he bear the full burden of the harm he has done—which includes all the giving that he *didn't* do, not just all the taking that he did.

Don't buy into these misguided philosophies. While it's true that not everything needs to be even and fair in a relationship every day or even every month, *over time a rough balance between giving and receiving is essential to a healthy relationship.* If one partner needs a lot of help and support for a few months because his elderly parent is in the hospital and facing death, that's fine, but he also needs to come through for the other partner when she struggles for a period because she was laid off from work. A sense of fairness, far from being immature, is actually a sign of wisdom in intimate partnerships.

All this is to explain why one of the Rules for Saving the Savable Relationship is that *the destructive partner needs to accept an extended period (again, probably two years or more) of imbalance, where he makes up for how self-involved he has been for so long.* He will need to be warmly and consistently supportive emotionally, he will need to not only contribute his share around the house but do more than his share, he will need to be prepared to put his own needs aside much of the time and focus on his partner's needs which have been getting short shrift.

One conflict that arises in this arena is your partner's need to be working on his change, and the time and effort that requires. A man who is overcoming substance addiction, for example, will typically be advised to attend at least one meeting *per day* of AA or a similar program. This represents a huge amount of time away from you and a heavy load on your shoulders of responsibility for the home and children. If you complain about the toll that his recovery is taking on you, he may respond quite defensively, saying that you are threatening his sobriety, or at least that you are being insensitive to how hard he has to work to deal with his addiction. He also may throw your own grievances back on you, saying, "All that time you were complaining about me drinking, and now you're complaining about my meetings! There's no way to get it right with you!"

The answer is that he is responsible for *both;* he's responsible for how his drinking affected you, and now he's responsible for how you are affected by his need to be off spending even more time focused on himself and his own recovery. The practical solution to this conflict is not simple. But the Rule for Saving the Savable Relationship is that *he has to be understanding and supportive about the impact that his recovery has on you, and he has to make space for you to express your resentment about it. Just as important, he has to do absolutely everything in his power to right the balance as much as possible, with a commitment to doing even more soon.* He can't, for example, come home from his AA meeting and declare that he is going to watch TV because it's all so stressful for him. He has to be spending constructive time with you (if you want that), and helping clean the house, fold the laundry, read to the children, communicate with their teachers, and all of the related work that goes into making a household run. At bedtime (for the adults) he needs to muster the energy—without being whiny about it—to rub your feet or make you tea, and to put effort and energy into intimacy and sexuality.

If he's saying that all this is too much for him, he needs to snap out of it and do what has to be done—just as he undoubtedly manages to do at various other points during his day to handle his work life and his recovery. If he can do it in other contexts, he can do it for your relationship and your family.

No Cheating

It may seem that stating a "No Infidelity" rule is too obvious to mention, but we don't think so. We live in a society where people often make light of affairs, and where all kinds of excuses for cheating are accepted by friends and family ("I was under tremendous stress"/"We were drifting apart, our relationship was crumbling"/"She was being cold to me and we hadn't had sex in a long time"/"I was drinking too much and didn't know what I was doing"/"My urges carried me away," and a host of others). The reality is that infidelity is profoundly hurtful. Selfish or self-centered people are far more likely than others to cheat, but they are also the most adept at making their infidelity sound like the other person's fault—like they were driven to it, in other words.

A corollary of the "No Cheating" rule is that if he had any affairs or inappropriate contact with other people during his destructive years, he has to reveal those *now* (unless you don't want to know about them). He can't come in a year or two from now and say, "I didn't have the courage to tell you, but the truth is . . . etc." You are entitled to have that information right away, for multiple reasons. One, it could have an impact on the difficult decision of whether to stay with him and invest more time or not. Second, you need to focus on your own healing, so you can't afford to be broadsided with more emotional injury down the road when you are finally feeling okay again. Third, if he doesn't come clean now, he's not serious about dealing with himself. Last, you need information about your possible exposure to STDs from him.

Now, what if you had an affair during his destructive phase? You need to come out with it, too, if you feel you safely can. (And if it isn't safe to tell him, then you aren't in a safe relationship.) You owe it to yourself not to live with the secrecy. Besides, seeing how he deals with the news over the months ahead will give you further information about his growth.

Does he have the right to be angry and upset about infidelity on your part? Not if you were living in fear of him; people who are trapped in relationships by danger sometimes have affairs to get some affection. But unless you have faced this kind of serious abuse from him, yes, you should acknowledge the wrong of your affair and be answerable about it. But he can't take up a lot of space right now with his feelings of hurt and rejection, because he has to stay focused on working diligently on his own change and on understanding how his actions have harmed you.

Physical Intimacy Needs to Progress

With occasional exceptions (meaning cases where neither partner finds it important), sexuality and other physical intimacy are central to a successful relationship. However, in a relationship with a history of abuse, cheating, addiction, or other violations of trust and commitment by one partner, building a healthy, satisfying sexual relationship is a loaded process. You may need quite a while for your partner to earn back your trust before you will even feel like being touched by him. If he has been violent or threatening, and all the more if any of those behaviors have been connected to sex, you will be struggling to figure out whether sexual contact with him is safe for you, emotionally and physically. He may be demanding or pressuring regarding sex, which will just push you further away. If he has a long history of selfish or addicted behavior, he may have been too self-involved or macho to ever learn properly how to make love to a woman in a sensual and caring way that could satisfy her. As with so many aspects of life, he may have to start learning at the beginning, correcting his years of stunted growth.

So when we say, "Physical intimacy needs to progress," we don't mean that you should move any faster than you are ready to—in fact, *he* needs to make the necessary changes in himself to make him trustworthy and sexually appealing to you again.

We often observe, however, that the destructive man is the one holding back from sexuality and intimacy, not his partner. Some of the issues we see go on with him (including a couple of points we discussed in earlier chapters) are:

- He still wants to punish you, even if he denies it.
- He's afraid of intimacy and of making a full commitment to the relationship, so now that he doesn't have alcohol or abusiveness or personality disorder to hide behind, he finds sexuality frightening.
- He has never learned how to relate to a woman as an equal and as a respected partner, so sexuality on an equal basis makes him very uncomfortable.
- He has sexual issues, perhaps related to his own experiences of trauma or abuse, which he has been avoiding dealing with.

None of these obstacles, whether on your end or on his, can be magically removed. But they need to be on the table where they can be talked about openly. He can't just be ducking the issue; nor can he be doing the opposite, pressuring and badgering you about it. He has to be working on open, caring communication—meaning that he discusses his own feelings without blaming you and that he listens carefully and thoughtfully as you express what goes on for you (which may indeed include some blame, given his history of destructive behavior toward you). And he needs to take responsibility for getting help for himself if his own emotional or sexual injuries are creating a block; you can certainly be supportive about pain and trauma that he may carry sexually, but he needs to be taking action toward making intimacy work.

HE NEEDS TO PRACTICE HIS CHANGE WITH OTHER PEOPLE

Although we care above all about how your partner changes the way he relates to you, that work is not entirely distinct from his need to develop new habits with everyone. If, for example, he has patterns of harshly criticizing other people and finding fault with them, those behaviors are going to keep triggering your memories of how he has been toward you. So he needs to pay attention in all situations to being more patient and less hostile with people, to taking a more sympathetic view of them rather than assuming the worst, to listening better, and to keeping himself calm and nonexplosive. If you have children, these changes in him will also be important to helping your kids feel safe with him.

He also needs to watch how he talks to other people about his past so that he's practicing owning his issues. If he says to friends or relatives, "I used to drink too much sometimes," or "I should have been nicer to my wife," he's still covering himself. He needs to get honest and say, "I'm an alcoholic and I've stopped drinking," or "I've been really abusive to my wife and I've got serious work to do on changing."

KEEPING YOURSELF ON TRACK

The principles at the beginning of Chapter 5 can help to keep a relationship on track while it is recovering from the destructive actions of one partner. You might benefit from going back over them from time to time, both to help in assessing your partner's behavior and in working on your own. (Chapter 5 was about abuse, but the principles fit all the kinds of relationship issues that this book is about.)

A FINAL THOUGHT

Practicing the concepts we have covered in this chapter won't guarantee that your partner's changes will go deep enough and will last, nor will it necessarily stop you from deciding one day that this relationship just isn't right for you.

But if your relationship does turn out to be savable, this is how you will find out.

EXERCISE 16–1:

Did you find it a relief to learn any of the principles in this chapter? Which ones? Write some about how reading these affected you.

Which principles do you think will be the hardest for your partner to follow? Are any of them hard for you to agree to?

EXERCISE 16–2 (TO DO TOGETHER WITH YOUR PARTNER IF YOU FEEL COMFORTABLE):

Go through the principles in this chapter, and see how many of them your partner is willing to agree to follow. Then make an agreement in writing about those points, and make a copy for each of you.

EXERCISE 16–3:

If your partner is refusing to agree to follow any of these principles, how does that make you feel? What do you think you might do about it, if anything? Does it affect your view of the chances for your relationship?

SEVENTEEN

How to Know When It's Time to Go

"What if I leave and it's the wrong thing to do?"

"I still love him. Isn't that enough? Isn't that the most important thing?"

"As long as he's changing and things are moving forward, I should be with him . . . right?"

S HANA HAD BEEN thinking long and hard about leaving Carlos. She had tried everything in this book, and more. Nothing had changed for two years. She watched her son playing and thought about how she wanted him to have a father. It wasn't even that she wanted Carlos in particular as a role model for her son; it was that she wanted somebody good to be his father. Shana puzzled for a long time until she came to the conclusion that for her, change was really hard.

Shana was playing on the floor with her son one day, and she thought how good it would be to see her own world from her child's eyes for a moment.

"Honey," she said to her son, "what do *you* think is the hardest thing about changing?"

Her son held his blocks for a moment in thought, until he had the answer for his mommy:

"When your feet get stuck in your pants leg."

Shana laughed and so did her son, though her son was laughing because Mommy was laughing and life is good when Mommy is laughing with him.

Shana's son was right. Changing is hard, and hardest when you can't get out of what you are in—which means you can't get into whatever is coming next. You have numerous things in the balance to weigh when deciding if you have had enough of your relationship and that it is time to go. In this chapter, we have gathered for you the insights that women who have successfully left unhealthy relationships have taught us about finally leaving. Each one of these suggestions has a very important requirement:

It must be as safe as possible for you. Safety is first.

It Is Time to Go When . . .

REASON #1: When the Only Thing You Are Waiting for Is for Your Loving Feelings to Go Away

This one applies to you if you have already accepted that your partner is not a good partner for you, he is not changing, and you don't feel that it will work even after all you have tried. It is natural for you to still have some loving feelings for him, or even to still care about him deeply. But the presence of these feelings can be confusing, and you may be wondering whether it really makes sense to end things before your love has completely faded.

In a healthy relationship where you are struggling, loving feelings would be a sign to stay, to keep working. When the dynamics between two partners are fundamentally sound, periods of conflict can be stressful but ultimately both people do some growing and adjusting. As we discussed in Chapter 1, commitments are reevaluated and renewed over time, periods of romance come back around, and struggles grow and change rather than always being about the same thing. But with the kinds of patterns we have described in this book, you have to go by what your "gut" is telling you, because your feelings could keep you trapped for years in a relationship that is not progressing, and where you are not getting what you deserve. If you have accepted that it is time to go, it is. Don't wait for loving feelings to go away.

You can love him for the rest of your life—you might—but not as his partner. You can always hold love for him and hope (or pray, if you do this) that he will grow and heal. It's okay to go, and go with love in your heart.

REASON #2: When You Do Not Recognize Yourself Anymore

This reason applies when your relationship has caused you to lose your sense of personal direction, your sense of who you are. When you have lost track of your values, your humor, and your hopes to the degree that standing back and looking at yourself, you do not recognize the person you know yourself to be inside, it's time to go. We're not talking about feeling off center and working back to yourself from a core that feels a little compromised; we're talking about when you have to work long and hard to remember and feel who you are at all. If you have become that much of a stranger to yourself, it's okay to choose to go. You are choosing to love yourself. Loving yourself helps everyone, not just you.

REASON #3: When You Don't Feel Love for Him and It's Not Coming Back

"It was as though there was a door to love between us. He kept slamming it closed when he'd act that way, and I kept opening it. I kept talking, working, pleading, asking, crying, trying. I kept opening that door to love. One day I reached out, and there was no handle on the door. It was just gone." If this is how you feel, do not feel guilty. It is your deep intuition speaking to you loud and clear. Respect your own sense of what it means to be loving; it *is* loving to walk away—loving toward yourself and loving toward the world. And in truth, it is even loving toward your partner; staying with someone who isn't willing to take the steps to get well doesn't help him. Perhaps losing you will be what finally gets him unstuck, and he'll live a better life as a result.

REASON #4: When He Uses Any Physical or Sexual Violence Toward You (Including Threats)

You have absolutely no obligation toward a partner who has been violent toward you physically or sexually (or who has used any method to force you to have sex, even if his method was not a violent one). You don't have to muster the desire to work with him on fixing these things if he has assaulted you; you can just go whenever you wish to, knowing you've given more than anyone has the right to ask you to give. You did more than enough. You tried hard enough.

REASON #5: When You Just Don't Want to Do It Anymore, Not Even "for the Kids"

We don't take your commitment lightly; we understand that you've committed yourself deeply to this relationship. We also know that women in destructive relationships work so hard and endure so much that if you finally reach the place of not wanting to do it, it's okay to honor that. This is not the same as simply not wanting to work hard on a healthy relationship; good relationships take work, but destructive relationships take everything. It's not supposed to be like that. It is okay to stop.

REASON #6: When He Breaks His Safety Commitments During the Change Process

After your partner has committed to and begun the process of change, and you have both clarified your expectations for the new phase, it is important to leave if he does any of the following (if you can leave safely):

- He hurts you.
- He threatens to kill himself.
- He breaks his plan to manage himself and then refuses to do the backup plan, too (see Chapter 11).
- He cheats on you.

Note that we aren't saying he has to be perfect as he works to change; of course he won't be. But a certain level of cruel and selfish behavior, and any decision on his part to refuse to be answerable for his actions, have to be made completely out of the question. It can be especially devastating to have one of the kinds of destructive behaviors rear its ugly head following a period when he had been doing a lot better and you were starting to let your guard down.

If this happens to you, it's important to get really good emotional support from a trusted friend or a counselor so that you can ride through the shock of it and come out the other end on your feet.

REASON #7: When You Have Lost All Sexual Attraction to Him

If it is important to you to have a sexually joyful life with a man, and you *do* have sexual feelings but you aren't feeling them at all toward your partner anymore, then this relationship is not going to work. It is possible for some people to have happy, emotionally intimate relationships with little or no sexuality *if that is satisfying to them,* but it won't work for someone to whom sexuality is a key need.

If there are reasons unrelated to your partner why you are in a time of not having much sexual interest—if, for example, you are recovering from damage to your positive sexual identity that was caused by earlier experiences—that is another matter. This is a common struggle for women (and for a fair number of men). This can be addressed carefully through "trauma-informed" therapies if you are interested in pursuing that kind of help.

(Also, we discussed earlier what it would take to repair a relationship sexually after being humiliated through affairs or sexual mistreatment by your partner. That is another challenge altogether.)

In short, if you come to find that you simply are not attracted to your partner—or perhaps even realize that you never have been—it is okay to choose not to be in the relationship for this reason; in fact, it makes sense to do so. A happy woman lives connected to her instincts. Listen to them.

REASON #8: When You Are Only Staying Because You Feel You Owe It to Him

You naturally want the best for your partner; you have had times of being close to him, you have probably had glimpses deep into him, you know about his history, his hurts, and his longings. You want him to be well.

At the same time, we want to keep asking you what you want for *yourself.* You deserve to be cherished, to feel loved and supported in your partnership. You give these things and you deserve them back. It is imperative that you live well.

We appreciate your compassion for your partner, and the weight you carry of concern about whether he is going to be okay (and all the more so if he has harmed himself or spoken suicidally in the past). Compassion is beautiful. Connected to your wisdom, it is a great source of healing. However, you are not with a client or at work on a project, you are sharing your life and giving your precious time. We don't want to see you martyr yourself to be there for a man who is not doing a good job of being there for you. It wouldn't be good for you, and it wouldn't be good for the world. You can remain concerned and compassionate, yet still give up the partnership when you can tell it isn't going to move forward. If the only reason left for your staying is out of compassion, and you can tell that a mutually strengthening relationship is not where this one is headed, it's time to go.

So choose authentically and from your instincts, drawing upon your deeper wisdom. It does not serve either of you for you to stay in a relationship that is not working for you out of a sense that you owe him.

(A note: If your partner is struggling with a prolonged physical illness or disability, the decision to leave can be even harder, since you worry about who will take care of him. If you were in a relationship where your partner was fundamentally kind and committed to you, standing by him through a long health challenge could be a transformative and deepening experience for your love. But where you are being repeatedly torn down or treated coldly, you have the right to let your caretaking job go and move on with your life when you feel deeply that it's time.)

REASON #9: When You Have Tried Everything in This Book and He Still Isn't Living by the Principles of a Healthy Relationship (See Chapter 5)

Let's say you've gone through all the steps: you've done the separation, you made your bottom lines clear, you gave him the exercises to read from the Web site. Maybe even he got some help, or got sober, or made some changes. But he still talks down to you, or gets bent out of shape if you don't do things in exactly the "right" way, or blames you for his problems. Look at how much you have already given. Look through the book at your goals, the impact this process has had on you, the life and hope and dreams that you still have. You deserve them. It's okay to move into your future, into the life that awaits you.

REASON #10: When You've Told Him That If He Does a Certain Thing You Will End the Relationship, and He Does It

If you have given him a warning about where your absolute limits are, and he has violated those, it's essential for you to keep your word. If you have said things such as:

> *"The next time you take a drink, our relationship is over."*
> *"If you ever raise a hand to me again, you'll never get me back."*
> *"I'm not putting up with your secret flirtations with women, and I'm done the next time that happens."*
> *"You stay in therapy or I go."*

. . . then, just like the parent of a two-year-old, you have to follow through. Your partner has to learn that a relationship is not a game, nor is it a power struggle; he has to absolutely and unconditionally respect his partner's boundaries and limits. His thinking may have been "Well, she said she'd leave me if I bought any more coke, but she won't really do it." And as long as he thinks that way, he'll stay stuck in his same ruts.

And, perhaps more importantly, you owe it to yourself to do what you promised you would do.

EXERCISE 17–1:

This might help you decide. Read the statements below one at a time, and take a moment to notice your immediate reaction. Are you relieved? Panicked?

> *"We think it's better for you to stay with your partner."*
> *"We think it is better for you to leave your partner."*

GIVE ME COURAGE—BUT NOT YET

If you are reading this and feeling a sense of recognition that it is time to go after all, you might not want to admit it. It takes a lot of bravery to look right at the truth of your situation. We remind you that you are still in charge of your own process. You still make your own decisions on your own timetable.

Sometimes it is hard to look at what you know to be true because it seems that you will not be able to face the overwhelming sadness of it. These kinds of sad feelings seem like they will never go away. It seems like life as you know it will end. That might be true—life as you know it might end. But you will go on and the sadness and grief will change over time. You will heal and be well once more. You can trust in what your insights show you. You can trust that a way forward will unfold for you. The efforts you put forth will open new choices. You will change and see things differently. You will see options you didn't see before. And you will have love in your life, first from loving and supportive friends, and eventually from a new partner.

When you make your choice to leave in these circumstances, inner resources will unfurl in you. New supports and opportunities will appear for you. Your future will be rearranged. Have courage.

RELIEF

It's okay to feel relief, too. It may come with a mixture of sadness and grief, but you also might just plain feel relieved, and that's okay. It is a relief to see what is true for you. You are touching your authentic self, and from this place come authentic grief and relief. Even authentic pain feels less hurtful than confusion from not feeling what is true for you.

This kind of courage leads to a life of authentic joy. That is what lies ahead for you, beyond the immediate pains of knowing what is true, of knowing when to go.

PART V

LIFE BEYOND

EIGHTEEN

Entering Freedom After a Destructive Relationship

"I'll tell you what I've learned from all of this: I am a woman who is very hard to confuse about things."

"I turned on my radio station. That was the first thing I did when I left!"

"I'm afraid if I start to cry about it all, I'll never stop."

Y OU ARE LEAVING. We are so sorry. And, congratulations!
Leaving brings a mixture of pain and hope. It moves you forward into a new life. In this chapter, we will help you plan for the life you are beginning, weaving in exercises and guidance about the grieving, planning, building, and rejoicing you will do as you move forward.

CONGRATULATIONS!

Leaving means creating a new container for your life that is built on the celebration of your many strengths and qualities. You are courageous! Only someone who has walked in your shoes knows just how hard a thing it is that you have done. You have entered the league of women who have embraced their own well-being. You have listened to your deep instincts, read the misleading, confounding, and confusing signs, taken into account the many practical and emotional factors, and have made your decision to move forward into a fuller and more nurturing life ahead. Well done.

Let's start reaping the benefits of your new perspective so that you can be sure to enter your new life strengthened by your insight. We will be asking you to create a new environment that specifically reflects your new wisdom, and that honors all of your gifts. Let's first remind you of who you are.

EXERCISE 18–1: YOUR RADIANCE

Take some time to write about the thoughtful, humorous, and loving things that you did and gave in your relationship. We are not reviewing these in order to find evidence of love in your past relationship, but rather:

We wish to celebrate what you brought and what you gave because these gifts and loving attributes are *yours*.

You may have been inspired by your feelings of attachment or love to act them out, but every loving and generous thought, every act of kindness, still exists for you in its own perfect radiance. Your loving heart is filled with the good you have given. Now, in your grief and reflection, your generous gifts are there for you to harvest, for yourself.

Make a list of loving and kind things you did in your relationship.

We want you to spend this next year reclaiming your awareness of the many gifts you brought to the table so that you feel how giving and creative, compassionate and kind, you are. We want you to see your gifts because it is so easy to lose sight of them when you leave your relationship.

Remember:

You are still "a good deal" to be in relationship with.

EXERCISE 18–2: HARVESTING YOUR WISDOM

1. In the beginning of everything are the seeds of its end. Let's look at how your relationship started. What moments of meeting and starting come to mind? Write about them.

2. When you look at them, is there anything in those moments, or ones that come soon after, that show you the seeds of the end of the relationship?

3. Keeping in mind your decision to leave the relationship, what is it that you would have wanted to have known at the start? Specifically, what events have meaning for you now in a way they did not then? What do you see about these events now that you have had so much more information to go on? In a loving way, that reaffirms your worth, what do you have to say to yourself now that you look at the beginning of your relationship?

4. What are the lessons about your relationship that you need to keep in mind as you leave it?

HONORING YOUR LOSS

We are sorry about the end of your relationship. We are sorry because leaving a relationship is always painful, and there is unique pain that comes from leaving an unhealthy relationship. Unlike the many people who leave a relationship when they realize they have nothing in common, or that they are no longer attracted to each other, or that they have grown apart, or that they simply don't like each other, when you leave an abusive, addicted, or emotionally unwell partner, you tend to face a more powerful set of emotions. You may well have to, for example, come to terms with leaving someone to whom you are still attracted, with whom you had much in common, and to whom you felt very bonded or connected when he was not destroying himself or being mean to you. This means having to say good-bye to much that you liked, were attracted to, or felt so connected to. We want to support you in grieving those losses.

Planning for Grief

Your emotional well-being is in your own good hands. This means you will need to embrace and structure time for grieving. Now that you have decided to go, let's make room for grief by naming some of the many things to grieve in leaving a destructive relationship.

We know that a relationship that has been so troublesome can lead your friends and family to offer a form of support that isn't really helpful, however well meaning it may be. It often goes something like this: "Thank goodness you left the bastard; now you can move on!" Just weeks later they may already be saying, "Are you still dwelling on the past? It's over!"

But that's not how grieving a destructive relationship works.

We know that there are many losses to grieve, and that there is much wisdom for you in this pain. We suggest that you plan for a year of grieving. It might take you shorter or longer, but we ask that you plan for support from a couple of trusted friends, or find wider support through a group for women recovering from abusive relationships, or Al-Anon, or a therapist, or a spiritual leader to help you through each of the four seasons of the year following your leaving. Planning for this as you get ready to go can make the entire journey not only more manageable, but fruitful and loving.

EXERCISE 18–3: NAMING WHAT HELPS

Circle the statements that feel most right for you, that you would most like to hear from other people.

"We are sorry that he wouldn't change."

"We are sorry that he threw it all away."

"We are sorry that he wouldn't step up, that he refused to 'man up.'"

"We are sorry that he decided he didn't want to go through all that work and that he chose what he knew already rather than risk a new way of being."

"We are sorry that he couldn't go any faster, or do any better."

"We are sorry that he can't offer to continue the lovely moments that you shared, because he is unreliable or unsafe."

EXERCISE 18–4: YOUR NEW ENVIRONMENT

Let's make a plan for what your new place will be like. Whether you decide to take advantage of a shelter, or you are renting a room, or buying a new home for yourself, or staying where you have been living but filling in the gaps that your partner's departure leaves, you will be creating a new container to nurture the beginning of the next part of your life.

First, what are you getting rid of? Have fun with this. Is there music, a certain chair, a game or a show that you know you are *not* having in your new place? Are there routines that you will no longer be oppressed by? What are they? Before we find out what it will look like, let's declare what it *won't* have in it:

1. Create a "NOT Happening" list.

   Now let's look at what your life *will* have in it, beginning with:

2. After researching your options for a physical place to go (if you need to move), what looks like it might be the best option?

3. Write below what you want for yourself in this space—what are your hopes for what your experience in it will be like?

4. What do you need to do to make it this way?

You deserve this beginning. All the energy and time you have committed toward someone else's well-being you deserve for yourself. You deserve a chance to feel filled up and hopeful again. You deserve the time to see what happens when you devote your energy to things that are fruitful. You deserve real intimacy and love.

5. What commitments can you make to yourself regarding the following:

   Care for your body
   Fun!

Connecting to Others

Feeding Your Spirit

Creativity

Grieving

Celebrating

Money

Nourishing the Children (if this applies to you)

This Was Not the One for You

You can grieve the lost hope that this was the nurturing partnership that was going to bring joy, companionship, and connection to your life. You have already lost the joy, healthy companionship and connection, but the loss of the *hope* that it will finally come to fruition, after you have invested so much, can be devastating.

But know that you are now free to find the joy that you seek. Your hope can slowly come alive again.

Having His Children

Leaving is the time for some women to grieve the hopes for bearing children with this partner. This may be a hope that your partner held out for you in his moments of well-being, and that promise of a deeply desired motherhood can be a viselike bond now. Leaving means grieving the loss of the image of the motherhood you thought you would have.

However, you have the chance to make this dream a reality in some way. There are many ways to have a family and to be a loving mother that are not limited to the one dream you had. You are only at the beginning of these new possibilities.

If you did have children with your partner, it is time to grieve the loss of the family life you thought you were going to have together. You won't get back those years and those significant turning points in the growth of the family. You won't have the supportive family life and shared parenting that you longed for. Your path will be harder than you'd hoped when you dreamed that family life would heal his wounds and adjust his beliefs and attitudes. We understand that you may be hurting as you think about the years you won't get back, and the milestones you won't get to share together in the future.

But please realize that through this relationship you have learned much and that your knowledge will be invaluable to your children. They will benefit from your understanding and skill in navigating their father's destructiveness. You will stand out as the other voice, the other way to exist in the world.

If your partner uses your children as a tool to continue his manipulation and cruelty toward you, you may have to struggle with him about their needs and interests for years to come. If, for example, you think there's any possibility that he will use legal action against you for custody, it's important to prepare yourself for that. (See the Child Custody section in "Resources" in the back of this book.)

It is a painful struggle, yet it is possible to maintain your own clarity, to enlist the right supports on your behalf, and to prevail. You will need emotional care and strategic care to address this. If this is your situation, please seek out regular support from the resources we've listed to help you grieve your feelings.

Releasing the Self-Destructive Partner

If your partner has been self-destructive, you can grieve the illusion of keeping him safe. Your staying may have held the ruinous momentum in abeyance, but it did not stop it. For some women, this moment of leaving can feel almost as if she is the one destroying him. Your grief is traumatic, since it is intertwined with cruelty and suicidal threats as your punishment for choosing loving health over impossible constriction.

You have to remember that you are not destroying him, nor is your leaving what causes his destruction. Your well-being formed a levee, but you know the levee was breaking and that the force of the pernicious and ocean-size pressures was straining against you all along. When you walk the way of health and abandon an annihilative path, it is a gift to everyone. Though it doesn't feel like it, it is a gift to the self-destructive person whose damaging choices you are leaving behind. We want you to know that this is not your fault (even if you seem to be the last supportive person standing between your loved one and death). You left because it was destroying your sense of love and wellness. Above all, that sense must be restored.

The Loss of You in Relationship

It is hard to let go of the loving way that you can be in a relationship. You miss all the creativity and energy that you bring in forming your coupledom.

However, there is great hope in this form of grief, because you can recapture that spirit of you for yourself. This kind of creativity may be inspired by being in relationship with someone, yet it is still your caring and thoughtfulness.

Wisdom Where Innocence Once Lived

You can grieve the loss of your innocence. If you are leaving a physically abusive partner, for example, you once were the woman who did not know what it was to look into the face of someone who knew he was causing you great harm and continued to do so anyway. How could he be so removed from your humanity that he would not hesitate to smash it? And for many women, the failure of police protection and intervention, the failure of prosecutorial effectiveness, and the lack of judicial insight are as deep a wounding as those inflicted by the abusive partner himself. Some women are betrayed by therapists who view them from a detached and mildly contemptuous stance, labeling them as "fixated" or "complicitous," missing the treacherous and inhumane barriers they must navigate.

We won't lose sight of the strengths you have gained. We plan to help you see and celebrate them. However, we want you to process your grief successfully along the way, because these suppressed and unrecognized pains can overwhelm you and confuse you, slowing your progress. We want you to know about your losses, and experience them, a little at a time, so that you will experience your transition with more love.

Once you see these patterns clearly, you will not be fooled by them in the same way. You will be keenly aware of misuses of power. You will spot manipulation a mile away. You will know what people are capable of and how they hide it. Once you integrate what you know, you will become a resource to others as well. You will have gained a keen ear for minimizing, denying, blaming, and distracting from clarity. You will spot the avoiding of accountability, the aggressive man who plays the role of victim, the shifting of blame onto the woman. You will be able to name it when someone denies the context in which something happened and why that matters, and any manner of discord between what is said and what is done. If his actions don't at all line up with what he preaches, you'll know it. These abilities will be resources that make you incredibly effective in sorting people out in your work and social settings. You may find you notice these behaviors and can name them in situations where others also feel uncomfortable about the person's behavior but can't put their fingers on why. You earned these skills.

OUTRAGE

Allow yourself the beautiful and clear sense of outrage for the injustices you have experienced. If your partner was abusive, holding attitudes that justified cruelty or violation toward you, if he persisted in sexual and emotional betrayals, if he stole from you, or put your children in jeopardy, or any host of assaults on your rights as a dignified human being, you have the right to sustain an appropriate sense of outrage.

Since you may react particularly strongly to these echoes of your destructive relationship in your first year apart, we recommend using your sense of outrage as a sign to *disengage* from dynamics that may repeat, even in a small way, what you are in the midst of healing from. A year from now it may still irritate you when, for example, a work colleague undercuts you in a conflict, and then ducks the subject afterward and acts like you are being unfairly attacking for bringing up what happened. But this same interaction might well affect you much more negatively now; you may respond with an outsize anger, since your colleague is triggering twisted maneuvers your partner used to pull. We want both to support your well-honed sense of injustice, and to caution you about how you respond while you are still freshly recovering from the very long injurious period you are overcoming.

HOW TO LEAVE SAFELY

Leaving safely requires knowledge of your partner's style of destructiveness, which you have. Following each section, we will give you some questions for you to use as a guide to map out your approach.

Leaving in Stages

Some women leave many times before they finally feel "done." Each time they leave, the reason why they are leaving becomes clearer. Leaving can help you experience relief from the constant pressure of being in the destructive relationship. Some women know they are leaving for good, but they need to tell themselves that they are leaving to "take a break." We encourage you to take this break and do the same grieving and celebrating work that you would do if you were certain you were leaving for good. Clarity, strength, and support cannot hurt you.

1. If you imagine yourself taking a break, how does this make you feel?
2. What do you think the break will lead to? Do you have any intuitive sense, having done the explorations in the earlier parts of this book?

Safety Through Appeasement

Some women with violent or destructive partners find that temporary appeasement—appearing to give him what he wants—is the way to safely leave the relationship. Just as some women find it soothing to take a "temporary" break as a way to come to terms with leaving for good, some of their abusive partners do, too.

"I told him I'm just taking a break, and that I found a place, and that I'm not leaving him, but just taking a break to get my head together for a while and that we'll see," says Sophie, who is planning on not returning.

This might strike some of you as indirect and manipulative. But Sophie knows her husband, who is actively using substances and is abusive to her. She knows that if she is very soft-spoken, gentle, and loving while removing her items, telling him she'll continue to pay his car insurance, she will avoid having him destroy all of her belongings and physically attack or viciously harangue her. She is not interested in pursuing divorce immediately, but she is certain that she cannot live the way she is living now, and she is interested in focusing on her own growth.

EXERCISE 18–4:

1. What is your intuitive sense of how your partner would respond to an approach like this?

2. How would he respond once you have let him know from a distance that you feel you would like to make the separation permanent?

Legal Protections

Many women with abusive husbands seek orders of protection as part of their strategy for leaving. However, a piece of paper has its limitations. Enforcement of the protection might be difficult and dangerous if police response times are lengthy or if the perpetrator is armed and dangerous. You might have a sense of whether an order would just enrage him further or if it would be something that would restrain him while you left. You must weigh the risks, considering if the order might help your children or work against you as you seek custody of your children (because some family court judges retaliate against mothers whom they perceive as "just getting the protective order to strengthen her position in the divorce").

Secrecy

Some women read about leaving and panic. They know that any hint of leaving is what inspires their abusive partner to act on his mentality of ownership and violence. This style of man feels justified in harming you, your property, your friends and family, and your reputation if he suspects you are moving apart. Women in this situation employ a number of strategies, such as creating a cover story so that they might arrange for a secret getaway.

Some women use their break time at work to turn their desks briefly into a headquarters for planning to leave (although many abusers continue their harassment and monitoring of women even while they are at work).

Other women feign joining a gym or some kind of women's circle and use that dedicated time to make phone calls on a disposable cell phone that will ensure no bill goes to the home.

Sometimes it is easier to call and order original copies of birth certificates, a marriage license, or children's medical and dental records than it is to find them in the house, remove them, and copy them. Financial records often pose a problem, though women do report that partners with substance issues are more predictably absent for longer periods and remain unfocused at home for sufficient periods that finding and keeping records to copy is less of a problem. (For more guidance on strategies for fleeing safely, we recommend that you use the book *Getting Free* by Ginny NiCarthy.)

EXERCISE 18–5:

1. What is at risk for you when you consider secrecy in leaving?

2. How do you know this?

3. What has he done or said that leads you to feel this way?

Distract Him

"When we first got together, he used to work long periods on the road driving a truck. He stopped doing that so that we could be more of a family. I've started to encourage him, really gently, to check out opportunities for driving, saying I know how unhappy he is with his job. He seems really interested. I want him to go back to it. I know him. Once he's got something else in mind, everyone else be damned. It'll be easier to leave him if he has something else to focus on, and if he's away for several days at a time," Tamara explains.

Maria used the same approach with her partner who had been with the merchant marines. Sonya did it with her partner who used to make more money working the third shift at a correctional facility. All three of these women encouraged their partners to absorb themselves in the work they used to do before becoming a couple with the plan to use the extended periods away to research their resources for planning to leave, and to ease his focus on her.

EXERCISE 18–6:

Is there something of these women's experience that resonates with your situation? If so, what might you try?

Public Persona

Some partners think very highly of themselves and care about their reputations as reasonable people. If they have emotional disturbances or personality issues, are dealing with trauma themselves, or simply are concealing their violent side, they are often invested in not having outsiders find out. For these partners, a strategy that includes lots of witnesses can work well when you are leaving. This can include having conversations in front of a third party, removing items with friends and neighbors present, and eliminating one-to-one contact during the time you are separating.

EXERCISE 18–7:

What friend or neighbors or others could you ask to help you manage the leaving process safely?

Money

Part of planning to leave means understanding your financial situation. Knowing you have a destructive relationship means that you might have a daunting time coming to terms with the state of your finances, which may have suffered from your partner's selfishness or irresponsibility.

Even if you are awarded a settlement by the courts through a divorce decree or separation agreement, the early stages can still be a period of upheaval and uncertainty financially, and your job performance may have been suffering because of your stressful home life and the extra pressures of trying to figure out how to leave. Think carefully about what you will need to manage the transition out. By thinking through your financial plan carefully, you will make yourself safer as well as increase you self-confidence.

Knowing what you are fighting for—the freedom and joys of being without a destructive force in your life—can help mitigate your distractions from your finances. Taking on what it means to care for yourself and not your destructive partner can be very freeing. As one woman said, "I started to realize that if I didn't have to pay for him, I would be able to get by. I don't know why it didn't occur to me before, but I buy all of the groceries and he likes these big, cooked meals. I started filling out the work sheets and realizing that though it takes a lot of money to get through the month, without him I can do it—he costs more than he brings in."

You are making an investment in the heart of you. You are giving yourself a chance to embody some of the ideas of freedom that you may have been considering in your daydreams for years. Think about your personal goals or mission. Include things you don't want to forget about yourself as you begin your new stage:

Congratulations. We believe in you.

NINETEEN

Choosing a New Partner

"Am I destined to end up with another guy who is like him?"

"Do you think I sought out someone with those kinds of issues?"

"How come I can't find a good man?"

"Are there things about him that I might have seen early in our relationship?"

S UCCESS STORIES DON'T create the kind of excitement that crises do; the evening news will rarely show you footage of a job well done, will not feature interviews with people who prevented a problem from ever arising, will not offer a ten-minute report analyzing the question "Why are so many people kind and generous?" As a result, you are unlikely to ever hear about all the women who extricate themselves from a relationship with an unhealthy or abusive man, and then move on to find a partner who is a great guy. But we meet these women all the time in our work.

You may feel discouraged by all the beliefs that are widely circulated claiming that women who find themselves with a destructive partner have some predilection in that direction and are likely to choose the same kind of man again. Worries about what will happen next time around are among the most common anxieties that women bring to us in sharing their experiences of leaving bad relationships. So let us say it loudly and clearly: *You are not fated to stumble into another unhealthy relationship.* You have the power to take what you have learned from love gone awry and apply it to taking charge of how your next relationship goes.

Preparing yourself to avoid trouble with your next partner involves the following pieces:

- looking carefully at ways society may have misled you into looking in the wrong places for love
- learning the qualities to look for in a new partner
- learning the characteristics to *avoid* in a new partner

In the pages ahead, we will take you point by point through the information you need to have in order to recognize a healthy partner—or an unhealthy partner—when you see one so that nothing has to be left up to fate. (And in the following two chapters you will learn approaches to strengthening yourself and to zeroing in on what you really want, making it even harder for a destructive person to draw you in.)

Examining What You Have Been Trained to Want

Movies, music videos, and pop songs are full of images of women falling madly in love with perfect men, and life is blissful from then on. It's easy, it's magical, and it solves all problems. And it isn't real. Back in Chapter 1, we looked at the Healthy Relationship Cycle, showing that while romance and thrills make a great beginning, lasting fulfillment only comes to those who are prepared to work hard on growth and communication. The initial magic of falling in love, as enjoyable as it can be, cannot by itself carry a couple through the years. There is simply no substitute for mature, respectful, and courageous relationship building.

Now it's time to look at another reason why we're concerned about "suddenly finding true love" images that are all around us: They can trick you into choosing the wrong partner in the first place. Consider the following list of qualities that many women have been conditioned by advertising and by other social messages to feel turned on by:

- a man who is suave and charming
- a man who brings romance and sexuality into the interaction right from the start
- a man who is emotionally mysterious, perhaps even seeming a little troubled, and who will need to be "brought out" to get him to open up about his feelings
- a man who is very masculine, decisively taking charge of things and afraid of nothing
- a man who drinks (which is portrayed as the gateway to having a good time)

You might think that this is a good list because you can use it to eliminate a lot of guys who might be boring or socially inept or unsexy, but you will also eliminate most of the best men, including many of the most lively, fun, and sexy ones. When you look closely at these thoughts, you'll discover they're not all that they're cracked up to be.

Charm, Instant Romance, and Instant Sexuality

It takes a lot of effort over a long period of time to develop a smooth, charming exterior, with just the right manners, the suggestive glint in the eye, the perfect phrase ready on the tongue, and the outfit to match. Who is going to work this hard developing what we might call "makeup for the personality"? Unfortunately, the answer is that it is often someone with a lot to hide—that's why he's willing to put so much of his energy into creating his cover. And what he is hiding is often a problem with addiction, with abusiveness, or with "womanizing" (meaning that he likes to keep a lot of women on the hook and play them against one another).

We're not saying that every charmer is bad news. What we do want to draw your attention to, though, is that if you are focused on looking for charm *above all other qualities*, then you are looking for trouble and it's looking for you. To find a satisfying and safe relationship, you have to be willing to look past superficial characteristics to see what kind of substance the person has underneath. And you should look sooner rather than later.

Some men take a little longer to get close to, perhaps because they have less of a suave routine going or perhaps because *they are interested in getting to know you as a friend;* in other words, because they are actually connecting to you as a person. A man of this style may turn out to be quite romantic and sensual, but he doesn't appear that way right from the beginning because he is making a genuine effort to take you in. He's not just playing the pickup game.

And while it can be flattering when a guy lets you know right from the start that he's turned on by you, it can also be a sign that he can't see much else about you.

We're not asking you to give up the thrill and magic, the chemistry, of falling in love. But we do want to see you take a close look at where you are looking for it.

Masculinity, Mystery, and Alcohol

We discussed, back in Chapter 11, the importance of a man examining his thinking regarding what it means to be masculine, especially if he has not been a good relationship partner and wants to become one in the future. Now we want to encourage *you* to reflect some on your outlook on manhood, and on what kind of man you find attractive.

Many of the qualities that are frequently emphasized in our social definition of masculinity are not, in themselves, a problem. If you are drawn to a man who has a strong body, who is athletic, who is self-confident and courageous, you aren't automatically skating onto thin ice. But the risks come when these images become exaggerated or distorted, and start to look like:

- a habit, or even an enjoyment, of intimidating people; a tendency toward aggressiveness or even violence
- a preoccupation with having a rippling body (as opposed to just keeping himself in good shape)
- a determination to show no fear
- a view of females as second class to males and therefore a fear of showing any qualities in himself that could be associated with femininity, such as gentleness or sensitivity
- a view of females as second class to males and therefore an outlook that women's role is to cater to men

- an insistence that any children he raises will need to accept and follow his definition of masculinity (which will make him a serious problem as a father, not only to boys but to girls as well)
- an association between alcohol and masculinity—in other words, he thinks drinking is part of what makes him a man

If you are attracted to very "manly" men, you don't need to change that about yourself; just make sure to stay away from guys that have the kinds of extreme and unhealthy gender views listed above.

The style of guy who comes across as emotionally mysterious, as different as he may seem on the surface from the above characteristics, often turns out to fit in with this unhealthy outlook. His darkness can be a way of making sure that a woman he is dating is focused on figuring him out and helping him open up so that he can always occupy the center of attention. We've seen a fair number of cases where Mr. Mystery later turned out to be a rager, even a scary one, and he would especially tend to pitch his fits when he felt he wasn't being catered to adequately.

Again, we're not saying that every guy who needs some drawing out is a bad catch. The distinction to make is whether the mystery is part of how he wants to be seen, a sort of chosen persona, and whether he is getting power in the relationship out of it. And notice whether he is taking a real interest in you, or if it's always the other way around.

Finally, a man who drinks can seem like tremendous fun, but can be a nightmare down the road. Moderate alcohol use can help some people release trapped energy and overcome inhibitions, but it tips easily into addiction in men who have tendencies in that direction. Beware of the man who can *only* have a good time if he's drinking, and who is in a great hurry to get to his first drink when he gets out of work or as soon as he meets up with you. If the whole basis of his connection with his buddies seems to be drinking together, that's not a good sign either. As we saw in Chapter 3, problems with alcohol tend to get worse, not better, unless the man himself recognizes that he is addicted.

In sum, the above qualities, so heavily promoted in ads for clothing and liquor, so big in romance novels, so well acted out by rock and movie stars, when taken together are actually a recipe for a long downhill slide. You may need to retrain your instincts some.

Some people ask, "But isn't it impossible to change what you find attractive in a man? Isn't that a deep, automatic reaction that is outside of conscious control?" The answer is both "yes" and "no." Yes, in the sense that you are not likely to change the "type" that gets your blood flowing. But also no, because by noticing and thinking about your reactions to people, you can lead yourself to a second response that is almost as automatic as the first. In other words, by monitoring and reflecting on what turns you on, you may find that a man whom you really found attractive at first suddenly starts to appear manipulative, and your feelings fade. And in contrast, a guy who didn't strike you as that thrilling right at the start is suddenly beginning to interest you.

We're not talking about forcing yourself to feel differently—you can't do that—but rather moving a little more slowly and with greater self-awareness, and discovering that your attractions shift in some subtle but important ways just from the increased reflection and attention you are bringing to them.

EXERCISE 19–1:

Write a description of the kind of man you tend to find most attractive. Then put down a few thoughts about whether these preferences have served you well or not. Lastly, what sort of man would you like to increase your openness to?

QUALITIES TO SEEK IN A NEW PARTNER

Now that we've spent some time examining the initial attraction process, let's move to some of the ins and outs of the beginning months of a dating relationship. What can you look for, as your connection with a man begins to grow, to discern whether he is capable of being in a healthy relationship? What qualities should be present, regardless of whether a man is super macho or super mild, into rock music or classical, a PhD or physically skilled, a blue blood or immigrant? While no formula, unfortunately, can work perfectly to steer you out of

The Good Signs

A good listener

Respectful of you

Has relationships with others that have lasted a long time

Can manage his own life

Follows what he preaches

Is respectful of his former partners

Can look at himself

Makes your wishes a priority

the path of a destructive partner—sometimes there's just no way to know until you've been with someone for quite a while—the majority of the time, unhealthy relationships could be avoided if society would equip women with proper information about what to watch for, both good signs and bad ones.

So we'll go with the positive indications first, and then go over the characteristics to sail away from.

A Good Listener

Does he focus well, setting aside distractions, when you are speaking to him? Does he value and remember the thoughts, the issues, the news about your life that you share with him? Or, rather, does he seem half present when you talk, eyes roaming, perhaps slightly bored seeming, and eager to get back to talking about himself?

Respectful of You

Love and respect are not exactly the same thing, at least not as those terms are commonly used. So even if you feel quite sure that the man you are dating loves you, keep asking yourself, "Yes, but does he respect me?" Is he willing to be influenced by your thoughts and opinions, or does he want all the influence in the relationship to go one way (from him to you)? When he is upset or angry, does he express his feelings appropriately, or does he become rude, demeaning, or insulting? Does he take seriously your wishes about intimacy, about how to spend time together, about plans for the future? As we asked earlier in the book, do you feel really *seen* by him, for who you are?

Has Relationships with Others That Have Lasted a Long Time

Look for a man who shows signs of being capable of staying close to someone over a period of years. Does he have any friends (not counting drinking buddies) whom he goes way back with? Does he maintain a close connection with any of his relatives? Have any of his previous intimate relationships (with a girlfriend or wife) lasted a substantial amount of time?

Can Manage His Own Life

You want to be a man's partner, not his mother. So look to see if he keeps his home clean and tidy. Does he have decent food in the refrigerator, or just pizza and beer? Does he get himself to the doctor and the dentist? Does he work (or make serious daily efforts to find work) and keep his finances in reasonable order? It can be tempting to find a man to take care of, but it leads to trouble later.

Follows What He Preaches

The word "integrity" refers not just to a person's honesty, but to the way the different aspects of his or her character fit together into a unified whole. People who do not have a solid ethical center can become unhealthy partners. Watch whether a man you are dating follows the values and beliefs he espouses. Do his views about what's right and wrong change with his moods or with the day of the week? Does he seem to apply double standards, so that actions that he would condemn in others he makes excuses for—or completely accepts—in himself? When he changes one of his opinions, does he then claim that his new stance is actually the one he has always had? Or, alternatively, does he demonstrate consistency, so that he judges everyone equally, including himself, and shows a commitment to living by his values?

Is Respectful of His Former Partners

Pay careful attention to this point, because it is almost entirely overlooked by people as they choose new partners: *it is crucial for a man to demonstrate basic respect and decency in how he talks about all of his former partners.* While it is natural for him to have some anger and resentment toward his past wives or girlfriends—most people have some bad feelings left over from earlier relationships—listen for whether he can talk about those issues in a way that shows that he sees the humanity of these women. The bad sign is when he talks about an ex as if she were a disgusting piece of garbage and as if she were responsible for everything that went wrong in their relationship, and he can't bring himself to say anything positive about her. You want to steer clear of a man who can reduce a woman to such a low level in his mind, because someday he will do this to you.

At the same time, you don't want to have to listen to him idealize any former partners of his, putting you in the position of having to compete or live up to that image. Balance is what we're hoping to see.

Be especially wary of the guy who is battling a former partner for custody of children. Although there are occasionally times when it may be necessary for a man to do so, more often than not custody actions by fathers are driven by desires for revenge, power, and control, and are used to drive wedges between kids and their loving mothers. (Research studies have found that abusive men are twice as likely as other men to fight for custody postseparation.)

Can Look at Himself

You can't have a lasting, intimate relationship with someone who thinks he is perfect. Does he sometimes mention mistakes he has made in the past, or does he pretend there haven't been any? Can he identify some of his own contributions to problems in past relationships of his? Does he show awareness of anything about himself that he needs or wants to work on? Does he have a sense of humor about himself?

Makes Your Wishes a Priority

Here's a tricky area that we would like you to watch thoughtfully in a new partner. On the one hand, you want a man who is able to focus on your needs and wishes, and gets behind your goals and dreams in life. It's important that he take seriously the direction of your life, and not try to make it secondary to his. A capacity for generosity is indispensable for a healthy relationship. On the other hand, it's not a good sign when a dating partner is overly dedicated to catering to you—doing everything exactly the way you want it, constantly asking you whether you're happy, appearing to have no needs of his own. Why is this a problem? Because it is a sure sign either of overdependence or of manipulativeness, either of which will lead to bad dynamics down the road. So even though it may feel great to be waited on hand and foot, don't give in to the temptation.

QUALITIES TO STEER CLEAR OF IN A NEW PARTNER

In the words of Sarah Buel, a law professor who gives lectures about abusive relationships, "When you're growing up as a girl, adults tell you all kinds of things to be careful of: Don't get too cold and catch pneumonia, Don't walk down dark streets, Don't eat too much junk, Don't get too close to the edge of high places. But no one ever says, *'Be careful whom you marry.'* They're overlooking the greatest danger in a girl's life."

Since this is a book about avoiding not just abuse but also a host of other tangles, we are going to encourage you to keep your eyes open for a fair number of warning signs. Above all, though, we want you to listen to your own intuitions. When you find a man attractive, or when you are feeling lonely and especially eager to have a partner, it is easy to convince yourself to overlook indications that a man has unhealthy patterns, disrespectful attitudes, or destructive tendencies. For the information we are offering to be helpful, you have to be prepared to apply these principles and move carefully, even when a guy looks great on the surface.

The Warning Signs

Self-Involvement and Self-Centeredness

Making Lots of Excuses

Making Lots of Promises

Having to Have His Own Way

Jealousy and Possessiveness

He Always Has to Have a Drink, a Toke, or a Snort

People Are Trying to Warn You About Him

He Pressures You

He Is Secretive

Self-Involvement and Self-Centeredness

As we discussed in our early chapters (which by now may seem long ago), a successful relationship depends on both partners' ability to maintain a balance between attending to themselves and focusing on the other person. A relationship that is based on one person doing almost all of the giving and the other being the constant center of attention is destined to be unhealthy. Does he talk on and on about himself? Does he fail to ask you many questions about your life and feelings? Does he forget (or ignore) important details of your life? Is he frequently lost in his own world and uncommunicative? These are signs of *self-involvement*.

A healthy connection also demands that partners have an ability to see themselves through other people's eyes. Does he exaggerate his own goodness and generosity, and perhaps seem taken with what a great person he is? Does he take severe offense when people have complaints or grievances about him? Does he have different rules for his behavior than for yours? If you don't like the way he is talking to you, does he tend to say that you just "took it the wrong way"? Does his generosity—which at times may seem very good—tend to suddenly vanish anytime your needs collide with his? Is he convinced the world is constantly being unfair to him? These are signs of *self-centeredness*.

Making Lots of Excuses

Justifying and excusing behavior is a slippery slope. We all have times when we need to give explanations about things we have done that weren't that great. But excuse making can also become a habit, and it's an especially unfortunate one when the behaviors being whitewashed are ones that have harmed another person. A man who is repeatedly trying to escape responsibility for his actions is one who eventually is going to be hurting you, and he'll be blaming it on his drinking, or on his emotions, or on his childhood, or on you. Look for a man who is prepared to own the choices he makes.

Making Lots of Promises

A guy who is looking for a woman to take care of him, or to take advantage of, sometimes presents himself as being "just about to" do all kinds of positive things with his life. A cousin has promised him a great job in the spring. A settlement from a work injury is coming in a few months, and then he'll pay off all his debts. He's going to stop drinking soon, and cut way down on cocaine. He's going to manage his temper better. He has several things he's "working on" and pretty soon one of them is bound to "come together." He's going to get that divorce finalized "any day now." He's going to introduce you to some people who can get you into that medical technician program you've been wanting to do. And on and on. Don't let the promises pile up; by the time he's on number three or four, it's clear that promising is his style for not dealing.

Having to Have His Way

Every relationship has disagreements and fights, and every relationship has times when both partners want something badly and they can't both have it. We'll talk more later in this chapter about what productive conflict resolution skills look like. But the short form is that both partners have to be able to fight fair, and not to win every time. Does he get enraged if you stand up to him?

Does his style of anger intimidate you sometimes (because, for example, he pounds the table or towers over you, punches the wall, gets his face or his finger too close to your face, screams and turns red, or uses other tactics to give you the message "Don't you dare stand up for yourself!")? Does he use a different style to accomplish this same goal, such as giving you the silent treatment, ruining plans that you had, or other passive-aggressive ways of retaliating against you for not giving in? Do you come out feeling afraid to say what you really think or really want? Do you end up ceding to him over and over?

Bear in mind that even though it's a relief to receive an apology, the man who is sorry is just as likely to repeat these kinds of behaviors in the future as the one who isn't. With or without an apology, there's more trouble coming, and it's best to keep your distance.

Jealousy and Possessiveness

Guarding you like a prized belonging is not a sign of love, although the two are often confused. A man can be head-over-heels crazy about you and not strive to take your freedom away—in fact, the more he genuinely loves you, the more he will want you to enjoy your life and have good friendships. Possessiveness actually proves that a man is not seeing you as who you are, but is viewing you as an owned object no different from his golf clubs or his motorcycle; it is the virtual opposite of intimate human love.

The jealous guy is sure to have excuses—that he's this way because his last partner cheated on him, or because his mother cheated on his father, or because he's never had such a beautiful partner and he's afraid you'll leave him. And that's just what they are: excuses. If he can't trust you, he shouldn't be with you.

(We have also observed, by the way, that the most jealous men are also the most likely ones to have affairs themselves. So if he doesn't trust you, don't trust him.)

He Always Has to Have a Drink, a Toke, or a Snort

Addiction doesn't always take the form of extremely heavy drinking or drugging. A fairly common form of alcohol or drug abuse is low levels of use, but pretty constantly (see Chapter 3). If he seems a little agitated until he's got an intoxicant in his system, you're probably seeing dependence.

Take his age into account in thinking about his partying. While heavy alcohol and drug use is a warning sign of destructiveness even in a sixteen- or eighteen-year-old, it becomes a much more worrisome red flag as a man gets up into his twenties and beyond.

People Are Trying to Warn You About Him

When your heart is fluttering with excitement about a guy you're getting to know, any words of caution that come your way from other people feel like flies that you want to swat away as quickly as possible. You may say to yourself, "Oh, that's just because of rumors that were started by a vindictive ex of his," or "People are just envious, so they want to find something wrong with our relationship." And you might be right on both counts. But listen carefully anyhow, and then keep your eyes open for glimpses of what they've been telling you about him. A man who has behaved destructively in past relationships will always have ways to cover what he's done, and to make the rumors of alcoholism or violence or cheating seem completely unfair. If it turns out the rumors are false, that's great for you; but if they prove to be true, you'll be a lot better prepared if you've heard, and filed away in your memory banks, the things that people say.

He Pressures You

Leaning on you to spend more time together than you are ready for, pushing for sex sooner than you want it, doing you favors that you haven't asked for (or have specifically told him not to do), trying to get you to change your job or any other aspect of your lifestyle—none of these have any place in the early months of a relationship. Failure to respect the other person's boundaries is a serious transgression at *any* point in the life of a couple, but it is especially telling when it rears its head right from the start. The pressure is a warning of two important characteristics about the person you are dating:

1. He is focused on himself and his own needs and desires, *not* on how to build a relationship that takes your interests into account and that works equally well for both of you.

2. He intends to mold you into the person he wants you to become, rather than accepting you as you are. And that effort to sculpt you will never stop once it gets started.

He Is Secretive

Without honesty and forthrightness, a relationship becomes a kind of sparring match. Secrecy is a power trip, and where there is one power trip, there are going to be others. If your partner has something to hide, you don't want to find out later what that is, by which time you may be deeply invested in building a life with him.

Secrecy and privacy are two different things. *Privacy* is a choice to keep certain aspects of your thoughts or your history to yourself, regarding issues that do not have direct impact on your partner and that he or she has no particular right to know. *Secrecy*, on the other hand, involves keeping your partner in the dark about actions of yours that have a direct impact on your partner's life, or that would change the decisions he or she is making about the relationship. It's secrecy, not privacy, when a man you are dating is hiding from you the nature of his connections with other women; is concealing his true use of alcohol or drugs; is telling you lies or misleading you about financial dealings that he's involved with; is involved in criminal behavior or is close to other people who are; or is making plans for the future and not telling you.

Be cautious of a dating partner who abruptly ends phone calls when you appear, who has questionable explanations for aspects of his life that you inquire about, or who keeps you from meeting important people in his life.

The characteristics we have reviewed here are general warning signs of various kinds of unhealthy partners. If you would like to read a detailed discussion of warning signs that are specific to avoiding verbal or physical abuse, see Chapter 5 of Lundy's book *Why Does He Do That?* That list includes some of the same points we have made above, but adds a number of others that you may find helpful.

WHAT DOES IT SAY ABOUT ME THAT I ENDED UP WITH SOMEONE LIKE HIM?

Nothing. It says nothing at all about you. His issues are his issues. Most or all of his issues were probably hidden early in your relationship, so unless you were taught the kinds of guidelines we've been offering in this chapter—and it's highly unlikely that you ever were—you wouldn't have known what to watch out for. Instead of blaming yourself for what happened last time, use your newfound knowledge—much of which you unfortunately learned the hard way—to make your next relationship a good one. And take your time.

Occasionally we talk to women who have had a number of destructive partners in a row. If you are leaving a relationship with your third consecutive alcoholic, or your third consecutive abuser, then *maybe*—just maybe—there are issues you might want to explore about:

- deeply believing you don't deserve any better
- feeling hooked on the drama and excitement, despite all the pain that comes with it
- feeling such a powerful need to have a partner that you refuse to see signs of trouble ahead
- suffering abuse in your childhood that you've never gotten a chance to heal from

However, our experience is that these factors are far from being the prevailing reasons why women end up with destructive partners. The far more common causes are that:

- There are so many people with these kinds of issues, which makes it tricky to avoid them.
- No one educates teens and adults about what to be cautious of when choosing a partner.
- Societal rules, many of them unspoken, about male and female roles in relationships help men get away with a lot.

So we discourage you from putting energy into suspecting yourself of being "attracted to unhealthy people" unless it is happening to you over and over again. And even if you do decide that there are pieces you need to look at, strive to do so with as little self-blame as possible, and stay away from philosophies that blame women for their difficulties. We think that believing in yourself will work better.

How Can I Be Sure I'll Make a Good Choice?

There is not, unfortunately, any completely guaranteed system for avoiding an unhealthy partner. Some people are simply too adept at hiding their problems, convincing everyone who meets them that they are sensitive, caring, undefensive, and humorous, and their dark side doesn't come out until someone stands up to them forcefully about an issue that means a lot to them, or until they find themselves in a relationship that is more intimate than they can handle.

But the good news is that the undetectable ones are a small percentage *as long as you have the right information about what to watch out for,* and of equal importance, *as long as you don't give yourself excuses to move forward with the relationship after the warning signs have appeared.* Your success at defending yourself from ending up in another destructive relationship depends to a great extent on your relationship with yourself; to the extent that you love yourself, trust yourself, believe that you deserve a good life, and take your own inner voices seriously, you become a more difficult person to take advantage of.

Maintaining a good relationship with yourself is not easy, however; almost every person in modern society seems to struggle in this area. So we encourage you to give plenty of time and serious effort to the exercises throughout this book, which can help you make a big change in how good a friend you are to yourself.

You can find a partner who wants to build you up rather than tear you down, and who makes healthful choices about his own life. Keep your eyes wide open, keep your heart open but not as wide as your eyes, and pay careful attention to your intuitions. Partnership need not mean combat, nor does it mean being a man's personal care assistant. You deserve to be valued, supported, and seen. Insist upon it.

TWENTY

Creating the Relationship You Want

FORMING A VISION, and then making that vision become reality, is what this next chapter is about. We are going to begin by asking you to do something a little different from what we've done before; rather than starting with explanations and then asking you to reflect, this time you dive inward right from the start, and the explanations follow.

EXERCISE 20–1:

Walk, climb, or drive to a place where you can find as wide a view as possible. Take a street that goes up on a hill, or find a building that you can go out on the roof of, or drive to a high place; the object is to get to a spot where you can see a long way. Focus your gaze on the farthest-off point, and if possible choose a natural object, such as a tree, hillside, or cloud, to settle your eyes on. Take a little while just looking.

Have you ever met a fiery five-year-old girl? She knows she is a warrior princess. She commands the world with a loving smile, a just heart. She has secret powers. She wouldn't be best friends with a boy who didn't know her true, fabulous identity while also being kind and able to have good adventures with her. Have that girl talk to you a little bit. Let her whisper to you her wisdom. Use what you have learned.

Then allow an image to form in your head of what your next relationship would be like. What do you imagine your partner will be like? How will you feel toward each other? What will it feel like to hold him? What kinds of things will he do that will let you know that he's on your side, that he's behind you?

Let this image dwell within you for at least a few minutes, feeling its warmth.

If you would like to, write a few thoughts down when you are done about what went on inside you.

It is natural, given what you have come through, to be concerned with what you *don't* want your next relationship to be like, and the kind of man you *don't* want to be with. But successful futures can't be built solely on the basis of what you strive to avoid; you have to keep returning your consciousness to the question of what you want to create, of what you *do* want to happen. In this chapter, we will work with you on centering yourself, and then developing a vision of the kind of relationship you want to build and nurture with a new person. You will still hold in mind the danger signs because you need that awareness, but the larger part of your attention will turn toward the future you want to wake up in.

GETTING YOURSELF PREPARED

Head, heart, and intuition: by preparing yourself on all three of these levels, you can almost guarantee that you will find your way to a much healthier and more satisfying relationship this time around. In fact, it will become difficult for anything to stop you.

The information we looked at in Chapter 19 covers the key ideas and concepts for avoiding destructive relationships; so you've already begun getting the "head" part ready. And over the course of reading this book, you have educated yourself about abusive relationships, addiction, and mental health, absorbing large amounts of information and insight during that process that will serve you in making your next relationship a healthy and rewarding one.

The next piece of work involves preparing your heart.

The first step we're going to ask you to take may well be the most difficult: *don't get involved with anyone right away.* We get how hard it is to follow this guideline. When you are just coming out of a destructive relationship, being single is extra difficult, given that:

- It may have been quite a while since you have experienced much physical affection or loving sexuality.
- Your experience may have left you feeling unattractive, especially if (a) your former partner was rejecting toward you, or (b) he was verbally abusive, perhaps doing such things as calling you fat or ugly or telling you that no other man would want you, or (c) he was physically or sexually violent or degrading.
- You may be afraid of how your former partner is reacting to your breakup, which may make it especially challenging to be alone.
- Your former partner may have left you in a hard economic position, so you have an urgency to find a new partner to help pay the rent and meet your bills.

Being single is not easy for a woman in our society anyhow, surrounded as everyone is by messages that say that a woman needs a man to complete her.

The collective impact of all these effects can make you doubt your ability to ever find a man, which ironically can propel you to search anxiously to turn one up right away. You also may have men move in on you quickly when they realize you are available, and their positive attention can be extra flattering to you because of how often you did not feel loved or appreciated in your last relationship.

But the risks of jumping quickly into seeing someone new are great; we've observed that those women who don't take some time to slow down have higher rates of ending up in another bad relationship.

Why does this happen? First, a man with destructive patterns is often attracted to a woman who is in a vulnerable position; he senses that she will be receptive to him and that she is hungry for male attention. A woman who is still feeling shattered inside from her last relationship may put up with more from him. He sees himself as able to take on the role of "helping" her through this tough time, which makes her less likely to notice that he's carrying a serious set of issues of his own, and makes her feel indebted to him. Many women report to us, with a sense of despair, "I can't believe I'm involved with *another* alcoholic [or abuser, or narcissist]. What is it with me? Am I attracted to these guys?" The answer is that it's more likely that they are attracted to *you,* precisely because they sense that you are at an emotional and off-balance time in life.

The second reason why moving quickly is risky is that if you are rushing into something new, you probably aren't going to keep your eyes as wide open for warning signs as you need to be (the kinds of signs we were discussing in the last chapter), and as you would be in a calmer period. It's very tempting at this stage to believe that you can "fix" the aspects of him that are worrisome, or just to overlook them altogether.

And third, you are *wounded,* as anyone would be in your position. Your last partner, whether he was abusive or not, made choices that hurt you deeply. His behavior was in no sense your fault, but you are carrying the effects, and it will take some time for the pain to pass. Starting a new relationship with injuries that are still so fresh from the last one makes it hard to have the kind of clarity you need in order to hear your inner voices well; you are still hearing echoes from the last relationship.

In short, the more eager you are to be with someone new right away, the more your deeper self is working to send you a signal that it's too soon, that you need to wait. Try to hear that signal. Muster your strength and take at least six months of either not dating at all or of keeping your dating relationships casual. (This includes that you make sure any guy you are seeing *keeps living in his own place.* If he needs a place to stay "just for a few days" or "just for a couple of weeks," don't bite—we've seen where it goes.)

During this period *focus your energy on healing.* Now is the time to:

- do a lot of journal writing
- participate in a support group, such as one for abused women (contact your nearest women's program or domestic abuse services); or for loved

ones of people with mental health problems (check listing in your town newspaper or call a local mental health center to see what groups are offered); or for loved ones of addicts and alcoholics (call the nearest substance abuse program and ask what groups are available for friends and family, or try a group such as Al-Anon or Co-Dependents Anonymous)

- spend time alone resting and reflecting, allowing the emotional processing to happen within you
- spend high-quality, calm, focused time with your children
- rebuild relationships in your life that may have suffered as a result of what you were going through; spend relaxed, enjoyable time with friends or relatives whom you love and trust
- cry through your sadnesses, and engage in other forms of grieving for your losses over the past years (such as writing about your feelings, sharing them with friends, painting or doing other kinds of creative or artistic expression that capture what you went through, or joining a group about grieving)
- cultivate your vision of what shape the next stage of your life is going to take
- work carefully through the concepts and exercises in the next and last chapter of this book, "Growing a New Heart"

One word of caution: Groups for loved ones of alcoholics and drug abusers sometimes send blaming messages. (The very term "codependent" can imply blame, in our view.) They may suggest that your own issues led you to choose an addicted partner, or that you are the one who needs to change in order to make it possible for him to change. Pick and choose which aspects of such a group are helpful to you, and don't internalize messages that hold you responsible for his choices or that say that you should hold your anger and resentment in so as to make life easier for him.

But What If the Perfect Guy Just Happens to Come Along?

It happens. We have known a few women who met a guy (or a gal) right at the time that a bad relationship was ending, and are still happily together with the new person many years later. We don't want to encourage you to walk away from a good match. But if he's truly the kind of person you need, he will:

- understand—and in fact support—your desire to move slowly
- not pressure you to live together or spend every night together
- be thoughtful and sensitive about what your needs may be about sex during this complicated emotional period in your life
- stand by you as you go through some powerful emotional ups and downs, as people naturally do when they are recovering from a profound set of losses and wounds

If the voice in your head is saying, in an urgent tone, "But if you don't scoop him up, someone else will," or "He's not going to be willing to wait long while you go through all your emotional crap," you can respond firmly to that voice that it shouldn't be talking to you in that tone, and besides it's wrong. The kind of man who is going to vanish because you won't dive headfirst into a deep involvement with him is too selfish to be a good catch anyhow, and it's best to let him go.

So take things very gradually, insisting that you not stay together more than once or twice a week, and reserve *plenty* of time for yourself and your kids so that you can be taking the kind of healing steps we listed above and that we discuss in detail in the next chapter. (If you feel the need for an excuse for being so cautious, tell your dating partner that you are working a program from a book, and this is how the program works.) Six to twelve months down the road, if everything is continuing to feel right, you can let it become serious.

Listening to Yourself

Much of your goal for this period is to strengthen your relationship with yourself. Practice paying close attention to what your inner voice is telling you: about what your healing needs are, about which people to trust, about what men to date.

Be kind to yourself, which goes hand in hand with developing and fostering your intuitive side. You know what is best for you, if you can tap in to your own deepest wisdom and live by it.

Exploring the Family You Came From

If you haven't already spent time drawing lessons from the family you grew up in, this would be an important time to do so. (And even if you have reflected on these questions in the past, you might seize this opportunity to go deeper.) How has your parents' relationship—or lack thereof—influenced your view of what kind of happiness a couple can have? If you grew up with a mother and a father, how did they shape your view of what the male and female roles are in a long-term commitment? Which of these messages were constructive and which were unhealthy? Has your choice of partners in the past been a reaction to your family experience—whether by trying to re-create the best aspects or by trying to avoid the worst? Did you grow up around abuse, addiction, personality disorder, or some combination of these?

Dating Women

You may find yourself interested in going out with a woman, even if you never have before; this discovery is not uncommon for women who are in the midst of intense personal growth—and you are growing rapidly, whether you realize it or not. These feelings toward women may fade after a while, or you may find that they strengthen and you want to pursue them. Follow what is right for you. If you do choose to become involved with a woman, though, it's important that you still apply the concepts and watch for the warning signs from this chapter before getting in deep; there are women who are harmful to other women, for the same reasons of addiction, abusiveness, or mental health problems. Falling for a woman won't automatically bring you a healthier relationship. Build your new connection with the same kind of care and awareness that you would use with a man.

BUILDING THE FULFILLING RELATIONSHIP

You can have an intimate relationship that is mutually trusting, full of good companionship, and fulfilling, and that remains passionate over the years. These are *not* pie-in-the-sky desires, the products of some fantasy world.

While very few relationships are easy, many are rewarding and healthy for both partners. Don't settle for less.

Nurture a Close Friendship

A satisfying and successful romantic relationship is constructed on a foundation of friendship. Your partner doesn't have to be your *best* friend—though that happens sometimes—but he needs to be a *good* friend. The two of you need to not only love each other but also *like* each other. Be cheerleaders for each other, rooting for mutual success and happiness. Your partner should have your back, knowing when you need him and coming through for you, and you should do the same for him. Stick up for each other (except when one of you is really out of line) and be a team. Each of you should show an interest in the endless process of getting to know and understand the other more deeply. Share common interests and joys, look forward to spending time together, laugh and cry, play. The mistaken notion that a close friendship is not compatible with romance and sexiness is one of the biggest obstacles to successful partner relationships.

A partner does not necessarily have to be the same as you to be a good friend. Some people like to choose a partner who balances them, who brings in certain aspects of character that they have less of, who is yin to their yang. What matters is to respect and enjoy each other's attributes, and not to be with someone who wants to turn you into what he is.

Fair Fighting

Learn how to fight fair, it you don't already know. Here are some principles of fair fighting:

- no name-calling, and no ridiculing of the other person's statements or opinions during the argument
- no telling the other person the "real" reasons behind what they are saying or doing in the argument, no discrediting
- no scary body language, including no getting so loud that it intimidates the other person

- each person gets to talk for roughly the same amount of time in the argument
- no interrupting, even when you're really mad (unless the other person is taking up way more than their share of the argument)
- try seriously to understand the other person's thoughts and feelings, even when you're angry and even when you feel sure that your partner is wrong
- look for solutions that would work for both of you, instead of just single-mindedly insisting on getting your way
- neither partner gets to insist that their way is the only "right" way to talk about the conflict or resolve it (except for following the Fair Fighting rules)
- be prepared to sometimes let go of some parts of what you were hoping for

The principles of fair fighting have to apply equally to both partners; if one person insists on continuing to fight dirty, the other person cannot single-handedly create a healthy relationship. However, it's important not to use your partner's behavior as an excuse for your own, saying, "You're fighting dirty, so I'm going to also." Otherwise, the whole conflict escalates rapidly, with both partners blaming the other for their own actions and no one accepting any responsibility.

So what is the solution if your partner's arguing style is an unhealthy one? First, explain that you aren't willing to be in a relationship that doesn't follow rules of fair fighting. Next, put the rules down in writing so he can read them and think about them, and keep pressing him to agree to change his style.

Some people will complain that these rules are too restrictive, claiming that they don't allow for enough emotional expression and angry outbursts, that they are too "nicey-nice," that they are products of a repressed culture. But if you look at the rules carefully, you will see that there is nothing that says that people can't speak angrily, can't raise their voices, or can't be emotional. They just demand decency and kindness, prohibit taking the stance that the other person is stupid, and prevent the use of bullying or intimidating tactics. In other words, *the person who hates these rules is the one who most needs them.*

Either person in a couple may need additional fair-fighting rules, based on their own history, culture, and personality. For example, the rules we listed do not prohibit yelling, but some people really can't stand to be yelled at, so yelling has to be off-limits in that couple. Any restriction you are going to add to the other person, though, you have to be prepared to follow yourself; double standards are off-limits. (And if one person's additional rules for fair fighting—beyond the ones we've given—are so very strict that the other person isn't willing to live within them, the relationship may need to end. But that doesn't change the fact that each partner has the right to set the limits he or she needs, and the other person has to respect them.)

The bottom line is that if your partner is not willing, even after extensive explanation and negotiation, to live with these fair-fighting rules *as a bare minimum,* you may be forced to choose to move on.

In general, we find that too much emphasis is placed on the *amount* of fighting that happens in a couple—people commonly believe it should be as little as possible—when the far more important question is the *kind* of fighting that happens. Couples in which both partners are willing to fight fair have the potential to build deeper and more lasting closeness; in fact, they will usually do better than couples that avoid fighting. And a partner who insists on using insults, demeaning facial expressions, frequent interruption, or intimidation will do greater and greater harm over time.

So make an ability to fight fair, or at least a willingness to work hard to learn how, one of your highest-priority characteristics in choosing a mate. In fact, we recommend reserving any early discussions of commitment until after you've had some good fights!

Growth and Challenge

Relationships don't stand still very well; when they aren't growing and developing, they tend to be slipping into routine and losing their vitality. Either deeper closeness is being achieved over time, or the connection is fading and the partners are growing distant. New levels of sensitivity and mutual understanding are being pursued, or resentment and silence are building and more things are being kept private and unshared. In short, a steady state seems only to settle into a relationship if it's already at a pretty low level, with most of the real zip already gone.

It is worth your while, therefore, to seek out a partner who challenges you and who is capable of growth himself. Does he inspire you (but not pressure you) to try new things in life that you might not have done before? Does he feel that you, in turn, open up new aspects of life to him? Does he view a relationship as a project that requires effort and attention (as opposed to expecting effortless bliss of the Hollywood movie variety)? Is he prepared to talk about feelings, both his and yours?

Comfort and Serenity

Look for someone who is content with his life, even if there are some changes he hopes to make. Especially after what you've come through, being with someone who is calm and centered, and who is capable of joy, will be a healing antidote to all that self-destruction and negative energy that you've had to absorb.

Consider Being in a Lighter Relationship for a While

You might find that the best step for you right now is to choose a relationship that feels less serious and more temporary, but where you feel safe and have fun. Depending on how you are feeling, this style of connection might feel restful and healing to you. There is no need to focus on finding a new life partner for now if you don't feel called in that direction yet.

Joy

Two people sometimes just "click" in a certain way that can't really be explained, and it can happen when the objective measures don't look exactly right. We hear women say sometimes, "I don't know why we're so happy together, but it just works." As long as your relationship is mutually respectful and supportive, as long as you like each other's values and ways of living, the rest doesn't really have to matter that much. It can be that you both find nothing more fulfilling than walking on a country dirt road together. If you get the feeling of "I wouldn't want to be anywhere else right now," that is your insight into joy. You could be together at a book reading three blocks from home, or sharing a trip on a dusty, chicken-filled bus on the other side of the world, connecting to people you've never seen before, but either way you are feeling the joy of each other's presence. So in addition to the fair fighting, and the principles of a healthy relationship, and the good signs and the bad signs, look for the sense of:

smells good
feels good
"I like you"
"this is right," and
centeredness.

Love and intimacy, honesty and authenticity, companionship and camaraderie, protection and encouragement, these are not special privileges; these are the basic stuff of emotional life, what every woman (and man) should be able to expect from a life partner. If these are what you are looking for, then you are only asking for your due. We believe that the world has these forms of heart to offer, and that you will find them with time. Whether you can feel it now or not, you have what it takes.

TWENTY-ONE

Growing a New Heart

We gathered together the flowers that grew after the fields were razed.
We made them into a tincture called Possibility.
Drop by drop, we serve this tincture—each drop says,

It is possible:
To grow a new heart. Like a womb that has carried a baby, it will
*   secretly be bigger.*

It is possible:
That the cement and stone that has become your body will crumble
*   softly, the doors will open, the light and air quietly dancing through.*

It is possible:
That though the lion is long gone, you can stand on the tongue in the
*   mouth of the one that still lives in your head and say, "You can't bite*
*   me anymore."*

It is possible:
To laugh again, with the brand of humor that honors everything outra-
*   geous and absurd about our losses—like the woman in a shelter sur-*

rounded by her worldly possessions encased in Hefty bags who
remarked, "At least I've finally got matching luggage."

It is possible:
Though it is a bargain no one willingly strikes
To have wisdom where innocence once lived.

It is possible:
To accede to ethical leadership without losing your freedom.
To taste the sour fruit of mistakes but to remain at the feast, knowing
     there's still a place at the table for you.
To hold up to the light the prism of an opposing viewpoint without feel-
     ing the press of moral vertigo against your person.

And finally, it is possible:
To find gratitude, as we have for each of you now.
We are grateful for the healing that has shown us
yours is a fire that can't be put out.
And because the world is incomplete without you well and whole,
survivors among you, all of you,
keep going
keep going.

JAC PATRISSI

Do we believe that you can truly leave behind the experiences of bullying
and cruelty? Can the pain of lost hope and unmet needs fade, and eventually
even disappear altogether? Can you forge new relationships that are nothing
like the old ones, find new friends, and enjoy partnerships that are truly trustworthy? Can you just feel *good* again?

Our answer is, emphatically, "Yes!"

Okay, you might be a little skeptical reading that. Hopeful, but skeptical.
Even if you leave the relationship that was not good for you, feeling the mixed
emotions of joy and grief, you undoubtedly still worry, "Will I ever really get
over it? I can get him out of my life, but how do I get him out of my head? I
want the pain to go away." In some cases, you might hope: "I want the longing
for him to go away. Can that happen?" If you stay with your partner and he

does successfully develop into the kind of companion you deserve, you will still need to heal, and you will still have these questions.

You might worry that we don't really know how hard a fight it is. Jeri Martinez, an advocate for abused women, puts it succinctly when she says, "It's like fighting an enemy who has outposts in your head."

We do know how hard the fight is. And yet we believe that in time you will find yourself at ease, happy, and joyful. We believe that you can come to love life again. You can build a new life. You can find expansive joy and creativity where constriction, fear, and frustration once were. We have known women who have not only escaped the pain of being let down and rejected, derided and hurt, but have also driven the man's negative voice out from inside of themselves. They have built close, trusting friendships and found kind, supportive partnership. They have nurtured lives that bloom in every color.

Your good work began before you even picked up this book. You have fought hard to preserve your sense of self while under siege, and you have gained more strength and wisdom than you know. The toll on you has been great, yes, and healing will take some time; but when you combine the many abilities you already possess with the tools that you have gained within these pages, your recovery will become an unstoppable force.

BREAKING FREE

At one dark point in the satire *Gulliver's Travels* by Jonathan Swift, Gulliver finds himself awakening on the isle of Lilliput. He is bound tightly by the thousand tiny ropes the Lilliputians have fixed there while he slept. He is awake, but unable to move. He is a giant compared to the diminutive natives of the island, yet they are able, for a time, to keep him prisoner because of the number of ties they have around him.

You, too, are a giant. You have been temporarily bound by the thousands of verbal, mental, or physical assaults you endured from your partner, or his devaluing messages, many of them subtle and invisible to other people. One of these hurts alone would not contain the strength to keep you from reaching freedom, but in their large numbers, they did hold you. You are breaking free. Your work in this book undoes each of these binding ropes. As you struggle, we are not forgetting that you are, in truth, a giant among the small.

The insights, exercises, and the fiery sense of determination that we have shared in this book grew in part from the "Growing a New Heart" weekend retreats that JAC has created for women recovering from destructive relationships. We know that the approaches we offer work because we've been honored to witness their power in transforming women's lives before our eyes. Here are some of the inspiring experiences that women have shared with us after the retreats:

"I was greatly blessed, beyond measure. I have a passion inside. A passion to see 'truth' set people and children free, to live as love created them to. Love does not always win, at first, and love suffers so much abuse, before it rises like the dawn. I AM HERE, I WILL REMAIN. Always . . ."

"I had healing goals for myself, but I never dreamed I would also leave with hope for my children. I now believe that they, too, can be freed from the concentration camp of abuse and I will not rest until they are free."

"I never anticipated that I would have a miracle-like transformation. What happened to me was awakening from a sense of deadness and fear. This experience was as personally transformative and liberating as abandoning a wheelchair where you watch life from the sidelines. It's been at least two years since I felt this alive, and believed I might never get well again. I began to understand that I no longer need 'what's-his-name' to bring about happy feelings, that I have them all by myself just by feeling love for life itself. The workshop reopened my ability to trust. I began to feel clean and clear and free of self-doubt. I experience deeper, kinder love and generosity toward everyone in my life, particularly those who have been difficult for me. The most freeing, powerful feeling was to know that I will be happy again because I am so full of love. I have more than hope; I have belief based on my own experience."

Even if you find it hard to believe in this kind of healing for yourself right now—or if any form of hope at all eludes your grasp at this point in your life—we hold for you this certainty: light will come to the dark; joy and freedom will return. You are on the path to reclaiming your very heart and soul.

You can experience the healing power of the principles we teach without coming to a retreat. We ask that you:

Give Yourself Time to Stand Up

Even if your partner has stopped his destructive behaviors toward you, or even if you have already left, keep in mind that your healing process will take time. Friends and family who don't understand how much time it takes to heal can be impatient with your process. They'll insist, "Come on, you should be over it by now. Put him behind you."

It takes time to heal from mistreatment. Remember that you are going through a normal process for someone who has been so badly treated in her relationship, or at the very least dramatically undervalued. You will, in time, break those thousands of ropes that bind you. You will stand up large. The healing process simply takes as long as it takes. Yes, you can speed your recovery along, but not by trying to "be tough" or to "just forget about it," or by rushing through it. In fact, healing needs to begin with being kind to yourself—and others in your life being kind to you—about the wounds, in all their depth, left by twisted emotional aggression or even outright abuse.

What you feel can be a complicated mixture of emotion. The worst part for you may be that your otherwise decent partner cannot come to terms with his trauma and its impact on you. For someone else, the worst part may be living with the way he hurt himself after she left him. For yet another woman, her greatest pain may come in accepting that someone she loved was selfish, careless, and cruel toward her. Your own growing insight into the mixture of feelings you have in your situation will become one of your greatest strengths. Look *with love* at what is hardest for you. You need kindness and compassion about the things that have torn at your heart.

Find Supportive People

At important points in this book, we have asked you to share your dreams or thoughts with a trusted person. If you are in circumstances where you don't have such a person in your life, you might feel frustrated by these assignments. You are not alone in this feeling; an unhealthy partner can make it very difficult to create and maintain a support system. We encourage you to call one of the hotline resources we have listed in "Resources." Ask if the program has a support group where you can share your struggle to decide whether to stay or go.

But if you do have a trusted friend, show her this book and ask her if she'd be willing to talk with you about it.

EXERCISE 21–1: THIS NEW HEART

That heart of yours is already rejuvenating itself. We will now ask you to identify ways in which you feel wiser, stronger, or more capable now than you did before. These are some of the signs of your resilience, that powerful tendency in the human spirit to refuse to give up.

Check all that apply.

_____ I feel like a wiser or smarter person.

_____ I am buying in less and less to the lies he told me about myself.

_____ I have become more assertive.

_____ I understand more now about how important it is to have a voice.

_____ The things he did to me hurt less than they used to.

_____ I fight hard to keep a good relationship with my children.

_____ I know more about the kinds of destructiveness a partner can bring to a relationship.

_____ I know more now about places to go to find help.

_____ I know now some characteristics that are signs of trouble to watch out for in a new dating partner.

_____ I know now that I have some really good people in my life, because of how some friends or relatives (or at least one person) really came through for me when times were tough.

_____ I have discovered that I have more inner strength than I realized before.

_____ I feel that others could learn from my experience.

_____ I have become more outspoken about injustices that I see around me.

_____ I understand more now about what other women go through.

_____ I now recognize some of the risks involved in being what society says a woman should be in relationship.

_____ I have become a harder person to stop when I set my mind on something.

_____ I have developed a closer relationship with myself.

_____ I am a little better at seeing, naming, and being with my feelings.

_____ I understand more about what healing looks like for me.

_____ I understand more about what my partner's healing looks like.

_____ I understand more about what to expect from a healthy relationship.

Add any additional thoughts you have about ways you have grown stronger, or other signs of your resilience or healing that we didn't include in the list above.

Anything you put a check next to above, even if it was just one item, is an indication of the strength you have for healing, learning, and moving forward. (And if you left every item blank, you are still going to discover healing power inside yourself.)

Take a minute to notice how you feel after working with this list. Do you feel a little more hopeful? Or did the opposite happen, where your discouragement actually grew? Any number of emotions could be going through you right now: relief, grief, renewed energy, determination.

EXERCISE 21–2: WRITE ABOUT WHERE YOU HAVE FOUND YOUR SOURCES OF STRENGTH

1. What, or who, has kept you going?

2. How has your soul been fed?

3. What has made it possible for you to continue believing in yourself?

As you have worked through the ideas and exercises in this book, you also practiced an important set of skills. You have repeatedly observed your own feelings and physical sensations. You have named them for yourself in your writing and lists. You have practiced allowing these feelings and sensations to be what they are, practicing self-acceptance of all the different emotional reactions that you may have. Healing has already begun for you. And you deserve it.

Life Beyond "What's-His-Name"

If you are leaving, or have left, there *will* be a day when you don't think about "what's-his-name." Not fondly, not with regret, just not at all. Okay, so maybe he'll come to mind occasionally. But, eventually, it will be like watching a movie that you were in a long time ago. Thoughts of him or the return of some echo of the old feelings will be the exception to the rule. The new context will be you: your wisdom, your insight, and your strength.

If you stay with your partner because he is changing, this good news will still be true for you. You will be in the relationship but learning how to do so while also staying centered in yourself. You may struggle with this on and off for years even if things go really well in your relationship, so know this is normal and be kind to yourself if you slip. You can get up again. You can quit the tiresome old job of managing his barriers to joy for him. If your partner is truly healing, you can quit that job as many times as you need to. Each time you find yourself there, you can hand his responsibility for himself right back to him.

You will, eventually, have so much more kindness available in yourself to give to others. As you lovingly come to understand the amazing strengths you have and what you have endured, you will come to appreciate both your vulnerability and your power. You will see these things in others. You will hear in their stories things that were hidden to you before. (Sometimes it happens in reverse; you see it in others first, and then, you reflect, "Oh, this is true for me, too.")

You will, eventually, deeply feel your value and your beauty. It will become part of your awareness, as easy to see as the changing color of the sky. You will know that you are, altogether, a good deal.

You will be flexible again. It will be okay to be wrong, because it will be just your idea that is wrong, and not you. It will be interesting to learn to see what you don't see now, and not fraught with fear and pain.

You will be funny again. The creative you will burst forth. There will be friends who will rock in laughter with you at the absurdities of your losses. And it will be okay, because you will be big enough to contain all of it, with compassion and love for yourself.

Tanya related to her friends exactly how it was she had tried to join her partner in his obsessive interest in taxidermy as a way to avert the rigidities he imposed and the privileges he assigned to himself. Their laughter demonstrated their compassionate understanding of the things we each try as we are attempting to figure out what helps promote change in one's partner and what does not. This did not.

You will befriend grief and tears. Your tears will lose the hopelessness that made them so unsatisfying. It will be a relief to you, because your tears will open and soothe you, just as your laughter does.

Your body will be your home. Perhaps this is one of the longer projects for some, but it will always be moving in that direction, as you move through your experiences and deeper into the center of you.

You will be hard to fool. No one will be able to easily shift blame to you, minimize what he or she has done, deny actual events and patterns of fact, or otherwise distract you from the clear unfolding of events. This will be very useful.

You will have a voice and use it well. That sense you had that no matter what you said or how you said it, you could not get heard, accepted, or understood tinges the voice with desperate notes. But now you will have heard, accepted, and understood yourself, and your actions will prove that to you. Your voice will ring accordingly.

You will use the talents that you are meant to use. There will no longer be a weight on you, holding you down, keeping you back. You will live free from those barriers to your own fulfillment. The world—which is to say the friends you don't even know, the people you can't even imagine—eagerly awaits what you alone can bring.

You will, eventually, relax into life again.

Sandy sat in her therapist's office with her eyes closed, noticing what was going on in her body after thinking about how far she had come in her healing journey. Her therapist suggested that she invite an image of an animal into her thoughts. She describes what happened:

"Before I knew it, the image of a large lioness appeared, circling around me. I caught my breath really fast and my therapist asked me what was the matter. I told her that I had the sensation of the lioness jumping into my belly! She asked me, after I was quiet for a minute, if I wanted to tell her anything that was happening. I told her that I imagined looking down at my hands and seeing giant paws, claws and all."

You will be like Sandy's lioness, stretching sleepily at nap time. Those claws will be for you a terribly handy thing to have if you need them. You will not need to be vigilant or stressed, but you will have sharp tools of discernment at the ready if you need them.

You will become more connected to more people. You will have so much more energy available to pursue your own joys and gather resources around you.

You will be joyful and well.

EXERCISE 21-3:

Remember back to Chapter 8, when we asked you to *find the thing that represented where you will be when you feel you've reached your healing goals and feel clear about your relationship.*

Now that you have come to the last chapter, let's see how you are doing.

Please take a look at the object that you chose earlier to represent these ideas, and look over what you wrote about this object and goal back in Chapter 8. Consider the following:

1. What are your thoughts now about your goal?

2. How does it look to you now?

3. How have your feelings and thoughts changed?

EXERCISE 21-4: MOVING IN, MOVING THROUGH

Notice any sensations in your body that come to your attention when you consider where you will be when your healing goals are fulfilled and you are clear about your relationship.

How are your head and shoulders positioned?

What is the feeling in your belly, or your legs?

Take several deep breaths, making a sound with your voice as you exhale. Think for a moment about the force or image that you find most deeply sustaining. It might be a favorite place that you like to go to where you feel happy or at peace; it might be a spirit that accompanies you, or a vision from your religious beliefs; it might be a person, alive or dead, whom you feel inspired or loved by; it might be your children; it might be any seen or unseen entity that brings you a sense of expansive power and protection, that makes you feel loved and well. Call this sustaining force to come and join you now. Close your eyes for a few moments if this helps you to focus.

Imagine that presence coming very close to you where you are now. Imagine it entering into your chest, your belly, down your hands, down to your feet. Let it rise to your forehead. Notice the sensations in your body.

Allow your body to move, as you notice the physical sensations you are experiencing. You might:

- Go for a walk for ten minutes (or longer if you want), focusing on the sensation of your feet hitting the earth and feeling the soft swinging of your arms. Feel your body moving through the air.

- Lie in a private space on a pile of pillows on your stomach, or on an exercise ball if you have one, and GROWL. Go ahead. Allow your laughter to pour forth if that's what comes up for you. If you wind up howling, you are not alone.

- Find some water—a sink, a shower, a tub—hot or cold—and feel it on any part of your body for ten minutes or so. Feel the water on your head and on your feet.

- If you have some privacy, shout whatever you feel like shouting, completely uncensored, for as long as you feel like doing it.

When you are finished with the activity you chose, return to your journal and write answers to these questions:

1. What did you notice about your feelings and reactions to your stated healing goals?

2. What sensations do you notice in your body?

3. Is anything unfamiliar or unusual happening in your body or in your thoughts?

EXERCISE 21-5:

Finally, building on what you did in the last exercise, ask yourself, "What do I still need to say right now?" Answer by writing your thought down, or by expressing it as a drawing, poem, or dance.

Is there someone who can share what you have created? We want you to share what you have accomplished so far. Whatever you create at this point in your journey is going to reflect what is courageous and beautiful in you. You deserve to be seen, if you want to be, by kind people who support you.

The Healing Ahead

First phase: "This is really happening. I can't live like this anymore."

Believe it or not, healing begins before your relationship has even ended (or changed for the better), with changes occurring inside you that you may not be conscious of. One sign of that healing might be, for example, that you start to think, "I can't take this anymore," or "I don't have to live like this." If you have children, your role as a mother may help you to see your value as a person despite your partner's devaluing of you. You may see how the disappointments and eruptions wound your children before you realize how much they are wounding you. Or perhaps you start to see your partner as if from a distance sometimes, noticing how vicious or absurd his nasty outbursts look. You may detect patterns that can only be recognized by observing them over time, as they play out repeatedly.

Other times a shift happens inside of a woman that seems geological, like tectonic plates moving within the earth, and she discovers a power inside of herself that just wasn't there a short while before. A way of life that was painful but tolerable suddenly turns unbearable, for no clear reason. And she starts to feel that she must take that wild leap through fear and sadness that is required to step out of the dynamics that an unhealthy partner sets up, without being overcome by the fear that refusing to go along with his patterns any longer could mean that she will lose the relationship.

So even though you are, naturally, limited in how thoroughly you can heal wounds when your partner keeps rubbing them raw again, the recovery process begins while you are still there with him.

At this very early stage, whether you are fighting with a drinking problem, or overeating, or struggling with your own tendencies to hurt yourself or lash out at others, feeling stuck in chronic uncertainty about what choices to make in life, your self-involved or bullying partner is like a lock ensuring that things stay stuck and that any gains keep slipping away, so that you no doubt have many times of coming out feeling—unfairly—like a failure.

At the same time, go ahead and pursue healing in any way that you safely can until the day when you can be free of mistreatment. With time, a way forward will appear to you even if none seems possible now. In the meantime, you can strive for a life that is as good as possible under the circumstances.

Second phase: "I left him . . . and I'm on an emotional roller coaster."

Whether you are leaving as a strategy to insist on his change, or whether you have left for good, you are likely to have times of feeling tremendous relief. "Oh my God, this is so much easier!" We have even heard women say that the sensation felt as powerful as escaping from jail. As you lay your head down peacefully on the pillow at night, or as you begin to make life's simple choices without his constant interference—what radio station to listen to, which clothes to wear, how to spend time with your children—you can feel as if someone has finally stopped suffocating you; it feels good just to breathe.

But more complicated feelings tend to follow behind, sometimes quickly. The grief of saying good-bye to the hopes you had for a partnership can pour down and become overwhelming. As we discussed earlier in Chapter 18, you can find yourself surprised at how much you yearn for a reunion with your partner—just the good parts of him, though. Sometimes the grief mixes in with the traumatic bond, a process that we explained in Chapter 10. It is so confusing to feel so sad about a relationship that was so unsatisfying or injurious much of the time. In fact, after taking some distance, it can become hard to remember that it was really that bad. The grief can sometimes be enough to drive you back, with you hoping that somehow his good side will magically take over from the bad side, even though your experience has taught you this won't happen.

This "newly-out-of-the-relationship" phase can include some times of fear, anxiety, and loneliness. In some cases, a woman finds she has to give up almost everything she had in order to get this space for freedom. Some women don't fully realize how traumatic the relationship has been for them until they get a break from the daily stress and drama. As what was unpredictable in your life becomes reliable, all the feelings you had that you weren't in touch with can rush in. Despair can loom, as you say to yourself, "I thought that getting away from him would solve all of my problems. Why am I feeling so bad?"

Dealing with the feelings about what you have experienced is work best not done all alone. You need to be connected to people who understand what you are going through and who will not hurt your feelings even more. You may need to dig deep for inner strength and reach out for support from others in order to avoid falling into depression during this critical time, or going back to your toxic partner before your demands have been met. Remember that the worst will indeed pass; hang in there, use this book as a guide, and don't give up. There is a wide circle of women who know this place; try to feel them surrounding you, and hear them telling you that they need you to go on through this place and join them.

Third phase: "I would never go back to that life, but I have so much healing left to do."

Women who are moving away from an unhealthy relationship describe a corner they turn where they wake up one morning and realize that they are finished; the struggle about whether to consider being with him is gone, replaced by a sense of "There's no way I would put myself back in that atmosphere. It's just not worth it, and I am going to be okay without him." Some considerable periods of peace and contentment tend to come into her life at this point, and she may feel herself reentering the world with increasing confidence.

This phase can also, though, be the time when you start to notice some of the ways you feel held back in life by the emotional wounds you are carrying from the relationship. You also may find that some concrete damage your partner did is fouling up your life, including ways he took advantage of you financially, damaged your credit, or derailed your career. He may also be fighting you for custody of the children, making you wonder if real peace will ever come.

During this phase we find that women's day-to-day worries lessen, but their anxiety about the longer term sometimes grows. You may, for example, find yourself struggling with a sense that, following a difficult but forward-moving period full of personal growth and empowerment, you have gotten bogged down and progress has started to slip away. You may notice some traits within yourself that surprise or disappoint you. The fear may begin to creep in that perhaps your wounds are permanent, that your partner's destructiveness simply destroyed something at the core of you that cannot be fully repaired. We are eager to assure you that you are experiencing a typical aspect of recovery, and that your healing will jump forward again soon.

If you are staying with your partner because his progress is looking significant and reliable, this phase of healing can be drawn out for you as you wait and watch to see if he will return to his old abusive values, addictive behaviors, or distorted perceptions. If there are times when he does relapse, be understanding toward yourself about the way your progress can feel shaken up, since you had started to settle into trusting him. Healing well from past injuries depends on feeling quite safe—not just physically but emotionally—in the present.

Fourth phase: "It's (almost) all behind me. I hardly think about those days anymore."

Yes, this phase does come! We talk to, and work with, hundreds of women who feel that the mistreatment and its effects are truly over and done. The destructive man has been kicked out not just from her home but also from her head. (And sometimes, though far less often, the man has taken on the lifelong process of change and has become a safe and loving partner.) Her days now belong to her again, the pain is gone, and she loves her current life. She often describes having a new partner who is kind and loving, worlds away from the ugliness or rejection she was tormented by before. You can get there, too.

Women who are in this fourth phase don't necessarily want to focus any-more on the cruelty they were subjected to (unless it serves as a reminder to their changing partner). Sometimes, though, you might find that you do want to go back to reflect some, from the comfortable emotional distance you have now, to gain some additional insights into what happened, or to see if you carry any lasting effects that you weren't noticing consciously. Some women have told us that their specific reason for doing more exploration of the past was to try to ensure that none of the old patterns would reappear in their new relationships. Another motivator can be the desire to assist their children with their own struggles resulting from their father or stepfather's twisted or scary behavior. Women who remain with partners who are working on changing may want to explore the lessons of the past to sharpen their intuition for rec-ognizing signs that he is his slipping back into old patterns.

Most interesting, what becomes so enriching about this phase is how the ordinary things of life feel extraordinary. You will be conscious of feeling really well and really happy . . . regularly.

EXERCISE 21–5: YOUR HEALING GOALS

Where are you in the stages described? Please take this moment and under-line the parts of each stage that you most want to remember. Write a note of encouragement for yourself that you can look at as you come back to this section, which we will be asking you to do in the next step. What do you most want to say to yourself?

Over the next few months, come back to these stages, as well as the checklist at the beginning of this chapter. Review how you are doing, and add to the statements above. You will, over time, have a good collection of wise reminders that you can post on your mirrors or your dashboard. They can bolster you for all your days ahead.

Shower yourself with as much gentleness as possible during this time. Please start talking to yourself, even silently, to cheer yourself on. Tell yourself that you are a light. Let yourself know that you can do it. You are doing it. If you have time to sleep a little more, or rest a little more during this time as you process so many emotions, please do. (Excess sleeping would be a concern— use your wisdom to guide you.) During this time of exploring, clarifying, growing, and healing, do everything you can to allow true sources of inspiration and love in your life. Get yourself a tiny stuffed lion, or refresh your altar (see Chapter 6) regularly. Cut out inspiring pictures related to your No-Matter-What Goals (see Chapter 10) and stick them to a bulletin board. Listen to songs that make you feel what you need to feel. Listen to other songs that make you feel what you really wish you were feeling.

Your well needs filling. We want to encourage you to keep digging for the water. The water is there.

We offer you our stories, ideas, and questions with the hope that they will help you find your way through until you feel clear and are living the life of safety, love, and fulfillment that you deserve. We hope that our ideas grow in you over time, supporting your opening and healing. We see you flourishing in a creative and joyful life, with the partnership you deserve. It is our honor to be part of your journey in some way. It is our deepest hope that we are of use to you as you move headlong into everyday happiness and joy.

RESOURCES

This is a list of books, organizations, and Internet resources for you on a wide variety of subjects that we have discussed. These can help you to understand your partner's issues or your own. *We don't recommend giving these to your partner,* for a range of reasons. If he starts to show a serious interest in examining his problems, you can find materials to offer him at ShouldIStayOrShouldIGo.net, under "Resources For Your Partner." That list includes many of the same listings you will find below, but also avoids offering him pieces that we believe he could easily misuse or turn against you. That list also includes some additional items that aren't included here that are specifically aimed at men who are working on making positive changes.

Abuse and Violence

HOTLINES
National Domestic Violence Hotline for the United States and Canada: 1-800-799-SAFE.
Call this number to receive a referral to the closest hotline for abused women in your area.

Rape, Abuse, and Incest National Network Hotline (Rain): 1-800-656-4673.
Call this number if you have been sexually assaulted or sexually abused by your partner or ex-partner (or by anyone else), and you will be connected immediately to the
sexual assault hotline closest to you.

BOOKS

Why Does He Do That?: Inside the Minds of Angry and Controlling Men, by Lundy
    Bancroft (G. P. Putnam's Sons, 2002). The book that answers the twenty questions
    that women most commonly ask about controlling or abusive relationship part-
    ners, including why he treats other people so much better than he treats you, how
    he came to be the way he is, why his good periods don't last, and how to tell if he
    is really going to change or not.

Getting Free: You Can End Abuse and Take Back Your Life, by Ginny NiCarthy (Seal
    Press, 2004). This is the essential book for women who are seeking guidance on
    how to cope with a controlling partner and how to move toward freedom and
    recovery. It is practical, down to earth, and accurate, and covers in detail a wide
    range of issues that women face.

It's My Life Now: Starting Over After an Abusive Relationship or Domestic Violence, by
    Meg Kennedy Dugan and Roger Hock (Routledge, 2000). Despite the title, this
    book is equally valuable for women who are still involved with an angry or con-
    trolling partner and for those who have left. This is a wonderful, warm, compas-
    sionate book by authors that deeply understand both emotional and physical
    abuse.

The Verbally Abusive Relationship: How To Recognize It and How To Respond, by
    Patricia Evans (Adams Media, 2010). Evans's book takes the reader through the
    details of verbally abusive tactics in relationships, and how to understand their
    effects on you. She offers terrific insight and practical advice.

Into the Light: A Guide for Battered Women, by Leslie Cantrelli (Chas. Franklin
    Press, 1994). This booklet is short and simple, with accurate information and
    good advice. This is a great resource for a woman who does not have the time or
    energy for the longer books listed above, or who wants to have quick inspiration
    handy.

When Dad Hurts Mom: Helping Your Children Heal the Wounds of Witnessing Abuse,
    by Lundy Bancroft (Berkley Books, 2005). If you have lived with a partner who
    yelled at you, tore you down verbally, threatened you, or assaulted you, this book
    offers you insights into how those experiences have affected your children—
    including events that you don't even realize they heard or saw—and how to help
    them bounce back.

Not to People Like Us: Hidden Abuse in Upscale Marriages, by Susan Weitzman (Basic Books, 2001). A valuable expose of abuse among the wealthy, with important guidance for abused women. Weitzman's descriptions of abusive men are accurate and helpful (though a couple of the myths slip in).

What Parents Need to Know About Dating Violence, by Barrie Levy and Patricia Occhiuzzo Giggam (Seal Press, 1995). The essential book for parents who are concerned that their daughters or sons may be involved in abusive dating relationships. Compassionate, insightful, and highly practical, written by people who grasp the wide range of anxieties and challenges that parents face.

Chain Chain Change: For Black Women in Abusive Relationships, by Evelyn C. White (Seal Press, 1995). This excellent book remains the key reading resource for any African-American woman who is involved with a controlling or abusive partner. It provides general information combined with guidance that is specific to the black woman's experience, and includes a section speaking to abused black lesbians.

Mejor Sola Que Mal Acompañada: For the Latina in an Abusive Relationship, by Myrna Zambrano (Seal Press, 1993). Zambrano's book for Latina women in abusive relationships is available in a bilingual edition, making it readable for women who use Spanish or English as their primary language. This excellent resource speaks to the cultural context in which Latinas live, and offers specific validation and recommendations.

Black Eyes All of the Time: Intimate Violence, Aboriginal Women, and the Justice System, by Anne McGillivray and Brenda Comaskey (University of Toronto, 1991). The experience of abused indigenous (native) women is told largely in their own voices in this wonderful and groundbreaking volume. Although there are a few portions where the writers use some difficult academic language, the great majority of the book is highly accessible and moving.

Woman To Woman Sexual Violence: Does She Call It Rape?, by Lori Girshick (Northeastern University Press, 2002). With the stories of survivors of sexual assaults by same-sex partners woven through, this book reports on an important survey and helps bring to light a seldom-examined aspect of intimate partner abuse.

Lesbians Talk: Violent Relationships, by Joelle Taylor and Tracy Chandler (Scarlet Press). This is a short book that draws from the voices of women themselves to describe the problem of abuse in lesbian relationships and offer solutions.

Same-Sex Domestic Violence: Strategies for Change, by Beth Leventhal and Sandra Lundy (Sage Publications, 1999). This well-written and insightful book offers guidance to community members who want to address the needs of abused lesbians and gay men, explaining the structuring of service provision and the overcoming of institutional barriers.

ORGANIZATIONS

Mending the Sacred Hoop
202 E. Superior St.
Duluth MN 55802
(218) 722-2781
www.duluth-model.org, (select "Mending the Sacred Hoop")
This project of Minnesota Program Development focuses on addressing the abuse of women in tribal cultures.

Institute on Domestic Violence in the African-American Community
Univ. of Minnesota School of Social Work
290 Peters Hall
1404 Gortner Ave.
St. Paul MN 55108-6142
(877) 643-8222
www.dvinstitute.org
This organization's website includes resources for abused women themselves, while also reaching out to policy makers, researchers, and other concerned community members.

National Latino Alliance for the Elimination of Domestic Violence
P.O. Box 22086
Ft. Washington Station
New York NY 10032
(646) 672-1404
www.dvalianza.org
Mostly oriented toward research and policy. Extensive listings.

Asian and Pacific Islander Institute on Domestic Violence
942 Market St., Suite 200
San Francisco CA 94102
(415) 954-9964
www.apiahf.org, then select "Programs", then select the Institute

Family Violence Prevention Fund
383 Rhode Island St., Suite 304

San Francisco CA 94103-5133

(415) 252-8900

www.endabuse.org (Select "Immigrant Women," then select "Help is Available")

FVPF helps abused immigrant women to get information about their rights and options and to find referrals to programs in their area.

Abuse and Child Custody

ORGANIZATIONS AND WEBSITES

Resource Center on Domestic Violence: Child Protection and Custody,

Operated by the National Council of Juvenile and Family Court Judges: (800) 527-3223. The Resource Center offers a free packet of information for abused women in custody and visitation litigation. It does not become involved in specific cases or provide legal advice. They also offer a book called *Managing Your Divorce* that helps women prepare for the process of resolving child custody, visitation, and child support.

www.batteredmotherscustodyconference.org

www.custodyprepformoms.org

www.protectivemothersalliance.org

More resources on abuse and violence can be found at LundyBancroft.com, including extensive information on child custody litigation with an abusive ex-partner.

Parenting

HOTLINES

National Parent Helpline 1-855-427-2736

www.nationalparenthelpline.org

BOOKS:

How To Talk So Kids Will Listen and Listen So Kids Will Talk, by Adele Faber and Elaine Mazlish (Harper, 1999).

Siblings Without Rivalry, by Adele Faber and Elaine Mazlish (Avon, 2004).

The Courage to Raise Good Men, by Olga Silverstein and Beth Rashbaum (Penguin, 1995). Consider this book a must read for any parent of a son, especially one who has been exposed to a man who mistreats his mother.

Reviving Ophelia: Saving the Selves of Adolescent Girls, by Mary Pipher (Riverhead, 2005).

Real Boys: Rescuing Our Sons from the Myths of Boyhood, by William Pollack (Random House, 1999).

How to Mother a Successful Daughter, by Nicky Marone (Three Rivers, 2006).

How to Father a Successful Daughter, by Nicky Marone (Fawcett Crest, 2006).

ORGANIZATIONS
The Love and Logic Institute
Provides simple and practical techniques to help parents have less stress and more fun while raising responsible kids.

www.loveandlogic.com

Alcoholism and Drug Addiction

BOOKS
Eating for Recovery: The Essential Nutrition Plan to Reverse the Physical Damage of Alcoholism, by Molly Siple (Da Capo Press, 2008).

AA: Not the Only Way—Your One Stop Resource Guide to 12-Step Alternatives, Second Edition, by Melanie Solomon (Capalo Press, 2008).

Alcoholics Anonymous: The Story of How Many Thousands of Men and Women Have Recovered from Alcoholism, by Alcoholics Anonymous World Services (author and publisher).

Tales of Addiction and Inspiration for Recovery: Twenty True Stories from the Soul, by Barbara Sinor (Modern History Press, 2010).

Sober . . . and Staying That Way: The Missing Link in The Cure for Alcoholism, Susan Powter (Fireside, 1999). This book is largely aimed at women, so it's a particularly valuable resource if you are concerned about your own drinking.

WEBSITES
www.addictionrecoveryguide.org
Lots of information and resources, including where to find drug and alcohol abuse treatment in your area.

www.helpguide.org/mental/alcohol_abuse_alcoholism_help_treatment _prevention.htm
Excellent web resource on recovery from alcoholism.

Mental Health and Trauma

BOOKS

Dialectical Behavior Therapy Skills Workbook: Practical DBT Exercises for Learning Mindfulness, Interpersonal Effectiveness, Emotion Regulation, & Distress Tolerance, by Mathew McKay, Jeffrey Wood, and Jennifer Brantley (New Harbinger). For people whose emotional reactivity, impulsive behavior, or problems dealing with interpersonal conflict are disrupting their relationships or leading to poor behavioral choices; includes people with "personality disorders."

Healing from Trauma: A Survivor's Guide to Understanding Your Symptoms and Reclaiming Your Life, by Jasmin Lee Cori (Da Capo Press, 2008).

Healing Trauma: A Pioneering Program for Restoring the Wisdom of Your Body, by Peter Levine (Sounds True, Inc., 2008).

When Someone You Love Has a Mental Illness, by Rebecca Woolis (Penguin, 2003).

Overcoming Depression One Step at a Time: The New Behavioral Activation Approach to Getting Your Life Back, by Michael Addis (New Harbinger, 2004).

The PTSD Workbook: Simple, Effective Techniques for Overcoming Traumatic Stress Symptoms, by Mary Beth Williams and Soili Poijula (New Harbinger, 2002).

Resurrection After Rape: A Guide to Transforming from Victim to Survivor, by Matt Atkinson (R.A.R. Publishing, 2008).

The Courage to Heal Workbook for Women and Men Survivors of Child Sexual Abuse, by Laura Davis (Harper, 1990).

WEBSITES

www.borderlinepersonalitydisorder.com
Humane, supportive website for people believed to have borderline personality disorder and their loved ones.

www.depression-recovery-life.com
Balanced, supportive information on depression, with a range of avenues to recovery.

www.nami.org
"Choosing The Right Treatment: What Families Need to Know About Evidence-based Practices," published by the National Alliance on Mental Illness

www.NCTSN.org
"Trauma-Focused Cognitive Behavioral Therapy Fact Sheet" from the National Traumatic Stress Network.

www.emdr.com (Choose "Find a Clinician")
Eye Movement Desensitization and Reprocessing
A sensory based treatment approach which has been empirically validated in over twenty randomized studies of trauma victims.

Gambling

WEBSITES
www.recovery-world.com/Anonymous-Recovery-s.html
Select Gamblers Anonymous, and then, "Gam-Anon:Help for Family and Friends."

Overeating

BOOKS
The Twelve Steps and Twelve Traditions of Overeaters Anonymous, by Overeaters Anonymous (author and publisher).
Food for Thought: Daily Meditations for Overeaters, by Elisabeth L. (Hazelden, 1980).
Fat and Furious: Mothers and Daughters and Food Obsessions, by Judi Hollis (iUniverse, 2002).

Sex Addiction and Pornography Addiction

HOTLINES
Sex Addicts Anonymous 1-800-477-8191 USA/Canada Toll free

WEBSITES
www.saa-recovery.org
Offers online and written resources such as "Sex Addicts Anonymous—A Pathway to Recovery" by International Service Organization of SAA, Inc. and "Abstinence." ("Abstinence in SAA means not acting-out achieved through the support of working a program of recovery. We suggest considering acting-out to be any sexual behavior which is abusive, high risk, painful, costly or compulsive"—from "Abstinence".)

ORGANIZATIONS

Sexual Recovery Institute
www.Sexualrecovery.com Toll free at 866-585-9174
Has tools, resources, and support group information, including video educational tools and discussion of the addictive use of pornography.

Your Own Healing

Women Who Run With the Wolves: Myths and Stories of the Wild Woman Archetype, by Clarissa Pinkola Estes (Ballantine Books, 1996).

Authentic Movement: Essays by Mary Sarks Whitehouse, Janet Adler, and Joan Chodorow, edited by Patrizia Pallaro (Jessica Kingsley Publishers, 1999). A collection of reflections on healing relationships with your body through a therapeutic form of movement called Authentic Movement.

A Woman's Book of Life: The Biology, Psychology and Spirituality of the Feminine Life Cycle, by Joan Borysenko (Riverhead Books, 1997).

Coming Home to Myself: Reflections for Nurturing a Woman's Body and Soul, by Marion Woodman and Jill Mellick (Conari Press, 2001).

Financial Planning

WEBSITES:
www.ncadv.org/programs/FinancialEducation.php
NCADV offers a free workbook called "Hope and Power for Your Personal Finances," which you can download from http://shop.ncadv.org/publications. We recommend this guide whether or not there has been abuse in your relationship—it is full of general economic empowerment information for women. (Even though the guide is free, you will need to go through the steps to "checkout" as if you were purchasing an item, but you will not have to actually provide a credit card number at the checkout. A box will appear that says "click here to download file.")

www. MyMoney.gov
Includes free videos and worksheets for increasing financial literacy.

www.ConsumerFinance.gov or toll free 1-888-MyMoney.
Call for guidance and resources.

www.dol.gov/ebsa/publications/nearretirement.html
Department of Labor sponsored planning information and tools for people 10 to 15 years away from retirement.

Safety Planning

HOTLINES
National Domestic Violence Hotline at 800-799-SAFE.
If you are concerned about your safety, whether or not your partner has been violent or threatening in the past, we urge you to call your local abuse hotline and work with an advocate on confidential safety planning. To be connected to the program closest to you, call 1-800-799-SAFE.

WEBSITES
www.thehotline.org/get-help/safety-planning/
The National Domestic Violence Hotline has various kinds of information on safety planning whether you are attempting to leave the relationship or not. Materials include a printable personal safety plan.

www.ctcadv.org
Click on "Get Help", then "Safety Planning", then "Sample Safety Plan."
This resource (from the Connecticut Coalition Against Domestic Violence) gives you an easy to use and detailed written form for safety planning.

www.ncadv.org/protectyourself/gettinghelp.php
The National Coalition Against Domestic Violence website, including safety planning information.

BOOKS
Safety Planning With Battered Women, by Jill Davies, Eleanor Lyon, and Diane Monti-Catania (Sage Publications, 1998).

INDEX

Page numbers in **bold** indicate tables; those in *italics* indicate figures.